D1090087

# Time Past, Time Future

## An Historical Study of Catholic Moral Theology

JOHN A. GALLAGHER

PAULIST PRESS
New York and New Jersey

*BJ1249*
*.G26*
*1990*
*Cop. 3*

*0 20723477*

## ACKNOWLEDGMENTS

The publisher gratefully acknowledges use of the following selected excerpts: *The Law of Christ*, by Bernard Haring, copyright © 1963 by The Newman Press, Westminster, Maryland. Permission granted by Paulist Press, Mahwah, NJ. *Catholic Theology in the Nineteenth Century*, by Gerald McCool, copyright © 1977 by Seabury Press, New York, NY. Reprinted by permission of Harper and Row Publishers, Inc.

Library of Congress Cataloging-in-Publication Data

Gallagher, John A., 1940–
    Time past, time future: an historical study of Catholic moral theology/by John A. Gallagher.
        p.   cm.
    Includes bibliographical references.
    ISBN 0-8091-3142-0
    1. Christian ethics—Catholic authors.   2. Catholic Church—Doctrines—History.   I. Title.
    BJ1249.G26        1990
    241'.042—dc20                                                          89-48607
                                                                              CIP

Published by Paulist Press
997 Macarthur Blvd.
Mahwah, N.J. 07430

Printed and bound in the United States of America

# Table of Contents

Preface . . . . . . . . . . . . . . . . . . . . . . . . . . . . . . . . . . . . . . . . . . . . . . . . . . . 1

1. The Historical Antecedents of the Manuals of Moral Theology . . . . . 5

2. The Emergence of the Manuals of Moral Theology . . . . . . . . . . . . 29

3. The Theology of the Neo-Thomist Manuals of Moral Theology . . . . 48

4. The Moral Theory of the Neo-Thomist Manuals
   of Moral Theology . . . . . . . . . . . . . . . . . . . . . . . . . . . . . . . . . . . . 75

5. The Casuistry of the Neo-Thomist Manuals of Moral Theology . . . . 98

6. The Tradition in Crisis and Transition . . . . . . . . . . . . . . . . . . . . . 123

7. European Catholic Theology from World War II to Vatican II . . . . 140

8. Four Alternative Manuals of Moral Theology . . . . . . . . . . . . . . . . 162

9. Theology and American Catholicism . . . . . . . . . . . . . . . . . . . . . . 184

10. The Impact on Moral Theology of Post Vatican II
    Theological Developments . . . . . . . . . . . . . . . . . . . . . . . . . . . . . 203

11. Moral Theology and the Situation Ethics Debate . . . . . . . . . . . . . 223

12. Proportionalism and Contemporary Moral Theology . . . . . . . . . . 245

Afterword . . . . . . . . . . . . . . . . . . . . . . . . . . . . . . . . . . . . . . . . . . . . . 269

Index . . . . . . . . . . . . . . . . . . . . . . . . . . . . . . . . . . . . . . . . . . . . . . . . 275

# Preface

In *The Making of Moral Theology*[1] John Mahoney studiously discussed what he considers to be the eight most significant factors in the history of moral theology. As important as Mahoney's book is, it fails to inform its reader of the answer to one fundamental question: what was moral theology? This work attempts to provide an answer to that particular question.

The first five chapters trace the historical formation of the manuals of moral theology. In Chapter One the penitential handbooks of Celtic monasticism, the *Summae Confessorum* as instruments of papal and episcopal ministry, and the university theology of Thomas Aquinas are initially examined as distinct theological genres each of which contributed to the formation of moral theology. The second chapter briefly investigates the formation of the manuals of moral theology in the post-Reformation era and then focuses on the creation of the neo-Thomist manuals of moral theology which flourished in the aftermath of *Aeterni Patris* (1879), the papal requirement that the writings of St. Thomas serve as the basic texts for seminary education. The third, fourth and fifth chapters outline the theology, moral theory and casuistry which constituted neo-Thomist moral theology.

The first five chapters define a very specific theological genre in terms of its structure, content and sociological setting. The next seven chapters discuss alternative theological and moral paradigms employed by various theologians between 1879 and the present. Chapters Six, Seven and Eight survey alternative theologies and moral theories developed by neo-scholastics, modernists, and the theologians of the *nouvelle théologie*. The impact of the manuals and neo-Thomism on the developing American Church, particularly with regard to the formation of the Catholic University of America and the aftermath of Americanism, are examined in Chapter Nine. The final three chapters trace the manner in which revisionist theologians have altered both the theological premises and the moral theory of the traditional neo-Thomist manuals of moral theology.

The first five chapters seek to define what will be called "the received

1

tradition." What did the majority of authors who wrote neo-Thomist manuals of moral theology understand the nature of their discipline to be? What
were they about, what interests and concerns shaped their work? The next
seven chapters seek to discern the sources of change, development, and
eventual collapse of neo-Thomist moral theology. They seek to grasp what
was going forward: the change which would originate a new routine and its
dissemination.[2]

The (thesis) of the present volume is that the neo-Thomist manuals of
moral theology constituted a specific theological genre and that for theological, cultural, and sociological reasons that genre has simply disintegrated.
Both the theologies and moral theories employed by contemporary revisionist theologians are so different from those of their neo-Thomist predecessors
that one must begin to question whether the present state of the discipline is
more accurately portrayed as the beginning of a "new routine" or a revision
of the old. If the theological ethic outlined in the first five chapters of this
study accurately portrays the discipline of moral theology, then the use of
the same nomenclature for the work of revisionist theologians is ambiguous
at best. The theological discipline which continues to be called moral theology is currently either in the process of discovering the manner in which the
remnants of its theological past can serve the needs of contemporary Catholicism or is in the process of creating a new theological genre to meet
those same needs. It is the contention of this study that the latter is the case.
Perhaps liberation theology has done this already for large sections of South
and Central America; perhaps political theology has done something similar
for German Catholicism. Although few expect to see the emergence of a
monolithic system such as neo-Thomist moral theology was, there certainly
must be a theology to guide the ministry of the Church within a given culture
as well as a means of investigating the relationship between a religious
tradition and a culture. But such a theological system has not yet been
developed for American Catholicism. We continue to remain dependent upon
European theology and, increasingly, Latin American theology.

A subsequent study will attempt to make a contribution to this theological vacuum within American Catholicism. It will argue for two distinct types
of Catholic theological reflection on moral issues. The first is a specifically
Catholic form of Practical Theology[3] designed for seminary education and as
a guide to Catholic ministry. The second is a university-centered theology
concerned with the implications of culture for a theological tradition and the
ability of a theological tradition to illumine the anomic dimensions of a
culture. The remaining chapters will develop the theology and moral theory
appropriate for such a university-centered theology.

I am indebted to Loyola University of Chicago for a semester sabbatical
during the Fall of 1986. During the 1986–1987 academic year I was a Fellow

at the University of Chicago's Center for the Advanced Study of Religion. I remain grateful to my colleagues at the Center and to its former Director, Bernard McGinn, for their comments on an early draft of the first five chapters. The National Endowment for the Humanities provided a Summer Grant in 1988 which enabled me to complete the final chapters of this study. James Gustafson, John McCarthy, William French, Susan Ross and Robert Harvanek, S.J. have read all or portions of this book; I am grateful to each of them for their helpful comments and suggestions. The librarians of Loyola University have been of enormous help in ferreting out old manuals and the *Raymundina* from storage areas of the library. My graduate assistants over the past two years, Rick Hudgens and Alison Lidstad have been of enormous assistance at various stages of the preparation of this manuscript. I am especially grateful to my wife, Susan Pangerl, and our children, Liam and Siobhan, who kept me aware of the fact that there was more to life than reading another manual. For their affection and support I am deeply grateful.

This book is dedicated to three men who first exposed me to the traditions studied herein, who taught me that to know the past was the first step toward understanding the present and possibly seeing the future. In grateful memory this book is dedicated to Michael Mary Montague, S.J., James Doyle, S.J., and Joseph Wulftange, S.J.

## NOTES

1. John Mahoney, S.J., *The Making of Moral Theology* (Oxford: Clarendon Press, 1987).
2. Bernard Lonergan, *Method In Theology* (New York: Herder and Herder, 1972), 178.
3. Several recent studies of Don Browning have been particularly important for the retrieval of the notion of "practical theology." In particular see: Don Browning, "Pastoral Theology in a Pluralistic Age," in *Practical Theology*, Don Browning, ed. (San Francisco: Harper and Row, 1983); Don Browning, *Religious Ethics and Pastoral Theology* (Philadelphia: Fortress Press, 1983). For a specifically Catholic approach to practical theology see: Regis Duffy, O.F.M., *A Roman Catholic Theology of Pastoral Care* (Philadelphia: Fortress Press, 1983).

# 1.

# The Historical Antecedents
# of the Manuals of Moral Theology

The manuals of moral theology constituted a significant element in the pastoral education of Roman Catholic priests from the late sixteenth century until the Second Vatican Council. The early authors of these texts did not create them *de novo*. There were three previous genres of Catholic pastoral and ethical reflection which significantly influenced the formation of moral theology: the medieval penitentials, the *Summae Confessorum*, and the systematic theological ethics of Thomas Aquinas' *Summa Theologiae*.

This chapter attempts to develop three points. First, it will explain why the patristic literature was not the definitive factor in the creation of moral theology, whereas the medieval manuals, the *Summae Confessorum*, and the systematic ethics of Thomas Aquinas were to be decisive elements in its formation. These central topics provide the structure of the chapter. Second, it will portray the significant transition which occurred between the eleventh and thirteenth centuries as Christian ministry was removed from the monks and placed in the hands of the pope, bishops, and diocesan priests. This significant alteration in the manner in which the mission of the church was carried out was justified by the emergence of canon law. The monastic theology of the penitential handbooks yielded to the canonical foundations of the *Summae Confessorum*. Third, these theological alterations occurred, in part, as a result of cultural developments. The medieval handbooks, the *Summae Confessorum*, the systematic ethics of Aquinas were each the product of distinct cultural environments as well as distinct institutional settings. The one was the product of the monastery, another the product of the cathedral, the third the product of the university. The one was the product of the early middle ages, the next was produced between the eleventh and thirteenth centuries, the third in the flowering of the golden age of Catholic theology, the thirteenth century. It will be argued that each of these

5

theologies was in part the result of its cultural and institutional setting as well as its understanding of the pastoral mission of the church.

## I. The Patristic Literature

Cyprian, Ambrose, Jerome, Augustine, and Gregory the Great, as well as numerous other authors of the patristic period, addressed questions arising out of Christian ministry and the moral requirements of Christian life. They were compelled to deal with the notion of unforgivable sins as well as the more concrete issues of Christian involvement in the military, the reconciliation of apostates and of murderers. Perhaps the most consistent theme in patristic literature was the effort to portray authentic Christian existence in relation to a non-Christian society or one imminently threatened by heresy, schism, or barbarian invasions. The contemporary reader of these classical texts cannot but be impressed by the intimate unity between theological reflection and Christian life and experience which they display. Despite their significance within the history of Christian theology and their potential for contemporary theological reflection, the patristic writings were neither direct antecedents for, nor the major influence on, the composition of the manuals of moral theology.

The most important reason for this is the long history of the theological and pastoral development of the sacrament of penance. As Karl Rahner has commented, "the institution of confession, with all its substantial stability, has undergone many changes which have been so far reaching that, if it were not a fact, most dogmatic theologians would *a priori* declare these changes to be impossible because they seem to go counter to the substance of the sacrament."[1] Although a detailed account of this history is beyond the scope of the present study, the evolution of the sacrament of penance was too central to the emergence of theological genres such as the penitentials, *Summae Confessorum*, and manuals of moral theology to permit a complete exclusion of the subject.

The sacrament of penance throughout the patristic period was celebrated once in a person's life, usually as part of preparation for death, and involved the public confession of sins and performance of penance. Since it was generally believed that the sacrament could be received only once, it was thought that one should wait till late in life to receive it so as to minimize the likelihood of relapse and to ensure a peaceful death. Although there was something of a consensus that apostasy, murder, and adultery were sins of sufficient gravity to require public penance, there was no clear agreement with regard to other sinful practices. The theological distinction between mortal and venial sins had not yet emerged. Penances were imposed for long periods of time and were fulfilled publicly.[2] The manner in which penance was conducted and the role of the minister in it did not require the sort of theological reflection which gave rise to the penitentials, the *Summae*, and the manuals of moral theology. What does tie the patristic literature to later types of theological reflection pertinent to the celebration of penance is the tight relation between the way in which Christian life is lived and experienced, in this case its self-understanding of a particular sacrament, and the types of theological reflection which have arisen within the church.

There is little evidence to suggest that the authors of the penitentials, the *Summae Confessorum*, and manuals of moral theology were primarily influenced by patristic theology. There was very limited reference to the Fathers in the penitentials. There are more references in the *Summae*, yet by far the primary influence upon their authors was the newly codified canon law. The manuals also cite the Fathers, but in doing so they were generally following Aquinas; there is no evidence that patristic theology was directly shaping or altering the content of the manuals of moral theology.

John Mahoney has quite correctly pointed out the importance of the writings of St. Augustine for moral theology and especially its sexual ethic.[3] However, Augustine's influence has been so pervasive in Catholic theology that it cannot be used to distinguish one strand of Catholic theology from another. During the 17th and 18th centuries when eclecticism characterized Catholic theology, the spirit of Augustine was one of the few common strands. But Augustine's theology did not directly set the form or the tenor of the manuals of moral theology.

## II. The Penitentials

The Celtic or medieval penitentials form a unique and fascinating theological literature. The penitential tradition was begun in Ireland and transported to the Continent by Irish monastic missionaries. It flourished from the 6th to the 10th century. Simply stated, the penitentials consisted of a series of concise definitions of sins which were correlated with specific penances. Thus *The Penitential of Theodore* stipulated that with regard to avarice:

1. If any layman carries off a monk from the monastery by stealth, he shall either enter a monastery to serve God or subject himself to human servitude.
2. Money stolen or robbed from churches is to be restored fourfold; from secular persons, twofold.[4]

In this vein the author continued to describe the requirements of restitution of stolen goods, the need to provide for the poor from an excess of goods, and the penance appropriate for the theft of consecrated things. The same penitential contains twenty-two entries with regard to fornication. Throughout the penitentials, fornication included an array of sexual sins. Penances were assigned depending upon whether specific sexual sins were committed with a virgin or not, a married woman or not, with a man or a beast, or alone. The author continued in the same vein to allot penances for homosexuality, lesbianism, pedophilia, and incest. The penalties assigned were periods of penance ranging from one year (fornication with a virgin) to fifteen years (bestiality and homosexuality for one who is over twenty years of age).[5] Thus, as McNeill has proposed, the penitentials should be considered as "practical manuals for the use of confessors; . . . [they] were designed to equip their users to deal with all sorts of persons in all moral and spiritual predicaments."[6]

The penitentials were to be used as guides in the administration of the sacrament of penance. They enabled the confessor to determine the specific kind of sin being confessed. They facilitated his questioning of the penitent, and guided him in the imposition of the appropriate punishment. The existence of these lists of sins and corresponding penalties was indicative of the changes which had occurred with regard to the sacrament itself. The penitentials were, Oscar Watkins has argued, instruments of "the new system of private penance. That system is administered by a priest, and the reconciliation which follows is effected by the priest."[7] The older practice of public confession and public penance had fallen into abeyance for a number of reasons. In its place the practice of private (auricular) and repeated celebration of the rite had become the common practice. At least this was the case in Ireland and on the Continent north of the Alps. Public penance remained the norm in Rome, however, and this divergence of practice was to be a factor in the decline of the penitentials and the rise of the *Summae Confessorum*.

What made the penitentials such fascinating documents was the religious and cultural world out of which they arose. Their "ideal was founded in monastic asceticism; their reality in primitive barbarity."[8] The penitentials played a significant role in the Christianization, first of Ireland and England, and then of the peoples of northern and central Europe. Their origins were Celtic. The significance of their geographical origin cannot be overstated. Ireland had been left virtually untouched by the Roman conquest; it possessed neither traditions nor remnants of Roman law, government, philosophy or literature. What Christianity confronted in Ireland were primitive, tribal barbarians. But what was of equal importance in the origins of the penitentials was that the Christianity which came to Ireland was monastic, not Roman (papal) Christianity. The penitentials, therefore, were the product of a monastic conception of Christianity and primitive Celtic culture.

Pre-Christian elements in Celtic culture, McNeill has contended, "made for the rise of the penitential literature and gave it some of its permanent features."[9] Celtic society prior to the advent of Christianity possessed traditions similar to some found in Buddhism, which required confession, repentance by austerity, and the singing of hymns. The religious dimension of the culture also provided for spiritual guides who required persons to perform penances proportionate to their sins. The primitive legal system provided for compensations by which restitution could be made to injured parties. "The penitentials promoted the substitution of pecuniary satisfactions for revenge, thus coming to the aid of the progressive movement in customary law."[10] These features of pre-Christian Celtic culture were assimilated into the penitential literature.

The penitentials, however, were also the product of specifically Christian assimilations of Celtic traditions. They were originally a part of the internal discipline of Irish monasteries. As the monks began to minister to those in the immediate environs of the monastery, the penitentials became central tools in their cure of souls. The remnants of the penitentials' monastic origin can been seen in the Christian sources which were drawn upon in their compilation. The writings of Cassian, one of the founders of Western monasticism, and Gregory the Great, one of the popes who prayed to be allowed to remain a monk, provided the authors of the penitentials with basic lists of vices.[11] Thus the discipline of the monastery was moved into the village; the Christianity of medieval Ireland was monastic Christianity. Authority and church discipline were the prerogatives of the monastery and the abbot, not the Pope or local bishops.

The function of the penitentials within Celtic and later continental society was not just religious. The penitentials had social, political, and legal functions as well.[12] Indeed *The Penitential of Theodore* proscribed and imposed sanctions for sacrifices to idols and diabolical incantations, an undeniably religious function, but it also regulated the conditions of marriage and the responsibilities of spouses within marriage as well as duties to and obligations of slaves,[13] more specifically social aspects of life. As ministers of the penitentials, the monks were involved in functions which would today be considered political or part of the legal system. The penitentials imposed sanctions for murder, theft and other acts which can be construed as both sins and crimes. In this context the penalties of excommunication and banishment came together; the punishment became deprivation of membership from both the religious and civil community. In such a society, however, it was not only the monk or religious leader who possessed multiple public roles; the emperor or the political leader also performed a dual role. When Charles the Great called his five synods, he consulted neither Rome nor the bishops. "He regarded the whole of the interests of his empire, spiritual no less than temporal, as coming within the scope of his office."[14] For it was the emperor, not the pope, who held the office of Vicar of Christ.

The intellectual and cultural world of the penitentials has been brilliantly depicted in Harold Berman's *Law and Revolution: The Formation of the Western Legal Tradition*. Berman portrays European society prior to 1050 as characterized by:

> ... the presence of a sense of the wholeness of life with all other aspects of life, a sense that legal institutions and legal processes as well as legal norms and legal decisions are all integrated in the harmony of the universe. Law, like art and myth and religion, and like language itself, was for the peoples of Europe, in the early stages of their history, not primarily a matter of making and applying rules in order to determine guilt and fix judgment, not an instrument to separate people from one another on the basis of a set of principles, but rather a matter of holding people together, a matter of reconciliation.[15]

Law, religion, myth, economics, as well as other aspects of early medieval life were simply elements in the warp and weft of society. Religion and law and politics could indeed be distinguished, but it would have occurred to none of its participants to separate the different aspects of society. How could the economy of such a society function apart from the land holdings and estates of the monasteries? How could the élan of the culture thrive apart from the dual function of the emperor as defender of the empire against enemies from without as well as holder of "the spiritual task of maintaining the Christian faith of the empire against a reversion to paganism?"[16] When the Celtic missionaries journeyed to the Continent with their penitentials, they brought with them not just a discipline for the church, but an order for society as well, the beginnings of a civic and legal order.[17]

In the world of the penitentials not only were the diverse functions or elements of society not yet differentiated, there was also no differentiation between the realm of theory and that of common sense. There were priests and monks, but no theologians; there were courts and judges, but no lawyers; there were workers as well as means of exchanging goods and sustaining the economic aspects of life, but there were no economists. As one reads Berman's depictions of the legal procedures of this epoch, which determined guilt and innocence on the basis of ordeals and compurgations, one is made vividly aware of the immediacy of that social order. Myth and religion were more important elements in such procedures than notions of tort and evidence. Other than their *de facto* function within the social order, there was no justification for such procedures nor for the notion of crime. So also with the penitentials. They were immediate and concrete instruments of monastic ministry. They were the products of neither theological reflection nor ethical theory. Rather they were the result of the syncretism of monastic Christianity and Celtic traditions.

## III.  The Transition to the *Summae Confessorum*

The brief historical sketch with which Bernard Häring begins *The Law of Christ* refers to both the penitentials and the *Summae Confessorum*, but the opening sentence of his discussion of moral theology from the seventh to the thirteenth century is indicative of his attitude towards this period: "The period from 600 to 1200 was barren."[18] F. X. Murphy's contribution to the *New Catholic Encyclopedia* suggests a similar appraisal: "From the years 700 to 1100 not a single work on moral theology appears."[19] The previous discussion of the penitentials has already suggested that these centuries were not as religiously and intellectually desolate as these commentators would portray them. They were the years in which Christianity was taking hold among the peoples of Europe north of the Alps, years in which the initial outcroppings of some important strands of Western, but not Roman, civilization were to emerge.

The world of the penitentials was one in which differentiation between functions and offices within society had not yet transpired; nor had the differentiation between common sense and theory occurred. The *Summae Confessorum*, however, were the product of a later cultural world which was the result of what Berman has called "the papal revolution." The central figure in this revolution was Pope Gregory VII, who in 1075:

> . . . declared the political and legal supremacy of the papacy over the entire church and the independence of the clergy from secular control. Gregory also asserted the ultimate supremacy of the pope in secular matters, including the authority to depose emperors and kings.[20]

The implications and consequences of this papal decision were to have a significant impact on the development of Western culture, particularly its legal, political, and religious structures. First, the papal decree initiated the process of differentiation of functions and offices within society. Second, it occasioned the burgeoning of law as a discipline, an instance of theory differentiated from common sense.

Gregory VII's position presumed a distinction between the function of the pope within society and that of the emperor, and that a similar distinction could be made between the office of bishop or priest and that of a king or lord. That these distinctions were made in previous centuries is only too obvious. But what occurred here in a new manner was not just the distinction

of these offices and functions, but their separation. It is important to understand carefully what was occurring. The dominating and organizing category which was to emerge first was "church," not society or the secular. The
reason that Gregory VII could claim such important prerogatives over emperors and kings was that they were simple laity; they were not ordained.
Emperors and kings could wield the temporal or secular sword, but they in
turn ought to be subordinate "to those who wielded the spiritual sword and
were responsible for spiritual affairs . . . for the laity were inferior to the
clergy in matters of faith and morals, and the secular was less valuable than
the spiritual."[21] The spheres of the religious and secular, spiritual and temporal, the priestly and the kingly were now both distinct and separated. Just
as importantly, the relationship between these spheres was construed not
horizontally, but vertically. These were not two "separate but equal" realms
of power, but rather two realms within a hierarchy with the papacy at
the apex.

One could reflect upon these events and come to the conclusion that this
papal initiative was the first step in the process of secularization. Such a
conclusion, however, presumes a univocal understanding of the word "secular." Peter Brown has provided at least two distinct meanings associated
with this word. In his essay, "Society and the Supernatural: A Medieval
Change," he suggested that a result of the Gregorian Reform was the
"disengagement of the sacred from the profane" which:

> . . . opened up a whole middle distance of conflicting opportunities
> for the deployment of human talent compared with which the
> society of the early Middle Ages appears as singularly monochro-
> matic.[22]

This usage of the term suggests a realm of human activity and creativity
which was neither governed by the divine nor understood in relation to divine
governance or plan. This notion of secularism, which of course is similar to
the contemporary meaning of the term, would allow not just for the distinction and separation of the spiritual and the temporal, but also for the possible
trivialization of the spiritual in relation to the temporal. But this certainly
was not Gregory's intention, nor does it suggest the paradigmatic relationship between the spiritual and the temporal that was to characterize the late
Middle Ages. "In a world where heretofore the sacred and profane had been
almost inextricably mingled, the Gregorian Reform proclaimed both the
unique character and the supreme importance of the spiritual mission with
which the Church was entrusted."[23] As construed by medieval popes, this
mission extended to papal supremacy in temporal affairs. The difference
between the medieval and the modern conceptions of the separation of the

spiritual and the temporal is that the latter has trivialized religion in order to enhance human agency within the temporal, whereas the former subjected the temporal to norms enunciated by the papal office.

Elsewhere Brown has elaborated the notion of secularism which is found in the writings of St. Augustine. The word *saeculum* in Augustine, he has argued, should be translated not as "the world" but as "existence," meaning "the sum total of human existence as we experience it in the present, as we know it has been since the fall of Adam, and as we know it will continue until the Last Judgement."[24] The *saeculum* meant to Augustine the scope of human existence in the world, an existence of pain and separation from what alone can give peace to the hearts of human beings, the City of God. The *saeculum*, however, ought to conform to the divine order. Human activity "can only reach fulfillment when it can take its place in a harmonious whole, where everything is in relation to God."[25]

What is important according to this conception of the secular is what lies beyond this period of human existence. The church and princes might provide human existence with some glimmerings of the divine order so that life might be lived somewhat less painfully, but the fulfillment and satisfaction of life ought not to be sought within the *saeculum*. This world of human existence was construed by Augustine as really of no ultimate or even significant value in itself. His ethical theory, Brown contends, was not concerned with what human beings could achieve, but rather "for what [they] must live in hope."[26]

Such a view will strike many modern readers of Augustine as a trivialization of the temporal on behalf of the spiritual. In relation to this notion of the *saeculum*, Gregory's reform would have yet another significance: it would concede greater importance to the temporal as a realm of human achievement and for the enjoyment of important values. Indeed the papacy reserved to itself the ultimate determination of what should constitute such achievements and values, but it also rejected the earlier monastic view of life which suggested that Christians should emulate the angels and seek fulfillment solely in what lies beyond this life. Gone was the ideal of the Christian as a monk dead to the world, gone was the desire "to make mankind over into a veritable monastery, joyous and active, living in expectation of the heavenly reward."[27]

A theory of the relationship between the spiritual and the temporal, the religious and the secular or profane, was not among the outcomes of the Gregorian reform. Such a theory could arise only with the emergence of philosophy and theology as intellectual disciplines distinct from the religious life of medieval Christians; it was to be among the accomplishments of late medieval scholasticism. Gregory and the papal reformers were neither philosophers nor theologians, but rather men sufficiently reflective of the legal traditions of their era to realize the need for a theory which would reconcile and harmonize the vast array of elements within that tradition. What was going forward in the Gregorian Reform was the assertion of the *legal* dominance of the Papacy over the empire, not the *philosophical* or *theological* justification of that dominance. Thus the second consequence of Gregory VII's claim to papal preeminence was the rise of the academic discipline of law and the legal profession.

The pre-Gregorian legal world of medieval Europe has been succinctly described by Berman:

> Secular law as a whole was not "disembedded" from general tribal, local and feudal custom or from the general custom of royal and imperial households. Similarly, the law of the church was largely diffused throughout the life of the church—throughout its structures of authority as well as its theology, its moral precepts, its liturgy—and it, too, was primarily local and regional and primarily customary rather than centralized or enacted. There were no professional judges or lawyers. There were no hierarchies of courts.[28]

The thesis of Berman's book is that the reform, from his perspective the revolution, which began in the papacy of Gregory VII and culminated in the reign of Gregory IX, totally and rapidly transformed the legal as well as the entire cultural dimensions of European society. The catalyst for these developments was the claim of papal supremacy, and one of the immediate and most important consequences of this claim was the development of first canon and then secular law.

Prior to his ascent to the papal throne, the archdeacon Hildebrand had proposed that all the prerogatives appertaining to the Roman church should be collected into one concise volume.[29] The need for such a collection arose from the legal history of the papacy prior to the twelfth century. The basic instrument of law in those areas of Italy and southern Gaul where papal influence was significant had been the Justinian Code. This compilation of Roman law was assembled in the early sixth century and was for all practical purposes accepted as the law of the land in those areas swayed by papal authority. The Code was supplemented over the years as new issues emerged, such as the rights of clergy, by decretals, that is, legal decisions emanating from the papal chancery. Addressed to individuals and groups, to bishops and princes, the decretals were "authoritative papal statements concerning a controversial point in doctrine, liturgy or discipline—in short any matter which the papacy considered relevant for the well-being of the whole Christian body public."[30] Over the centuries (the earliest extant decretal is dated from 385) a vast number of statements had been issued, but there had been no systematic attempt to order them. What existed was a hodgepodge of conflicting and inconsistent positions taken by the papacy in response to different situations and changing circumstances. What Hildebrand proposed was a codification of the decretals which would clearly and accurately demonstrate the prerogatives of the church.

Such a document was published during the reign of Hildebrand as Gregory VII. The *Dictatus Papae* (Statements of the Pope) drew upon the decretals to demonstrate the privileges of the papacy and "presented the theme of papal monarchy as the only permissible government in a Christian society."[31] The *Dictatus Papae* provided Gregory with the legal basis for his claim to papal supremacy, as well as the legal foundation for the investiture controversy. There remained, however, a vast number of decretals dealing with other matters which had not been codified. That task was to be the work of legal scholars in Italy during the next century and resulted in the *Concordance of Discordant Canons* of Gratian (1140).

There were predecessors to Gratian throughout the last half of the eleventh and the first part of the twelfth centuries. Bonio of Sutri, Ivo of Chartres, and Bernhold of Constance were among the more prominent. An important element in their task was the discovery and creation of a method which would enable them to assemble, relate, and provide a rational justification for the enormous number of decretals. What were appropriate categories by which they could be grouped? How were the elements within such a group to be related and how was one group to be related to all the others? Was there a theory, a jurisprudence, which could justify the groupings and provide a rational justification for individual decretals? The achievement of Gratian was that his *Concordance* responded to these exigencies of the legal system. But what made Gratian's task possible, and what was in fact the achievement of his predecessors, was the development of the scholastic method and its application to the study of law.[32]

In both law and theology, Berman has written, the scholastic method:

> . . . presupposes the absolute authority of certain books, which are to be comprehended as containing an integrated and complete body of doctrine; but paradoxically, it also presupposes that there may be both gaps and contradictions within the text; and it sets as its main task the summation of the text, the closing of gaps within it, and the resolution of contradictions. The method is called dialectical in the twelfth-century sense of that word, meaning that it seeks the reconciliation of opposites.[33]

The *Concordance* was divided into three parts. Part One consisted of 101 distinctions. The first twenty dealt with the nature and sources of law as well as the relationship between the various kinds of law: divine, natural, human, ecclesiastical and civil. The remaining 81 were concerned with the jurisdiction of various offices. Part Two addressed specific cases which were analyzed in relation to patristic, papal and conciliar teaching. The third part reverted to the elaboration of still further distinctions.[34]

The significance of the *Concordance* can hardly be overestimated. Stephan Kuttner has written:

> As a methodical treatise, which submits the thousands of *auctoritates* to the analysis of reason, it became the starting point and fundamental text of a new science in the schools as well as the foundation for the juristic reasoning by which the popes since the mid-twelfth century, in particular, since Alexander III, created in their responses and judicial decisions, the new laws of the decretals.[35]

The *Decretum*, as the *Concordance* is most frequently called, was to become the major text in the law schools which began to arise at this time. The process of compiling the *Decretum*, both for Gratian and his colleagues as well as for his predecessors, had produced a line of students of the law with a body of knowledge to convey to the subsequent generation. It provided the papacy with a coherent body of law by which to distinguish ecclesiastical and royal authority as well as a set of standards by which a wide variety of disputes might be adjudicated.

What the *Decretum* accomplished was the possibility of what we know today as canon law. The term "canon," Ullmann has reminded us, means "norm of right living."[36] In the century following the completion of Gratian's work, the papal chancery was to issue a vast array of new decretals. The *Decretum* continued to provide the theoretical and practical framework from which new papal decisions were to be construed. The development of papal legislation and its codification reached yet a further point of development in 1234 when Gregory IX issued a *Decretum* in his own name which became the canon law of Roman Catholicism until 1918.

The significance of these developments, from Gregory VII's assertion of papal supremacy through the emergence of canon law under Gregory IX, for the evolution of Catholic theology, ethical theory, and ministry were to be vast. The first differentiation, the first separation of one aspect of life from the wholeness and integratedness of life which characterized the early middle ages was the differentiation of law and legal theory. Philosophy and theology were also beginning to mature. The scholastic method which made possible the *Decretum* would also give rise to the differentiation of philosophy and theology from the immediacy of experience and religion. The fruits of this movement, however, would not ripen until the thirteenth century. The theory which primarily contributed to the church's understanding of its role in society and its ministry during the twelfth century was legal theory.

The period from 1075 till 1234 witnessed the theology of Anselm and the Victorines; it gave rise to the transition from theology stemming from the monastic tradition to that originating from within first the cathedral chapters and then from within the Franciscan and Dominican houses of study. The same era witnessed the use of the scholastic method in the hands of Abelard and the creation of the first theological analogue to Gratian's *Decretum*, the *Sentences* of Peter Lombard. These theologians, however, were not the voices of the Lateran Councils held throughout these years. The dominant voices were those versed in the law and eager to facilitate papal authority both within and without the church. The first Lateran Council (1123), for instance, was largely concerned with the removal of the cure of souls from the monks and the establishment of episcopal and thus papal dominion over this pivotal ecclesiastical function.

Legal theory had emerged, theology was on the way, but ethical theory became trapped in these two more sophisticated disciplines. Canon law as the norm of right living provided detailed accounts of proper Christian conduct within marriage; it dealt with issues of inheritance, property, and contracts. If not exhaustive in its ordering of Christian moral life, canon law certainly addressed its greater and more significant aspects. These issues, however, were understood in legal rather than ethical categories. Such a context for ethical reflection presumed that moral questions were capable of the same objective resolution as might be the case with legal matters. The theology of this period ranged from the systematic concerns of Anselm to the more concrete attempts to reconcile the divergent patristic writings and the development of sacramental theology. There was little in the way of theological ethics. The one exception was Abelard's *Scito Te Ipsum*. What was perhaps most interesting in Abelard's work was his emphasis on intention, "his concern for the inner point of view in moral discussion, the attitudes of a man rather than the nature of his deeds."[37] Abelard's emphasis on intention was probably a reaction to the objective treatment of moral matters in the penitentials as well as a response to the psychological requirements of auricular penance in which the penitent's efforts needed to be taken into account. At best, Abelard's ethics remained incomplete. He never finished the project, but the beginning of Book II, which dealt with the vices, suggests that he would have balanced the emphasis on intention in Book I with a normative aspect to his ethical theory.

## IV. The *Summae Confessorum*

The emergence of papal dominance, the codification of canon law, the incomplete differentiation of theology, and the entrapment of ethical theory within jurisprudence provided the backdrop for the creation of the *Summae Confessorum*. The *Summae* were eleventh and twelfth century pastoral handbooks which provided guidance to confessors in the administration of the sacrament of penance, a sort of "systematic exposition of doctrine concerning the sacrament of penance and its administration."[38] The authors of these works drew upon the canonical and theological achievements of their contemporaries. Although there was something of a legal bias which ran throughout this literature, there was also a significant attempt to assimilate theological developments. Allan of Lille and Peter Cantor were among the better-known authors of these texts. The *Summae* reached their high point of development in the *Raymundina* composed by Raymond of Penaforte between 1220 and 1245, a *Summa* which continued to be published until the end of the fifteenth and the beginning of the sixteenth century.[39]

The *Raymundina* consisted of four books. The first two considered sins against God and sins against one's neighbor. The third was a treatise on the priesthood and the sacrament of penance. The last consisted of an exposition on marriage. The sins against God ranged from simony, sacrilege, the swearing of oaths and lying to divination and defilement of graves. With regard to lying, for instance, Raymond attempted to distinguish deception, false speech, and lying; further he established when lying was a mortal sin as opposed to a venial sin, and under what conditions there might be doubt with regard to its sinfulness. Following St. Augustine, he proceeded to classify eight kinds of lying.[40]

Book Two, which dealt with sins against one's neighbor, discussed homicide, torture, duelling, warfare, abduction, theft, usury, and secular business (*negotium*). War may be waged, Raymond contended, against pagans and persecutors of the faith. War between Christians, however, must follow the just war theory outlined by St. Augustine. The penalty imposed for waging unjust war was a canonical one, excommunication *latae sententiae*, i.e., the penalty was incurred when the crime was committed.

The third book was primarily an effort to elevate the moral and spiritual life of the clergy. As the pope and bishops became the center of Christian ministry from the eleventh through the thirteenth century, one of their central concerns was the reform of the clergy. Attempts were made to enforce the rule of celibacy among the secular clergy and to provide for their support by the church. Raymond discussed in Book Three the qualities which the clergy ought to possess and their privileges. His concern was that clerics should be proper ministers of the sacrament of penance. He also discussed significant characteristics of penitents which might affect the administration of the sacrament. He concluded with a consideration of the canonical penances associated with specific crimes. The final book was essentially concerned with the canonical aspects of the sacrament of marriage.

The Dominican John of Freiburg was instrumental in maintaining the significance of the *Raymundina* into the fourteenth and fifteenth centuries. His *Summa Confessorum* was closely modeled on that of Raymond of Penaforte; John of Freiburg followed the basic division into four books and dealt with substantially the same content within each. He complemented the work of Raymond with more recent developments in canon law and provided as well a more comprehensive theological framework for specific moral teachings. His work was an early attempt to relate Thomas Aquinas' systematic theological ethics to the concrete moral issues relevant to the sacrament of penance. His *Summa* was more theological than Raymond's, but like its model it too was "a mixture of practical theology and canon law."[41]

How, then, can the *Summae Confessorum* be compared and contrasted to the Celtic penitentials? They had two common features. First, both were legalistic in their approach to Christian moral behavior as well as the administration of the sacrament of penance. The penitentials consisted of lists of crimes and appropriate penances; the *Summae* created definitions and categories of sins, e.g., mortal and venial. Second, both the *Summae* and the penitentials presume repeated, auricular confession. This was one of the significant, abiding contributions of monastic theology to the modern Western church.

There were, however, also significant differences between these two theological genres. The penitentials were the product of monastic theology and Christian ministry exercised principally by monks. The *Summae* differ in two important regards. They were originally prepared to facilitate the administration of the sacrament by secular priests, i.e. priests who did not belong to an order and whose ministry was under the control of a bishop. The monastery was no longer the center of Christian ministry nor the primary context for the celebration of the sacraments. The bishops, assisted by their clergy, had become the persons chiefly responsible for sacramental ministry. The theology which gave rise to this development was first associated with cathedral chapters. More specifically, it produced the concept of sacraments as means to grace, mediated by the hierarchical church, which was controlled by a strong papacy and an increasingly powerful episcopacy. However the *Summae* of both Raymond of Penaforte and John of Freiburg were indicators of the developing role of the new mendicant orders, the Franciscans and Dominicans, in the sacramental ministry. As they had limited and controlled the ministry of the monks in the twelfth century, so now in the thirteenth the seculars were concerned that "no order . . . be established

whose goal is preaching and the cure of souls for this right belongs to the
bishops and their clergy."[42] The *Summae Confessorum* were aids to both
secular and mendicant clergy in the administration of the sacrament of
reconciliation.

Second, the penitentials represented a world of immediacy and common
sense. The functions and duties of personages within that world overlapped,
conflicted, and complemented one another. The *Summae Confessorum* were
made possible by the differentiation of law as well as the efforts of philosophy and theology to achieve differentiation. Although the penitentials were
more legalistic than the *Summae*, the *Summae* themselves were most directly the product of the *Decretum* and the emergence of legal science. The
penitentials list crimes like items on a shopping list. The *Summae* reflect
legal sophistication. In them, crimes are carefully distinguished. The *Summae* impose the traditional sorts of penalties: periods of fasting, prayers,
etc., but also canonical penalties. The penitentials stipulate crimes; the
*Summae* reflect a jurisprudence and authority which stood behind the law to
authenticate and enforce it. Later *Summae*, such as that of John of Freiburg,
reflect the theological sophistication developed in the thirteenth century.
The monastic vision of indifference to this world had yielded to a sense of
responsibility for the culture and society within which Christian life
was lived.

## V. The Contribution of Thomas Aquinas and the University Theologians

The importance of the writings of Thomas Aquinas for the manuals of
moral theology can hardly be overestimated. The manualists drew upon the
*Summa Theologiae* in order to devise general moral theology and in many
instances to develop an exposition of the theological and cardinal virtues.
Both the structure and the content of the manuals of moral theology were
deeply reliant upon the writings of Aquinas. In Chapters Three to Five the
enormous influence Thomas' thought exercised upon the theology, moral
theory and casuistry of the manuals will be examined in detail. The purpose
of this section, therefore, can remain rather limited. The emergence of
theology as a discipline of the university rather than the monastery or
cathedral chapter, and the tenor of that theology—systematic rather than
directly related to a sacramental ministry—will be its principal concerns.

The thirteenth century marked a renaissance as well as a major epoch in
the development of Western civilization. It was a renaissance in the sense
that it drew upon classical and patristic thought as important sources to be
assimilated and then transformed into contemporary modes of comprehending and transforming the world. The thirteenth century, however, was not

anachronistic—it did not return to the past to live in the past. Rather it found in the writings of the classical and patristic authors elements which could advance learning, which could contribute to yet further refinements in culture and to the process of civilization. It witnessed the flowering not only of philosophy and theology, but also of art, architecture, music, and literature.

With regard to the theology of the thirteenth century, however, the emphasis on development must be carefully qualified. Jaroslav Pelikan has remarked that the "principal contribution of this period to the history of doctrine was to be summation and systematization, not further development."[43] One line of theological development prior to the thirteenth century, the transition from monastic theology to canon law and cathedral theology, has been traced in the previous pages. The role of the cathedral schools in the development of sacramental theology has also been alluded to. In the scholastic era theology initiated the process of detaching itself from exclusively pastoral concerns.[44] The theological task of the thirteenth century was the drawing together, the systematization of the achievements of prior centuries: patristic, monastic, and cathedral theology. As the scholastic method gave rise to the *Decretum* as a *Summa* of law, so too it gave rise first to the *Sentences* of Peter Lombard and then the two *Summae* of Thomas Aquinas.

The theological concerns of Thomas Aquinas and his contemporaries were markedly different from those of the authors of the penitentials or the *Summae Confessorum*. Monastic theology was focused on the cure of souls. In the *Summae Confessorum* the cure of souls was construed as primarily, though not exclusively, sacramental ministry. Unlike their predecessors, the great scholastics were not directly and immediately concerned with the pastoral implications of their theology. Rather their interest was focused on the meaning and consistency of the doctrines handed on to them by their predecessors. And the genius of St. Thomas as a systematic theologian can best be portrayed in the manner in which his *Summa Theologiae* marked a development beyond Peter the Lombard's *Sentences*. The systematic character of the *Sentences* consisted in Lombard's division of doctrines into "signs" and "things." The signs were those doctrines which dealt with sacramental theology. "Things" were divided into those that were to be enjoyed, those to be used, and those to be both used and enjoyed. The doctrines to be enjoyed were concerned with God as one in nature and three in person. All created things, the angels, humanity, the fall and last end of all persons, and redeeming grace constituted the things to be used. Among the things to be both used and enjoyed, Peter referred to the incarnation, faith, hope, charity, the gifts of the holy spirit and the ten commandments. Within the *Sentences* the relationship between things and signs was undeveloped and the designation "things" remained vague.

The vision of the *Summa Theologiae* was set forth in the architectonic notion of all things (beings, *entia*) proceeding from and returning to God (*exitus-reditus* schema). This organizing framework, which determined the context of each doctrine and effected the relationship between specific doctrines, also gave expression to Thomas' pivotal theological affirmation, the doctrine of providence, as well as his major philosophical affirmations of finality and intentionality.

The theological ethic of Thomas Aquinas ought to be comprehended in relationship to the systematic character of his work. As Weisheipl has commented, Thomas completely "revised Lombard's discussion of moral questions, synthesizing man's return to God through the virtues in much the same order as Aristotle treats man's search for happiness in the *Nichomachean Ethics*."[45] The discussion of the virtues, and indeed that of the law as well, receive their meaning in Thomas' theology, at least in part, because of the manner in which they are related to other theological affirmations. Thomas' theological ethic was not developed in order to facilitate the task of the confessor nor in relation to any specifically pastoral function. Thomas Slater has accurately characterized Thomas' treatment of these topics as a "dogmatic treatment."[46] Although the word "systematic" better portrays Thomas' theology than does "dogmatic," the insight is basically valid. His theology was far removed from the exigencies of a sacramental ministry.

The changed nature of theological reflection was not a sudden phenomenon. It was the result of the changing character of the institutions in which theologians were working as well as developing cultural contexts, which in turn gave rise to new notions of the function of theology and the role of the church within society, and thus, in turn, to new notions of ministry. The new institution in which theological reflection occurred in the late middle ages was the university. The transition from the monastery to the university as the institutional setting for theological reflection was mediated by the cathedral chapter.

As the influence of monasticism began to wane throughout the twelfth and early thirteenth centuries, and as the bishop with his priests became the principal agents of the pastoral office, the cathedral schools of the local bishops became the major centers of theological reflection. The new schools, Chenu has written, were a far cry from the monastic schools, "where the teaching personnel, inspired only by love of God, and without haste or personal ambition, or care for the morrow, prepared the young monk for the reading of the Bible and taking part in divine services."[47] What emerged in their place were "new city schools where the clerical teachers, under episcopal control, were fulfilling the needs and aspirations of students of their own kind, a clientele that could not have been assimilated intellectually any more than socially into the monasteries. These were no longer men of the cloister (*claustrales*) but scholastics, scholars (*scholastici, scholares*)."[48]

Theology was now under episcopal rather than monastic control; it was urban rather than rural; it had intellectual ambitions rather than purely religious or monastic goals. All these developments, however, cannot be attributed to exclusively ecclesiastical innovations. Indeed the shift from monastic to episcopal control of the setting in which theologians worked was the result of the growing papal power stemming from the reforms of Gregory VII and Gregory IX. However, the rise of the importance of the cities as places of commerce and thus the inevitable migration into the cities for employment gradually transformed them into the centers of late medieval life. "A widening of commercial enterprise, an increase in the circulation of money, the reopening of the Mediterranean to ship traffic, improved technical devices, a specialization of craftsmen's skills, a rapid increase in population—all had been factors toward the gradual development of urban centers."[49] With the exception of Oxford, universities would be founded in the cities. Finally, as learning expanded in other areas, in law, philosophy and science, there were new tasks set before the theologians, tasks not previously associated with the cure of souls. Cultural and intellectual values began to attract their attention. "The place of the masters in the church became increasingly difficult to determine as they organized theology into a science with its own rules, constructed within the faith and its premises to be sure, but according to criteria stemming from the intelligible nature of the subjects they were examining, and not according to the needs and opportunities of pastoral responsibility or of subjective pious intentions."[50]

From the cathedral schools of France and Italy the universities were to take their foundation. By 1200 the universities were beginning to acquire their unique definition: "a learned corporation or society of masters and scholars, *universitas societas magistrorum discipulorumque*, as it is expressed in the earliest and still the best definition of a university."[51] The university was organized around the chancellor of the cathedral "who alone conferred the right to teach, *licentia docendi*, in the guild or league of licensed masters or professors which became the university."[52] What most sharply distinguished the universities from the cathedral schools was that the former became centers for the study and investigation of the entire scope of Western knowledge and learning; they were not exclusively theological institutions. Also the study of theology in the universities generally required prior preparation in the arts. Thus the institutional revolution which led to the establishment of the universities went hand in hand with the intellectual revolution of the period.[53]

Three features of thirteenth-century university theology need to be noted. The universities, and thus the theological faculties as well, attempted to avoid control by both the crown and the papacy. "The university," Copleston has written, "was a largely independent and closed corporation, which maintained its privileges against Church and State."[54] Although the independence of the university was frequently challenged by both papal and royal interests, the universities attempted to defend their privileges of granting the right to teach as well as to provide the discipline necessary within the university itself.

The theology of the cathedral schools had largely been the product of clerks and cathedral chapters, i.e., priests under the rule of their bishops. University theology was to become increasingly the product of members of the new mendicant orders, the Franciscans and Dominicans. Although there was initially resistance from within the universities to the incorporation of the faculty and students of these orders into the university system, by early in the thirteenth century (1217) first the Dominicans and then the Franciscans were granted chairs within the University of Paris. Albert the Great, Alexander of Hales, Thomas Aquinas and Bonaventure were only a few of the prestigious members of these orders who were to teach at Paris. To the Franciscans and Dominicans "was to fall the lot and policy of being at hand, at the heart of the new civilization, and of ensuring a holy reaction to its intellectual intoxication or its moral disorders."[55]

Thus the first characteristic of the university theology of the thirteenth century was that it struggled for independence from both the monarchy and papacy. Second, it was increasingly the product of the work of members of the Dominicans and Franciscans. Third, as was indicated above, the typical theology of this period was more the result of intellectual than traditional pastoral interests. As Pelikan has argued, the primary intellectual drive behind this theology was the task of summarizing and systematizing the vast theological positions enunciated by the Fathers and monastic theologians. Differences and contradictions needed to be reconciled. Such was the first achievement of this theological epoch. A second task was the incorporation of classical and Islamic thought into the framework of Christian theology. Aquinas' use of Aristotle for the development of basic philosophical terms as well as for his comprehension of the enormous scope of reality encompassed by the notion of "being" was only one instance of such an undertaking. The era was characterized by Christian scholars engaged in reading and assimilating non-Christian sources. Their civilization or culture could be normative for there was no other. The philosophy and theology of this era were dominated neither by French, nor by Italian, nor by German or Spanish patterns of thought, but rather by the thought patterns of thirteenth century European Christianity. Indeed these authors knew of other cultures, especially the Jewish and Islamic, but held both to be inferior and in religious and intellectual need of salvation through Western Christianity. Finally, in the writings of the philosophers and theologians of the thirteenth century the differentiation of theology from religion and of philosophy from human experience came to the fore. The theology of this period was an attempt to find the organizing patterns and the inherent meaning within the doctrines which shaped and informed the religious life of Western Europe. One could live quite successfully without reflecting on the nature of being or the meaning of intentionality and finality; those categories, however, greatly facilitated the understanding of human experience throughout the thirteenth as well as subsequent centuries.

Although the theology of this period was not directly related to the sacramental ministry, it would be a mistake to think that it did not have any pastoral goals. The papal bull issued to the Friars Preachers (Dominicans) by Honorius III in 1216 confirmed the revolutionary character of this new order.

> Its mandate of preaching was intended to embrace every type of apostolic preaching—the communication of religious truth in the classroom, in writing, in pulpit and public sermons, and for the salvation of souls generally.[56]

This new orientation to Christian ministry introduced by the Dominicans and Franciscans was directed not just to the hearts of the men and women of the late middle ages, but to their minds as well. With the introduction of new ideas from both the classical and Islamic worlds, with the differentiations not only of law, but now philosophy, theology and science, the need for sophisticated theological reflection become more imperative. Weisheipl comments with regard to the writings of St. Thomas that they "should probably be seen as an act of apostolic service to the intellectual needs and requests of others."[57] This intellectual apostolate found its ideal environment in the university.

## NOTES

1. Karl Rahner, "Problems Concerning Confession," in *The Theology of the Spiritual Life*, vol. 3 of *Theological Investigations*, trans., Karl H. and Boniface Kruger (New York: The Seabury Press, 1974), 191.
2. For one account of this history see: Bernhard Poschmann, *Penance and the Anointing of the Sick*, trans., Francis Courtney, S.J. (Montreal: Palm Publishers, 1963), 35–121.
3. John Mahoney, S.J., *The Making of Moral Theology* (Oxford: Clarendon Press, 1987), Chapter Two, "The Legacy of Augustine."
4. John T. McNeill and Helen M. Gamer, *Medieval Handbooks of Penance* (New York: Octagon Books, 1965), 186.

5. Ibid., 184–186.
6. John T. McNeill, *A History of the Cure of Souls* (New York: Harper and Row, Publishers, 1951), 118.
7. Oscar Watkins, *A History of Penance*, vol. 2 of *The Western Church From 450 to 1215* (New York: Burt Franklin, 1961), 627.
8. McNeill and Gamer, *Medieval Handbooks*, 3.
9. John T. McNeill, *The Celtic Penitentials and Their Influence on Continental Christianity* (Paris: Libraire Ancienne Honore Champion, 1923), 107–108; see also, John McNeill, "Folk-Paganism In the Penitentials," *Journal of Religion* 13 (1933):450–466.
10. McNeill and Gamer, *Medieval Handbooks*, 35.
11. Ibid., 19.
12. Thomas Oakley, "The Cooperation of Medieval Penance and Secular Law," *Speculum* 7 (1932):515–524.
13. McNeill and Gamer, *Medieval Handbooks*, 208–212.
14. Watkins, *History of Penance*, 701.
15. Harold Berman, *Law and Revolution: The Formation of the Western Legal Tradition* (Cambridge: Harvard University Press, 1983), 78.
16. Ibid., 89.
17. McNeill, *Celtic Penitentials*, 152.
18. Bernard Häring, C.SS.R., *The Law of Christ*, 3 vol., trans., Edwin Kaiser, C.PP.S. (Westminster: The Newman Press, 1961) 1:10.
19. *New Catholic Encyclopedia*, s.v. "Moral Theology, History of."
20. Berman, *Law and Revolution*, 87.
21. Ibid., 111.
22. Peter Brown, "Society and the Supernatural," *Daedalus* 104 (Spring 1975):135.
23. Marc Bloch, *Feudal Society*, trans., L.A. Manyon (Chicago: University of Chicago Press, 1961), 107.
24. Peter Brown, "St. Augustine," in *Trends In Medieval Political Thought*, ed., Beryl Smalley (Oxford: Basil Blackwell, 1965), 11.
25. Brown, "St. Augustine," 7.
26. Ibid., 12.
27. M.-D. Chenu, *Nature, Man, and Society in the Twelfth Century*, selected, edited, and translated by Jerome Taylor and Lester K. Little (Chicago: University of Chicago Press, 1968), 212.
28. Berman, *Law and Revolution*, 85.
29. Walter Ullmann, *Law and Politics in the Middle Ages* (Ithaca: Cornell University Press, 1975), 120.
30. Ibid., 121.

31. Ibid., 135.
32. Berman, *Law and Revolution*, 131-151; Ullmann, *Law and Politics*, 138-139.
33. Berman, *Law and Revolution*, 131.
34. Ibid., 144.
35. Stephan Kuttner, *Gratian and the Schools of Law: 1140-1234* (London: Variorum Reprints, 1983), 495.
36. Ullmann, *Law and Politics*, 121.
37. D.E. Luscombe, *Peter Abelard's Ethics* (Oxford: Clarendon Press, 1971), xxxi.
38. Rev. F. Broomfield, ed. *Thomae De Chobham Summa Confessorum* (Louvain: Éditions Nauwelaerts, 1968), xvii.
39. Thomas N. Tentler, *Sin and Confession on the Eve of the Reformation* (Princeton: Princeton University Press, 1977), 31.
40. *Summa Sti. Raymundi De Barcinonensis* (Hants: Gregg Press Limited, republished 1967), 97-101.
41. Leonard E. Boyle, O.P. "The Summa Confessorum of John of Freiburg and the Popularization of the Moral Teaching of St. Thomas and Some of His Contemporaries," in *St. Thomas Aquinas, 1274-1974: Commemorative Studies*, ed., Armand A. Maurer, C.S.B. (Toronto: Pontifical Institute of Medieval Studies, 1974), 249.
42. James A. Weisheipl, O.P., *Friar Thomas D'Aquino* (Garden City: Doubleday and Company, 1974), 264.
43. Jaroslav Pelikan, *The Christian Tradition*, 5 vol. (Chicago: University of Chicago Press, 1978) 3:269.
44. M.-D. Chenu, O.P., *Towards Understanding St. Thomas*, trans., A-M Landry, O.P. and D. Hughes, O.P. (Chicago: Henry Regnery Company, 1964), 21.
45. Weisheipl, *Friar Thomas D'Aquino*, 220.
46. Thomas Slater, S.J., *A Short History of Moral Theology* (New York: Benziger Brothers, 1909), 39.
47. Chenu, *Towards Understanding St. Thomas*, 17.
48. Chenu, *Nature, Man, and Society*, 273.
49. Chenu, *Towards Understanding*, 14.
50. Chenu, *Nature, Man and Society*, 276.
51. Charles Homer Haskins, *The Renaissance of the Twelfth Century* (New York: World Publishing, 1957), 369.
52. Ibid., 382.
53. Ibid., 368.
54. Frederick Copleston, S.J., *Medieval Philosophy, Part 1, Augustine to*

*Bonaventure*, vol. 2 of *A History of Philosophy* (Garden City: Image Books, 1962), 2:242.
55. Chenu, *Towards Understanding*, 18.
56. Weisheipl, *Friar Thomas D'Aquino*, 23.
57. Ibid., 142.

# The Emergence of the
# Manuals of Moral Theology

The manuals of moral theology were instances of a theological genre developed within the context of the counter-Reformation. They served as major instruments in the theological and ministerial education of Roman Catholic priests for almost four hundred years. They continued to be a major element in seminary education until the eve of the Second Vatican Council (1963–1965). Just as the Council of Trent (1545–1563) occasioned the emergence of this new theological genre, so the theological, cultural, and ministerial concerns which were the catalyst for Vatican II occasioned the demise of the genre of moral theology.[1]

The purpose of this chapter is to define the manuals of moral theology as a specific theological genre. The first step in the development of such a definition will be to distinguish the manuals from earlier theological treatises concerned with similar issues. The *Summae Confessorum* and the systematic theological ethics of the *Summa Theologiae* were the immediate historical antecedents of moral theology.

The second step in identifying the genre of the manuals of moral theology must be to attend to their distinctive structure and content. The structure consisted of the division of the discipline into general and special moral theology as well as a presentation of the canon law of the sacraments. The structural distinctions between general moral theology, special moral theology, and the canon law of the sacraments constituted a defining characteristic of the theological genre. This tripartite form of the genre was the result of the merging of the systematic moral theology of St. Thomas with topics assimilated from the *Summae Confessorum*. A specific set of issues also contributed to the development of this theological genre. General moral theology consistently dealt with the nature of the human act, conscience, law, and sin. Special moral theology considered the nature of sins. Some manuals defined sins as violations of the ten commandments, whereas

GENERAL — SPECIAL — CANON LAW } ST. THOMAS
- NATURE OF HUMAN └NATURE
  ACT        OF SINS
- CONSCIENCE
- LAW
- SIN

} SUMMAE CONFESSORUM

29

others studied sins as acts contrary to the theological and cardinal virtues. Each of the manuals also contained an exposition of the canon law of the sacraments, an exposition heavily dependent upon the tradition of the *Summae Confessorum*.

Like the penitentials and the *Summae Confessorum* before them, the manuals can best be understood in relation to their cultural milieu, the orientations of theology at the time of their composition, and the basic conception of the cure of souls out of which they arose. Moral theology was a form of pastoral or ministerial reflection. The intellectual context of moral theology was the seminary, not the monastery, nor the university. Its most immediate concern was the preparation of future priests as ministers of the sacrament of penance. The manuals of moral theology also instructed seminarians with regard to the proper manner in which each of the sacraments was to be celebrated. They were thus concerned with issues of liceity and validity in the administration of the sacraments. The primary conception of the cure of souls presented in the manuals of moral theology was juridical. Ministry within the post-Reformation church was primarily a sacramental ministry; the manuals of moral theology were the principal and frequently the exclusive course which directly prepared seminarians for that ministry.

The manuals of moral theology were one of three major manners in which Catholic reflection on moral issues was mediated into the pre-Vatican II church. The encyclical letters of the papacy, especially since the pontificate of Leo XIII, as well as a strong philosophical tradition within Catholicism, were also important means by which Catholic moral reflection was brought to bear upon Western cultural developments. Calvez and Perrin[2] and more recently Hollenbach[3] have surveyed the development of papal teaching with regard to the "social question" from the 1890s to the 1970s. The encyclicals of the popes over this period of time were themselves an instance of a particular theological genre, in part the product of the new understanding of the papal teaching office which developed in the aftermath of Vatican I's declaration of papal infallibility. The philosophical strain within Catholic thought was yet another means by which the tradition addressed moral issues. Philosophical reflection on issues of morality became a major task of the great commentators on the writings of St. Thomas, John of St. Thomas, Suarez, et al., and found its most sophisticated modern expression in the works of Jacques Maritain[4] and Etienne Gilson.[5]

Although clearly influenced by the encyclicals and less directly by the philosophical aspects of the wider tradition, the manuals of moral theology need to be distinguished from both of these modes of ethical reflection. The manuals viewed moral issues from the perspective of the individual Christian and the moral requirements incumbent upon him or her, not from the wider, more comprehensive perspective of Christian philosophy or modern papal thought. The manuals were to provide guidance with regard to the concrete, immediate demands of day-to-day Christian living. Their concerns were immediately pastoral and ministerial. Moral theology and the papal encyclicals were exclusively clerical writings, whereas the philosophical tradition was carried on by both clerics and laity. The encyclicals of the popes were expressions of their unique and privileged position within the teaching office of the church; the manuals participated in that teaching office in a much more restricted and inferior manner.

The manuals of moral theology, therefore, constituted a distinct theological genre. Moral theology can be distinguished from earlier forms of similar theological reflection; the genre possessed a distinctive structure and content, and was primarily concerned with issues of pastoral care. Further, it can be distinguished from other forms of moral reflection within the Catholic tradition and can be identified with a particular historical epoch within the life of the church.

One further prefatory note is important. This examination of the manuals of moral theology does not claim to be exhaustive. The details of the origin and development of moral theology from roughly the late sixteenth into the late nineteenth century will be only briefly studied. What this scrutiny of moral theology intends to accomplish is an exposition of "what was going forward":

> By "going forward" I mean to exclude the mere repetition of a routine. I mean the change that originated the routine and its dissemination. I mean process and development but, no less, decline and collapse.[6]

The composition of the manuals of moral theology as an element within the counter-Reformation created a new "routine." A theological genre was created which, in the years following the 1879 publication of *Aeterni Patris*, would be largely assimilated into neo-Thomism. Ultimately, the neo-Thomist manuals would become the "received tradition," the body of knowledge conveyed to each generation of seminarians in their courses in moral theology. "The received tradition" represents the neo-Thomist theology which dominated Catholic thought from *Aeterni Patris* until the eve of Vatican II, what Vincent MacNamara has referred to as "the understanding of Christian morality which was in possession."[7] It was the theology taught in Catholic seminaries until the 1960s.

The manuals of moral theology composed or re-edited after the 1918 revision of canon law constitute the primary materials to be investigated below. Nor have all the manuals written during this period been examined. Manuals authored in English or translated into English, as well as Latin selections from the Jesuit, Redemptorist, and Dominican traditions have been used in the course of this study. They represent a reliable sample of the manuals which directly influenced the moral theology of priests and thus indirectly the Catholic laity of the pre-Vatican II church. Although more exhaustive investigations may modify and refine the conclusions drawn here, I am confident that the limited number of manuals examined in the research for this essay provide sufficient clues to the content of the theological genre to justify the findings offered below. As the literary critic Tzvetan Todorov has stated:

> ... scientific method proceeds ... by deduction. We actually deal
> with a relatively limited number of cases, from them we deduce a
> general hypothesis, and we verify this hypothesis by other cases,
> correcting (or rejecting) it as needs be.[8]

## I. The Historical Formation of the Manuals of Moral Theology

Moral theology was a genre of Catholic theology which arose in the counter-Reformation, originally within the Society of Jesus, and endured until the eve of the Second Vatican Council. The four-hundred-year history of these manuals can be conveniently divided into three overlapping periods. The first extends from 1540 till roughly 1650. During this period the manuals of moral theology were beginning to take form within the Jesuit order as it planned the course of study for its own students as well as for those in the seminaries under its direction. The second period arose from the 1577 commentary of Bartholomaus de Medina on the *Prima Secundae* of Aquinas' *Summa Theologiae* in which he wrote, "if an opinion is probable, it may licitly be followed, even if the opposing opinion is more probable."[9] This second period encompasses almost three centuries in which the issue of probabilism was the major question within the discipline, and Alphonsus Liguori was the single most important figure. The third period arose out of the growing return to the theology of St. Thomas Aquinas throughout the nineteenth century, and reached its apogee in the years following the encyclical *Aeterni Patris* (1879). The first and third periods are the more important ones for the purposes of this study.

In each of the three periods the common characteristics of the genre can be detected. The manuals had as their primary purpose the preparation of young men as ministers of the sacraments, in particular the sacrament of penance. Therefore, a concise presentation of the canon law of the sacraments, as this had been worked out in the pre-Reformation church, as well as of the developments in post-Tridentine theology were important goals of the manuals. Most of the manuals which existed in 1918 were re-edited as a

*— NEED TO KEEP ABREAST OF CHURCH LAW*

*\* 1. SEMINARY TEXTS*
*2. DIRECTED TO PRACTICAL TASK OF SACRAMENTAL MINISTRY; LIMITED THEORETICAL/ SYSTEMATIC CONCERN*

*\*3. DOMINATED BY THE THEOL. OF ST. THOMAS.*

result of the revision of canon law. In this regard the manuals of moral theology shared a common characteristic with the *Summae Confessorum*: a need to keep abreast of current church law. The manuals possessed three other characteristics which clearly distinguished them from earlier types of Catholic pastoral theology. First, they were seminary texts, thus related neither to the concerns of a monastic view of Christianity nor to the exigencies of the university. Second, although primarily directed to the practical task of preparing men for a sacramental ministry, they also possessed a limited theoretical/systematic concern. Third, and this was most characteristic of the manuals of the first and third period, they were dominated by the theology of Thomas Aquinas.

*COUNCIL OF TRENT : SEMINARY SYSTEM*

**(A) The Manuals from 1540–1650**

The origin of the manualist tradition in Catholic theology was an incidental outcome of the counter-Reformation. One of the important accomplishments of the Council of Trent was the establishment of the seminary system. Among the abuses within Catholicism attacked by the Reformers was the lack of theological sophistication and the scandalous moral life of a significant number of the clergy. "There was superstition, immoderate ambition among monks, excessive credulity in the cult of the saints, crass ignorance about Scripture, and need for instruction of the people (and by a better-educated clergy)."[10] In order to raise the level of theological sophistication and to improve the pastoral capabilities of the clergy, the Council mandated the establishment of seminaries. Their purpose was to provide an appropriately educated clergy who had systematically studied the major points of Catholic theology and had learned them in a manner consistent with the theology of the Council of Trent. The graduates of the seminaries, it was hoped, would be prepared to administer the sacraments wisely and competently. The manuals of moral theology, like the manuals dealing with topics of systematic theology, were developed to constitute the curriculum of the new seminary system.

Another decree of the Council of Trent was also to have significant implications for the manuals of moral theology. In its teaching on the sacrament of penance the Council stated that Christ had left priests "as his vicars, as rulers and judges to whose authority Christians are to submit all mortal sins that they have fallen into."[11] Penitents were required to confess all their mortal sins "specifically and particularly" in order that the priest might impose an equitable penance.

As has been suggested at several points throughout this chapter, and as Johann Theinner comments at the beginning of his detailed study of the manuals of moral theology, "the education of the clergy cannot be without influence upon the development of theology as a science."[12] Already in 1215

*PERIOD 1 : (AUGUSTRY*

at the Fourth Lateran Council, there had been efforts to enhance the level of clerical education. When the universities replaced the cathedral schools as the context of theological education throughout the thirteenth century, there was a growing sentiment for centers of theological education which would be focused on the practical needs of the clergy. Trent, therefore, had precedents to support its demand for seminary education. The Roman College conducted by the Jesuits would replace the University of Paris as the model of pastoral theological education. Such an education would be governed by neither the ideals of monasticism nor the theoretical, systematic orientations of university theology.

The pioneer attempts to create such an education were to occur within the Society of Jesus. Almost from the moment of its papal approbation (1540), the Society was at the center of the counter-Reformation. Several of its members were advisors to bishops at the Council of Trent. The most important aspect of the Jesuits' contribution to the counter-Reformation was connected with the educational system it established in the Catholic areas of Europe. A significant service provided by the Society was the development of a curriculum for the seminaries. The *Ratio Studiorum*, the plan of studies for men seeking ordination within the Society, became the paradigm of seminary education not only within the Society's own seminaries, but also in those institutions in which Jesuits educated diocesan clergy, and then in seminaries in general.

The *Ratio Studiorum* was to undergo several revisions between 1540 and 1599, the year of the last edition relevant for the purposes of this study. In each of its versions, the *Ratio Studiorum* outlined two distinct tracks of theological education. The first, the *cursus maior*, was intended to prepare the next generation of seminary professors. This track emphasized the theoretical, academic aspects of theological education. The preparation of these seminarians focused, according to the express wishes of the order's founder, Ignatius of Loyola, on Aquinas' *Summa Theologiae*. The first and third part of the *Summa* constituted the curriculum in systematic theology for these students; the second part of the *Summa* was the focus of their study of theological ethics. In order to prepare these students for the pastoral functions they might assume, *casus conscientiae*, i.e. cases of conscience, were held several times a week. In a *casus* a particular moral case would be presented which the students would be asked to resolve. After the discussion the professor would address the theoretical as well as the practical aspects of the case.

The *cursus minor* was intended to prepare men for the roles of confessor and pastor. It had a purely practical orientation. The students of the *cursus minor* did not directly study the *Summa Theologiae*. They had their own distinct faculty among whom was a professor of casuistry. The education of these students emphasized moral issues. They were to be trained both in the practical resolution of specific moral issues as well as the principles from which such resolutions could be deduced. The *cursus minor* also stressed the canon law of the sacraments. In fact the term "casus" was juridical in origin and derived from the *Raymundina*.[13] The *cursus minor* with its emphasis on pastoral issues was the program of seminary education which the Jesuits introduced into the diocesan seminaries.

Theinner's excellent study of the formation of moral theology gives an account of the numerous attempts to develop a handbook of moral and canonical issues principally for use in the *cursus minor*. The work which was to gain special recognition because of the clarity of its method and organization, and which was to provide the link to the second period of the manuals of moral theology, was Hermann Busenbaum, S.J.'s *Medulla theologiae moralis facili ac perspicua methodo resolvens casus conscientiae* (The Marrow of moral theology for resolving cases of conscience in an easy and perspicacious manner, 1650). The *Medulla* consisted of seven books. The first was concerned with the inner and outer norms of the moral act, i.e. conscience and law. Book Two was an exposition of the theological virtues as a prologue to its exposition of the Decalogue. Books Three and Four were treatises on the commandments of God and the church as well as commandments associated with specific states of life. The final three books were more casuistic in their orientation; they addressed the distinction of sins, the canon law of the sacraments, and canonical censures and irregularities.[14] The movement from the first two books to the remaining four presaged the later distinction between general and special moral theology. The influence of the *Medulla* was not limited to the seventeenth century. It continued to be reprinted into the subsequent century and was the text upon which Alphonsus Liguori would base his own manual in 1787.

The manuals of moral theology as they emerged from this early period already possessed several of the genre's definitive characteristics. First, they were seminary texts for the preparation of men for a sacramental ministry. Second, they were concerned with systematic theology and theoretical issues only to the extent that these were necessary for the resolution of specific cases. The first two books of the *Medulla* foreshadowed the clearer distinction to emerge later between general and special moral theology. The content of the manuals was also beginning to become clear. The law and the virtues in relationship to a series of preselected theological themes were becoming the chief ingredients in the first two parts of a manual. Third, the canon law of the sacraments continued to be an essential element. Finally, the influence of Aquinas was present in the early manuals. Although not as decisively as would be the case in the nineteenth and early twentieth century, nevertheless Jesuit theology, and thus the theology of the early manuals, was theology deeply indebted to the thought of Aquinas.

36                              Time Past, Time Future

## (B)  The Manuals from 1577 to 1879

The specification of moral theology into three periods does not intend to
be rigidly chronological. Medina's commentary on the *Secunda Pars* of the
*Summa Theologiae* (1577), for example, significantly predates Busenbaum's *Medulla* of 1650. Rather the periodization represents dominant
trends in the literature which mark significant transitions in the development of the discipline of moral theology. The chief issue of the second period
was the question of probabilism.

The probabilism controversy which dominated the seventeenth and
eighteenth century debates among Catholic moralists was concerned with
the binding force of moral laws and the opinions of theologians. From the
mid-1600s to the mid-1800s the literature portrayed an almost exclusive
interest in casuistry.[15] Discussion of the issue focused on how certain a law
must be in order to be binding upon an individual's conscience. Ought a
person to be understood as free to choose between two equi-probable opinions? Must one choose the more probable opinion, or may one choose any
probable opinion? The battle ranged from laxism, which would accept any
legitimate opinion, to rigorism, which would demand that the most restrictive and therefore safest opinion be accepted. The harshness of the controversy was heightened by the influence of Jansenism.

The contribution of St. Alphonsus Liguori to this controversy was twofold. His most significant service was an argument in favor of probabilior-
ism, that is, one must act in accord with the more probable opinion. Although
Alphonsus' position was to find growing acceptance throughout the late
eighteenth century, the smoldering embers of this debate can still be detected in the late nineteenth and early twentieth century manuals. His
second contribution was the composition of his own manual, which was
essentially a commentary on Busenbaum's *Medulla*. Alphonsus' moral theology was to go through numerous editions and become the source and inspiration for Redemptorist, Jesuit, and other manualists.

Bernard Häring's comment on this period is particularly appropriate.
"So thorough-going was the effort that the history of moral theology
throughout these two centuries is basically little more than the history of
probabilism. It is also true that such a limited perspective leads to a type of
abstract casuistry bereft of vital nourishment. For over a century moral
theology enshrouded itself in its own problems."[16] The importance of this
epoch, however, consisted in its emphasis on law and the determinations of
casuists regarding the formation of Christian conscience. What had been
latent in the first period of the manuals, what had been more and then less
explicit throughout the development of Catholic theologies of pastoral care
focused on the sacraments, was the specter of legalism. The issue was not
the question of antinomianism, but rather what justifications, what response

could be given to the question: why should Christians live in accord with the law? As this period was assumed into the third, the question on the minds of some theologians was whether a moral theology "presented not as an ethic of virtue, but as a law and duty"[17] was more like the law of Moses than the law of Christianity. The casuistry of the canon law of the sacraments was being transferred to a casuistry of morals. The intimate relationship between legal and moral categories which had marked earlier genres of Catholic thought persisted into the era of the manuals.[18]

✓ *(C)  The Manuals from 1879 to the 1960s*
 The distinctive characteristic of the manuals of moral theology during the period from 1879 to the early 1960s was their neo-Thomist orientation. The manuals which were composed or revised after 1918 can be further distinguished by their attempt to assimilate the new code of canon law promulgated under Benedict XV. The title pages of these works frequently claimed that their contents were "Based on St. Thomas Aquinas and the Best Modern Authors"[19] or *"Juxta Constitutionem Apostolicam Deus Scientiarum Dominus."*[20] Others noted that their teachings had been developed in relationship to the new code of canon law.[21] Each of the distinctive traits of the manuals of this period was a sign of their relationship to the teaching office and juridical function of the papacy. As were the manuals of the counter-Reformation period, so too these manuals were deeply affected by the theology developed by theologians of the Society of Jesus and by their concern for the curriculum of the Roman College. This section will examine the general cultural and historical movements which gave rise to this distinctive theological genre. Chapters Three, Four and Five will provide a more detailed study of their theology, moral theory, and casuistry.
 The neo-Thomist manuals of moral theology shared with their ancestors of the 17th and 18th centuries the fundamental characteristics of the manual genre. They intended to provide the theological basis for a pastoral ministry focused on the sacraments. The manuals of moral theology were seminary texts devoid of the wider systematic and theoretical concerns of university theology. They addressed theoretical and systematic issues only to the extent necessary to resolve issues of casuistry. Whereas the manuals of the 17th, 18th and early 19th centuries were eclectic in their choice of theological paradigms, the manuals published after 1879 were presented as summaries of the moral theology of St. Thomas. It would be with regard to this last point that the neo-Thomist manuals would embark upon a line of distinctive development
 Neo-Thomism had its origins in the developments of Catholic theology in the latter half of the nineteenth century. The dominant Catholic theology which would continue into the twentieth century was in part a product of

Vatican I (1869-70). It would be reflective of the uniqueness of the papal
teaching office as well as of the significance of the distinction between faith
and reason which emerged from the Council. However, early twentieth
century Catholic theology was also a result of the attempt by the neo-
Thomists to establish the teaching of St. Thomas as the authoritative basis
for Catholic thought. Their efforts culminated in the encyclical *Aeterni
Patris* in which Leo XIII sought "to restore the golden wisdom of St.
Thomas, and to spread it far and wide for the defense and beauty of the
Catholic faith . . . "[22]

Seventeenth and eighteenth century Catholic theology had been the
product of a rather unimaginative era in which the notion of dogmatism had
moved to the center of theological reflection. As Congar quoted one such
work:

> . . . [we understand as] dogmatic and moral, theology in which,
> having set aside all Scholastic questions and omitted questions of
> positive theology . . . only those things are treated which were
> defined or handed out as dogmas in the Council of Trent or ex-
> plained in the Catechism of this same Council.[23]

And, as Lonergan has commented concerning the theology of the same era,
the inquiry of the scholastic question was replaced by the pedagogy of the
thesis. Dogmatic theology "demoted the quest of faith for understanding to a
desirable, but secondary, and indeed, optional goal. It gave basic and central
significance to the certitudes of faith, their presuppositions, and their consequences."[24] This was a period in which the universities were declining as
centers of Catholic theological activity. The seminaries were increasingly the
exclusive setting in which Catholic theologians worked.

The seventeenth and eighteenth centuries were also periods of significant social and political change. The remnants of the feudal world were in
the process of giving way to modern economic, political and social developments. The age of colonization not only produced opportunities for the
increasingly powerful mercantile class, but also the possibility of a new
beginning to the adventuresome among the lower classes. As manufacturing
became the dominant economic activity, yet another understanding of what
constituted wealth would develop, along with new centers of wealth and
power. A study of the revolutions of 1688, 1776, 1789 and 1848 provides a
chronicle of events which led to the democratization of the West.

From the perspective of the development of Catholic theology, the
countries of France, Germany and Austria-Hungary were to be particularly
important. As the events which would give rise to the modern nation-state
were occurring within these countries, their respective governments at-

tempted to gain control of clerical education as well as the appointment of bishops. France experienced a vibrant Gallicanism; Austria-Hungary developed Josephism. In Germany, the government of Count Metternich would have many of the same aspirations. The shades of the investiture controversy were arising from the past, but this time new claims were being made on behalf of secular authority over the church.

This period also coincided with the development of Enlightenment thought. First in England and France, then later in Germany and Italy, new patterns of thought were shaping the intellectual community. The rejection of the authority of tradition, new claims of subjective authenticity in religion and politics, and the gradual emergence of modern science as the dominant interpreter first of the physical world and then of the specifically human world were each antithetical to many of the theological convictions of Catholicism. Perhaps as early as the counter-Reformation, Catholic thought had begun to distance itself from the dominant intellectual patterns of Western culture. The Catholic view of this world has been graphically depicted by Thomas O'Meara:

> The fear, almost panic, that spread in the years following the Reformation caused in the counter-Reformation a conserving reaction. This altered the intellectual life of what had been the Western church; the openness of discussion in the medieval church (where Thomas Aquinas and Albertus Magnus could disagree with papal views on Aristotle) ceased. From the point of view of Roman Catholic intellectual life, Immanuel Kant was Martin Luther applied to philosophy; both furthered the triumph of subjectivism. The scenario begun at the Reformation had two acts, and Luther and Kant were the protagonists. What Luther began, Kant completed. The haughty secularity, the mechanism, the natural rationalism of the Enlightenment seemed to Rome a strong argument that, whereas modernity might find congenial some form of contentless, subjective faith, it had nothing in common with a historical revelation, a powerful faith, a permanent church. The world of Protestantism and Enlightenment had brought down the curtain upon the richness and aesthetic sacramentality of the Catholic baroque. Rome, despairing of the direction of rationalism, retreated to the patristic and especially to the medieval.[25]

Such was the Roman and papal worldview from which neo-Thomism was to take its bearings.

The renaissance which the neo-Thomists hoped to accomplish had two tasks. "The first was the defense of the Catholic faith against the rationalism and the religious skepticism of the Enlightenment. The second was the presentation of positive Christian revelation in a coherent, unified system that could stand in comparison with the systems of Fichte, Schelling and Hegel without compromising the supernaturality and the unique, historical character of positive Christian revelation."[26] The first of these goals sought to establish a strong Catholic theology in opposition to the philosophical and theological strains of the wider intellectual community. It sought neither assimilation to, nor compromise with, the Enlightenment, but rather a clear alternative based on an understanding of St. Thomas' thought. The first task encouraged Catholic philosophers and theologians to direct their efforts outside their own community; the second focused their attention within the Catholic community. Previous attempts to respond to the Enlightenment from within the Catholic tradition were dismissed. The traditionalists who stressed the role of faith were dismissed because they denied that reason could know metaphysical first principles; the ontologists' position was rejected because it denied direct knowledge of God; the romantic Tübingen school of Drey and Möhler was to be discarded because its categories, such as the Kingdom of God, were insufficiently inclusive to serve as the basis of a comprehensive, systematic theology.

A series of distinctions, the neo-Thomists contended, were essential to the formation of a theology adequate to these tasks. Each of the positions mentioned above was considered inadequate because it failed to understand correctly or to make the proper distinction between the natural and supernatural, nature and grace, faith and reason, body and soul, philosophy and theology. In addition dogmatic and moral theology needed an architectonic idea such as can be found only in the writings of St. Thomas, "the idea of God, considered in his inner being and his exterior creative and redemptive work."[27] This notion of the unifying theme of Thomas' thought, as well as specific understandings of the distinctions noted above, became the identifying hallmarks of neo-Thomist theology and were to impose a distinctive stamp on the theology of the manuals written during this period.

Neo-Thomist theology became the basis of a virtually universal theological education throughout Catholic Christianity. Its victories over traditionalism, ontologism and romanticism meant that it would become the theology of French, German and Italian seminaries. Neo-Thomist moral theology would also be brought from Europe and incorporated into the burgeoning American Catholic seminaries. What had been at first the theology of the Jesuits' Roman College was now on its way to becoming the theology of the Catholic seminary system. The manuals of moral theology were culturally invariant texts; they were deemed equally appropriate for the seminaries of Italy and France, the United States and Germany. The only accommodation made as these texts migrated from one country to another was that they needed to be altered to reflect the specific canonical and legal requirements peculiar to each country, i.e. what the holydays of obligation and the days of fast and abstinence were, by what hour of the day in each area the priest's office must be read; the moral and legal obligations which Catholics incurred as a result of civil law in their homelands or as a consequence of papal concordats with their governments. Thus the Sabetti/Barrett title page states that their manual had been adjusted to the customs and law of the United States.[28]

The continuing reliance upon legal categories to interpret moral issues was a tendency in this literature which has already been discussed. The moral manuals of the late 19th and early 20th centuries took this danger to an extreme. Liberatore had argued as early as the 1840s for the need of a "sound scholastic philosophy to overcome the dangers to public order and to religious and moral life created by false notions of liberty and authority."[29] A fear of secular notions of liberty and of the dismissal of ecclesiastical authority lingered among the writings of the manualists and this fear gave rise to crisp, clear, and exceptionless determinations which possessed a legalistic character.

A trend which had developed already in the 17th and 18th centuries would become even more significant in the neo-Thomist manuals. As social, scientific, medical, and economic developments occurred, requests about how to resolve new moral issues were sent to the Vatican. In response to these questions either the pope or a member of his curia would provide an answer. In fact this was simply a continuation of the decretal tradition within Catholicism, a conviction that the church ought to provide legal guidelines for right living. As David Kelly has carefully documented, the drift toward what he has called "ecclesiastical positivism" would continue until the eve of Vatican II.[30]

These manuals were once again seminary texts intended for the preparation of young men for a sacramental ministry and especially as ministers of the sacrament of penance. They did not intend to give rise to speculation; they were not interested in assimilating the learning of the wider culture. To learn from these texts meant to learn their dogmatic positions. They were not university texts.

## II. Moral Theology as a Theological Genre

The discussion of genre by modern literary critics, philosophers, and theologians has become an enormously complex topic. Although it is impossible to enter into a full discussion of these issues or to provide an adequate response to the diverse positions taken by participants in this debate, nevertheless a discussion of moral theology as a genre must at least be set within the context of these ongoing discussions.

The traditional notion of genre referred to a system of classification of primarily written texts, although it originally included oral communications such as those with which Aristotle was concerned in *The Rhetoric*. Cleanth Brooks and Robert B. Heilman gave classic expression to the definition and classification of literary forms in their *Understanding Drama*:

> We can see . . . that drama, fiction, and poetry have certain common elements, characteristics which distinguish literature from such types of writing as history, biography, philosophy. All forms of literature, we may say, "present a situation," which stimulates the reader's imagination and thus leads him to apprehend the meaning or meanings latent in it.[31]

The authors then distinguish drama from other forms of literature. Such an approach argues that there are kinds, types, or genres of literature which can be discerned. It would further contend that there are subdivisions within genres, or subgenres of drama, poetry and prose. In a similar volume which Brooks co-authored with John Thibaut Purser and Robert Penn Warren, the authors stipulate that:

> . . . a piece of literature exists in its form. We shall be constantly concerned not only because questions of form are in themselves important, but because without an understanding of, and feeling for, form, we can never grasp the human significance of literature.[32]

Thus Brooks and his colleagues reveal the function of literary forms; they help the reader to understand the significance of a literary piece. Readers use literary genres or forms to distinguish kinds of literature and to facilitate their own comprehension of what a particular work intends to signify.

There are many reasons why such conceptions of literary genres have been challenged by contemporary authors. First, is it always possible to distinguish literary types, or might not a specific writing be a conflation or elision of two types? Could a theology be written in a poetic rather than expository form? Is theology fundamentally narrative, as some have suggested? Second, might not the acceptance of or the presumption of the presence of a particular genre mask or conceal rather than reveal the "human significance" of a particular piece? Do not such presumptions concerning genre deprive the reader of the discovery of his or her own significance, meaning, or truth within a piece of writing? These are each important hermeneutical and philosophical issues which cannot be adequately addressed here. A sensitivity to these questions, however, has shaped the understanding of theological genre to be offered below.

Genres, I wish to argue, are convenient ways of classifying particular forms of written and oral expression. Further, a genre should be understood as a form, as that which makes something to be what it is and which distinguishes it from other objects. Again, as in the classical notion of form, genres are related to the meaning of objects. As employed in this context "form" does not mean a principle of being, but rather pertains to Lonergan's metaphysics of knowledge. A form is what can be understood as a concrete and intelligible unity, identity, whole.[33] Like Lonergan's theory of knowledge in general, the notion of form is also the product of the isomorphic relationship between the knower and the known. Genres are the result of acts of understanding of written or oral expressions. The kind of genre something belongs to, therefore, is the product both of what has been written or said and of what has been assimilated by the reader or hearer. Such a conception of genre concedes to the text its own facticity and givenness, but it also acknowledges that what it is, is also the result of the minds that inquire into it. What the genre signifies is in part the product of what the author wrote or said; but its meaning is also the result of the interests and attentiveness of the audience. The meaning of the text is neither purely subjective nor purely objective, but rather the result of the interaction between the knower and the "to be known." Because acts of understanding are by their very nature public and shared, there exists the possibility of commonly acknowledged meanings of texts. Because acts of understanding are not static, but rather yield to further and more complete evaluations, forms and genres are not static. They are open to review and amendment and rejection.

It is in such a manner that theology should be understood. "Theology," Lonergan wrote, "is a product not only of the religion it investigates and expounds but also of the cultural ideals and norms that set its problems and direct its solutions."[34] This means that theology is the understanding of the possible meaning of a religious tradition within a specific cultural setting. The culture, in a sense, becomes a source for the inquiring mind; it sets the preconditions of what can be meaningful. The provocative characteristic of religious traditions, their "to be known," is their capacity to occasion transcendence for communities as well as individuals. David Tracy's exposition of theology as the interpretation of the revelatory capacity of classic texts to society, church, and the academy represents a similar understanding.[35] Both conceptions of theology presume that as culture changes, theology will change in response, and that religious traditions can be significant factors in cultural development.

The stipulation that moral theology, particularly that of the neo-Thomist manuals, was a theological genre seeks to highlight the structure, the threefold division that is found in virtually all of these texts. First, they each contain a treatment of what has been called "general moral theology." Under this heading were considered human acts, the nature of morality, conscience, law, and sin. To the extent that the manuals address systematic and theoretical issues, they do so within this context. Second, each of these manuals contains an exposition of particular sins which was developed in relationship to either the theological and cardinal virtues or to the ten commandments. This section of the manual genre was intended to assist priests in the determination of the nature and species of sin; it was keyed directly to the preparation of ministers of the sacrament of penance. The inherent weakness of this approach, it will be argued in subsequent chapters, was that its stress on acts and particular sins destroyed the emphasis which the neo-Thomist manualists intended to place on the role of the virtues. The first two parts of the manuals were attempts, largely patterned on Busenbaum's *Medulla*, to separate large sections of the *Summa Theologiae* from their original theological context, and to create a theological genre distinct from that of the *Summa*. The third part of the manuals consisted of a presentation of the canon law of the sacraments. Thus the second and third parts of the manuals of moral theology provided generations of priests with the preparation needed for their roles in a sacramental ministry.

Literary genres, however, are not only classifications of texts or utterances; they also facilitate an understanding of the human significance of the experience or vision which the author wishes to communicate. The common vision of the manuals of moral theology was the need of Christians for a sacramental ministry as the essential means of salvation. Life within the church as envisioned by this model was also asserted as a need of all persons. The institutional church had become the sole instrument of salvation. The meaning of human well-being was understood within this context. The wider Christian and cultural conceptions of authentic Christianity and human existence were dangers and aberrations rather than legitimate sources of complementarity.

New genres, Todorov has argued, come from other genres. "A new genre is always the transformation of one or several old genres: by inversion, by displacement, by combination."[36] The neo-Thomist manuals were the product of displacement and combination. Their first and second parts were separated from the unified vision of the *Summa Theologiae* for specific pastoral and pedagogical purposes. The concerns of the manuals were not the wider cultural concerns of university theology, but the more limited interests of a sacramental ministry directed to members of the church. The second and particularly the third parts of the manuals were assimilations of the *Summae Confessorum*; their focus was on the application of the law and questions of casuistry.

The chapters which follow will argue that changes in culture, a new understanding of ministry within Catholicism, and the development of more sophisticated theological paradigms and moral theories have each contributed to the obsolescence of this theological genre. A theological genre which had an illustrious history for almost four hundred years has become a purple patch when set against the fabric of contemporary theological, ministerial, and cultural concerns. As the penitentials, the *Summae Confessorum*, and the systematic theology of the *Summa Theologiae* were the preconditions for the development of the manuals, so the manuals themselves have become the antecedents to a genre of Christian ethical reflection which remains yet undetermined. The contemporary significance of the manuals, however, remains important. More than any other source they influenced how Catholics thought about moral issues. The anger, frustration, and incomprehensibility expressed at times by Catholics with regard to the moral teaching of their church are fundamentally reactions to the teachings of the neo-Thomist manuals. But as Catholicism's most recent memory of its moral tradition, the manuals may also contain latent possibilities for a vital theological ethic, drawn from the Catholic tradition, which would be illuminative of the moral issues which are important for contemporary North American culture.

## NOTES

1. Throughout this essay the manuals of moral theology and moral theology are used interchangeably. The manuals were the books which conveyed moral theology. Christian theology with regard to morality and ministry existed before 1545 and continues to occur after 1965. Although analogues existed both inside and outside of Catholicism, moral theology was a theological genre unique to Roman Catholicism from the counter-Reformation until Vatican II.
2. Jean-Yves Calvez and Jacques Perrin, *The Church and Social Justice*, trans., J.R. Kerwin (London: Burns and Oates, 1961).
3. David Hollenbach, *Claims In Conflict: Retrieving and Renewing the Catholic Human Rights Tradition* (New York: Paulist Press, 1979).
4. Jacques Maritain, *Integral Humanism*, trans., Joseph W. Evans (Notre Dame: University of Notre Dame Press, 1968); *Scholasticism and Politics* (Garden City: Image Books, 1960); *Man and the State* (Chicago: University of Chicago Press, 1951); *Neuf Lecons sur les Notions Premières de la Philosophie Morale* (Paris: Chez Pierre Tequi, 1949). These works serve only as an indication of Maritain's contribution.

5. Etienne Gilson, *History of Christian Philosophy in the Middle Ages* (New York: Random House, 1955); *The Christian Philosophy of St. Thomas Aquinas*, trans., L.K. Shook (New York: Random House, 1956).
6. Bernard Lonergan, S.J., *Method In Theology* (New York: Herder and Herder, 1972), 178.
7. Vincent MacNamara, *Faith and Ethics* (Dublin: Gill and Macmillan, 1985), 14.
8. Tzvetan Todorov, *The Fantastic*, trans., Richard Howard (Cleveland: The Press of Case Western Reserve University, 1973), 4.
9. Ignaz von Döllinger and Fr. Heinrich Reush, *Geschichte der Moralstreitigkeiten* (Nordlingen: Verlag der C. H. Beck'shen Buchhandlung, 1889), 28.
10. Jaroslav Pelikan, *Reformation of Church and Dogma (1300–1700)* vol. 4 of *The Christian Tradition* (Chicago: University of Chicago Press, 1984), 248.
11. *The Church Teaches*, ed., The Jesuit Fathers of St. Mary's College (St Louis: B. Herder Book Company, 1955), #793.
12. Johann Theinner, *Die Entwicklung der Moraltheologie zur eigenständigen Disziplin* (Regensburg: Verlag Friedrich Pustet, 1970), 57.
13. Ibid., 116.
14. Ibid., 314. see also John Mahoney, *The Making of Moral Theology* (Oxford: Clarendon Press, 1987), Chapter Four, "Teaching With Authority."
15. Edgar Hocedez, S.J., *Histoire de la Théologie du XIXe Siècle* (Bruxelles: L'Édition Universelle, 1946), 325.
16. Bernard Häring, C.SS.R., *The Law of Christ*, 3 vols. trans., Edwin G. Kaiser, C.PP.S. (Westminster: The Westminster Press, 1966), I:20.
17. von Döllinger and Reush, *Geschichte*, 13–14.
18. Harold J. Berman, *The Interaction of Law and Religion* (Nashville: Abingdon Press, 1974), 61.
19. John A. McHugh, O.P. and Charles J. Callan, O.P., *Moral Theology*, 2 vols. (New York: Joseph F. Wagner, Inc., 1929), title page.
20. Marcellinus Zalba, S. J., *Theologiae Moralis Compendium*, 2 vols. (Matriti: Biblioteca De Autores Cristianos, 1958), title page. *Scientiarum Dominus* required the teaching of the theology of St. Thomas in Roman Catholic seminaries.
21. Aloysio Sabetti, S.J. and Timotheo Barrett, S.J., *Compendium Theologiae Moralis*, 30th ed. (Neo Eboraci: Frederick Pustet Co., Inc., 1924), title page.
22. "Aeterni Patris" in *One Hundred Years of Thomism*, ed., Victor B. Brezik, C.S.B. (Houston: Center for Thomistic Studies, 1981), 195.

23. Yves M.-J. Congar, O.P., *A History of Theology*, trans. and ed., Hunter Guthrie, S.J. (New York: Doubleday and Company, 1968), 178. Congar is citing Noel Alexandre, *Theologia dogmatica et moralis* (1693), 178.

24. Bernard Lonergan, S. J., "Theology In Its New Context," in *A Second Collection*, ed., William F. J. Ryan, S. J. and Bernard Tyrrell, S.J. (Philadelphia: The Westminster Press, 1974), 57.

25. Thomas F. O'Meara, O. P., *Romantic Idealism and Roman Catholicism: Schelling and the Theologians* (Notre Dame: University of Notre Dame Press, 1982), 2–3.

26. Gerald McCool, S.J., *Catholic Theology In the Nineteenth Century* (New York: The Seabury Press, 1977), 32.

27. Ibid., 196.

28. Sabetti and Barrett, *Compendium Theologiae Moralis*, title page.

29. McCool, *Catholic Theology*, 232.

30. David F. Kelly, *The Emergence of Roman Catholic Medical Ethics in North America* (New York: Edwin Mellon Press, 1979), 311–320.

31. Cleanth Brooks and Robert B. Heilman, *Understanding Drama* (New York: Henry Holt and Company, 1945), 24.

32. Cleanth Brooks, John Thibaut Purser, and Robert Penn Warren, *An Approach to Literature*, 4th edition (New York: Appleton-Century-Crofts, 1964), 8.

33. Bernard Lonergan, S.J., *Insight: A Study of Human Understanding* (New York: Philosophical Library, 1957), 435.

34. Lonergan, "Theology In Its New Context," 58.

35. David Tracy, *The Analogical Imagination: Christian Theology and the Culture of Pluralism* (New York: Crossroad, 1981).

36. Tzvetan Todorov, "The Origin of Genres," *New Literary History* 8 (1976):161.

*3.*

# The Theology of the Neo-Thomist
# Manuals of Moral Theology

The previous chapter provided an historical account of the cultural, ministerial, and theological factors which gave rise to the manuals of moral theology. The manuals were developed within the thought patterns of the counter-Reformation and were intended as texts for seminarians preparing for a primarily sacramental ministry. The manuals of the neo-Thomist era were composed from shortly before 1879 until Vatican II.

Gerald McCool has proposed a further refinement of the neo-Thomist era in Catholic thought.[1] He has suggested that it be divided into five distinct periods: 1) turn of the century neo-Thomism from its origins until 1900; 2) 1900 to World War I; 3) the period between the wars; 4) World War II until Vatican II; 5) Vatican II to the present. The first period has been sufficiently discussed in the previous chapter; the fourth and fifth will be examined in subsequent chapters. The manuals to be studied in this chapter were products of the second and third periods; they were written or edited between approximately 1900 and 1960. The issues which McCool employs to divide this half-century into two distinct periods, the emergence of Maritain's traditional Thomism, Gilson's historical Thomism, and Marechal's transcendental Thomism,[2] were simply not factors which influenced the positions of the manualists. Indeed this is an important point in interpreting these writings. It implies that their neo-Thomist character was primarily influenced by the first period of neo-Thomism. The manuals give no indication that their authors were familiar with the works of Maritain, Gilson, or Marechal. It was, rather, the neo-Thomism of Kleutgen, Liberatore and other early members of this movement which most directly influenced the theology and philosophy of the manuals of moral theology. Although there were some early forebodings concerning the nature and orientation of moral theology prior to the end of World War II, it was only after the war that the historical

48

character of theology and the need for a transcendental basis for their task began to find expression in the writings of moral theologians.

In order to assess correctly the manuals of moral theology to be examined in this chapter it is necessary to distinguish neo-Thomism and neo-scholasticism. Both movements were the result of Leo XIII's *Aeterni Patris* and its emphasis on the theology and philosophy of Thomas Aquinas. Neo-scholasticism construed Leo's mandate as a return to Catholic medieval thought in general. It produced new editions of ancient and medieval manuscripts as well as massive historical investigations of them. Neo-scholasticism in general, as was instanced particularly in the writings of Etienne Gilson and Jacques Maritain, was open to dialogue and discussion with modern philosophy. Neo-scholasticism was a more significant movement among Catholic philosophers than Catholic theologians. Neo-Thomism was a more specific movement. It focused exclusively on the writings of St. Thomas. The basic positions of neo-Thomism were the result of Joseph Kleutgen's interpretation of the writings of St. Thomas; key aspects of Thomas' philosophy and theology as interpreted by Kleutgen became the fundamental tenets of the movement. Neo-Thomism intended to offer a coherent, unified systematic theology and philosophy as an alternative to the philosophy of Immanuel Kant and other modern philosophers. From 1879 till Vatican II neo-Thomism was the centerpiece of papal theology. It would be in relation to neo-Thomism that the papacy would evaluate the writings of the modernists as well as those of the theologians associated with the *nouvelle théologie* in the post-World War II era.[3] The manuals studied in this and the next two chapters are neo-Thomist manuals. Examples of neo-scholastic moral theology will be examined in a subsequent chapter.

There are six topics, included within virtually all of the manuals, which can serve as indices to the theology of these documents. First, what was the understanding of moral theology as a theological discipline? Second, in what manner was the end or goal of human existence defined? Third, on what grounds was merit to be attributed to human acts? Fourth, what was the function and significance of the new law? Fifth, what role was attributed to the virtues and to the theological virtues in particular? Sixth, what was the definition of sin according to these authors? The responses to these six topics indicate how the manualists understood the issues which McCool proposed as central to the theological vision of the neo-Thomists: first, the proper distinction between nature and grace, faith and reason, body and soul, philosophy and theology; second, the unifying theological theme of St. Thomas: "the idea of God, considered in his inner being and his exterior creative and redemptive work."[4]

Later chapters will assess the adequacy of the theology of the manuals of moral theology from the perspective of the pre-Vatican II era as well as

1. UNDERSTANDING MORAL THEOL AS A DISCIPLINE?
2. END OR GOAL OF HUMAN EXISTENCE DEFINED?
3. MERIT FOR HUMAN ACTS?
4. FUNCTION OF NEW LAW?
5. VIRTUES?
6. SIN?

the post-conciliar era. The task of this chapter is threefold. First, the identification of the genre's theology as instanced in the six indices will be noted. Second, the neo-Thomist imprint on the theology of the manuals will be examined in terms of the set of distinctions described by McCool as pivotal to this theology. The third part will seek to uncover the remnants of Kleutgen's unifying theological theme in the theology of the manualists. The last point will require an examination of that theme in the writings of Aquinas himself.

## I. The Theological Indices of the Neo-Thomist Manuals

### (A) *The Conception of Moral Theology as a Theological Discipline*

A number of distinct topics can be used to reveal the self-understanding of moral theology which existed among its early twentieth century practitioners. Some began their manuals with a definition of their discipline. They frequently alluded to the sources of moral theology and the methods appropriate to that discipline. Each of these factors can be used to portray the conception of theology operative throughout these documents.

Moral theology, Henry Davis wrote, "is that branch of theology which states and explains the law of human conduct in reference to man's supernatural destiny, the vision and fruition of God."[5] In only a slightly different vein, John McHugh and Charles Callan introduced the discipline as:

> . . . a technical and scientific treatise on human conduct, [dealing] exclusively or primarily with vice and sin, and that is intended only to enable the priest rightly to administer the Sacrament of penance . . . [it] has also a much higher purpose which is to enable man not only to know what is forbidden and how he may escape from moral disease and death, but also to understand what are his duties and how he may live the life of grace and virtue.[6]

Similar definitions can be found among other moralists.[7]

There were two key issues in these definitions. The most consistent element was that they understood moral theology as primarily concerned with human conduct in relation to the final end of humanity. A teleological orientation was introduced into this ethic from its inception. It should be noted however, as will become more evident in a subsequent discussion, that the emphasis was on conduct and actions conducive to that final end; the moralists did not provide an elaborate treatment of the end itself. Another consistent element was that the manualists construed their task to be primarily the determination of sins and duties in order to prepare seminarians for the proper administration of the sacrament of penance. The focus of this literature was on what one may not do, what constituted a violation of the virtues or the commandments; it did not emphasize positive moral duties inherent in Christian existence.

Revelation, reason, and tradition were the most frequently cited sources of moral theology.[8] The role of reason within neo-Thomist manuals will be examined in the context of the ethical aspects of their writings. Tradition seems to have been taken in a very wide sense. The neo-Thomist authors often referred to the Fathers of the Church; St. Augustine was the most frequently cited patristic source. The writings of Thomas Aquinas and Alphonsus Liguori were the two most frequently cited theological sources. Two other very important aspects of the tradition were the teaching of previous moralists and teachings of the church.

The importance of the teaching of previous moralists was a particularly significant factor in this theological genre. The double names that many of these volumes bear usually do not indicate joint authorship, but rather that the second person re-edited and modernized in some way a manual developed by a previous author. Some of these manuals were the consequence of authorship which went back four or more generations. In at least one case, the work of one theologian produced a series of different manuals. The writing of the nineteenth-century Jesuit John Peter Gury became the basis of manuals by Bulot, Buceroni, Balnerini/Genicot, Sabetti, and Noldin.[9] Noldin's work was revised to become Noldin/Schmitt, and Sabetti's *Compendium Theologiae Moralis*, a manual introduced to America at Woodstock College in Maryland and specifically adapted for American usage, became Sabetti/Barrett/Creeden. The authority of these writings was not the product of the talents or insights of a particular author, but rather the authority of a self-authenticating tradition. The manuals retain a medieval notion of authority residing in the text and the tradition, rather than in the authority of the author.

The teaching authority of the church was an especially important theological source; it probably provided the most significant catalyst for change. These manuals were post-Vatican I documents composed for a community headed by a papacy whose control within the church and among its theologians was unprecedented.[10] The previous chapter has already alluded to some of the dangers of ecclesiastical positivism. *Aeterni Patris* (1879) which introduced Thomism as the dominant theological system in the seminaries, was only the first of the modern attempts by the papacy to determine the direction of Catholic theological development. In fact, it was Joseph Kleutgen who first introduced the notion of "the ordinary magisterium" into Catholic ecclesiology and who advocated a position which made the natural law an appropriate topic of papal teaching. At least from the time of Pius IX,

there was a very close facsimile between neo-Thomist theology and that of
the papacy.[11] The decree *Lamentabili* (1907) and the encyclical *Pascendi*
(1907), issued by Pius X in response to Catholic modernism, as well as Pius
XII's *Humani Generis* (1950) in regard to the *nouvelle théologie* were each
instances of papal efforts to control the trends within Catholic theology. The
guidelines established by these documents were largely adhered to by the
authors of the manuals. The new code of canon law published in 1918 was to
occasion a major revision of all of the manuals. They now had to be brought
into accord with the new canons.

The casual contemporary reader of a manual of moral theology may
find it strange that these authors considered revelation, meaning by that the
scriptures, a significant source for moral theology. Indeed if one means by
that *sola scriptura*, or that Christian ethics begins with a biblical view of
morality such as "obedient love,"[12] then one will not find such a preconcep-
tion verified in these texts. Charles Curran has commented that "the failure
to find a basic orientation and grounding in the Scriptures frequently is
mentioned as a most important lack in the older textbooks."[13] And James
Gustafson has suggested that Protestant readers of the manuals have "good
reason to assert that scripture, when used, was generally cited to proof-text
an argument basically derived from the natural law."[14] The contentions of
both Curran and Gustafson, however, fail to comprehend adequately the
methodology of the manualists.

There were two methods consistently employed by the manualists,
scholasticism and casuistry. The latter was an approach to the resolution of
specific moral questions through the application of appropriate laws. Casuistry pertains more properly to the moral theory of the manuals than to
their theology. The scholastic method was the methodology most frequently
used by the manualists.[15] However, there seem to have been several notions
associated with this methodology among the manualists. Hürth and Abellan
construed scholasticism in a somewhat traditional manner. They refer to:

> . . . the scholastic method in which supposed norms are related to
> the positive sources of theology; it especially requires that the
> intrinsic nature of moral norms be explored; it investigates the
> ultimate universal norms of morality from which more particular
> norms flow, and it collects norms and principles in one scientific
> system whose individual parts, like the members of some organ-
> ism, are joined together as a composite.[16]

This definition retains the thirteenth century notion that the scholastic
method seeks the systematic ordering of authorities. Like their counterparts
among the medieval scholastics, the manualists considered scripture and the

patristic commentaries upon scripture to be among the positive sources of theology. In the *Summa Theologiae*, for instance, the *sed contra*—the turning point in Thomas' arguments—was frequently a quote from scripture or a citation from a patristic commentary on scripture.

Further, since for the manualists—and again they were following Aquinas on this point—the new law or the law of Christ adds no positive moral duties not already included within the natural law, the blending of reason and revelation as sources from which specific moral obligations could be deduced was consistent with the methodology. Hürth and Abellan's concern to relate moral norms to the positive sources of theology, to identify the ultimate sources of moral norms, and to relate universal and particular norms in a systematic manner was consistent with the scholastic tradition.

What was near the surface in Hürth/Abellan was much more clearly expressed in McHugh/Callan. Scholastic method, they state:

> ... is a scientific statement of moral teaching through accurate definitions of terms, systematic coordination of parts, strict argumentation and defense, attention to controversies and recourse to philosophy and other natural knowledge.[17]

This was dogmatic moral theology. The methodology made no appeal to the positive sources or universal principles of moral theology. Traditional scholasticism sought to create positions from a number of diverse authorities and to harmonize such positions into a systematic whole. The McHugh/Callan definition presumes the existence of a whole which stands in need only of clarification from within and defense against external opposition. Dogmatic theology, Koch/Preuss proposed, defined the rules to be believed (*regula credendorum*); moral theology defined the rules for what ought to be done (*regula agendorum*).[18]

### (B)  The Goal of Humanity

The teleological orientation of moral theology has already been alluded to in the definition of the discipline. The neo-Thomist conception of the ultimate goal or end of human actions provided the theological basis for a fundamental characteristic of the genre. The doctrine of beatitude as the ultimate end of human existence was fundamentally a theological conception of how the goal of human existence could be known and achieved, as well as its religious significance for human existence. The manner of conceiving and explaining beatitude was largely the result of employing Aristotelian/Thomistic categories.

The metaphysics which Thomas adopted from Aristotle spoke of formal, material, efficient, and final causality. These causes were purported to be categories in which the whole of reality, being, could be interpreted and explained. The end or goal of human existence as portrayed by the manualists implied final causality. Final causality attempted to explain the "why," the ultimate purpose of a particular kind of being. Formal and material causality accounted for what something was, its defining characteristics; efficient causality explained how it came to be. Final causality explained a being's purpose or proper function within (philosophically) the realm of being or (theologically) the created and redeemed order. Final causality could be further subdivided into ultimate and proximate: that which totally and completely fulfilled the purpose of a being, and that which was an appropriate partial completion of its nature.

The consistent understanding of the neo-Thomist manualists was that "the ultimate end of man is God himself so that in all his action man must direct himself to God."[19] Davis' treatment of this topic was particularly interesting because of the manner in which a philosophical interpretation was given to a theological doctrine. The ultimate end of human nature was interpreted both objectively and subjectively. The end in itself, objectively, was presented as God's intrinsic glory; subjectively, as experienced by human beings, it was eternal happiness through the vision and fruition of God. Since the ultimate end of human nature could neither objectively nor subjectively be experienced by persons while still on their earthly pilgrimage, the emphasis fell upon the proximate end of human nature which ought to be sought within earthly existence: the love and service of God which leads to the attainment of the ultimate end and which is both an obligation and a perfecting of human nature.[20]

The doctrine of the end of human nature was clearly considered by the manualists to be a theological doctrine. It could be adequately known only through revelation and was primarily mediated to the Catholic community through dogmatic theology. The destiny of humanity was construed in this manner so as to elucidate the religious significance of human acts. Indeed it was important to know the ultimate end of human nature, but within this life it was also extremely important to have a perspective from which a life of virtue could be construed as one of "love and service of God." Thus Merkelbach could express this insight in the following manner:

By his positive will and gratuitous goodness God has destined us to his supernatural glory which is procured through habitual grace and infused virtues here on earth and by an intuitive vision of God himself in heaven.[21]

"A life of love and service of God" and a life lived "through habitual grace and infused virtues" became synonyms for what is meaningful and purposeful within human life. This same conception, however, also pointed to the basic conundrum of human existence: the end of human beings is both an obligation of and a perfection of their nature, but its achievement is totally a consequence of God's gratuitous grace.

### (C) Merit/Grace

The concept of merit has been one of the most controversial topics in the history of Christian theology. In the era of St. Augustine it wore the raiment of Pelagianism and semi-Pelagianism. And like Augustine, Luther and Calvin, moral theologians were confident that when God rewarded human works, He was really setting a crown upon His gifts. The purpose of this section cannot be an attempt to resolve the profound and important differences between Protestant and Catholic conceptions of the manner in which God cooperates in human action. The goal must be the more limited task of exploring how divine cooperation in human activity was conceived by the neo-Thomist manualists of moral theology.

The manualists' discussion of the end of human nature portrayed the human situation as one in which persons have an obligation toward a supernatural goal which they are not able to attain apart from the free gift of grace. For a human action to be proportionate to its ultimate goal and fitting to the "love and service of God" it must be a supernatural act. The consistent position of the manualists was that three things were required for an act to be supernatural: 1) it must be a morally good act; 2) it must be supernatural, i.e. elicited by the help of a supernatural principle; and 3) it must have a supernatural motive.[22] These three characteristics of the supernatural/meritorious act are essential to an adequate comprehension of this system of morality.

First of all, the act must be morally good. As will be seen in more detail in the next chapter, the object, end, and circumstances were the objective determinants of morality within this system. The end pertained to the reason or intention of an act. The circumstances referred to accidental characteristics of the act: to whom, when, where, at what time, etc. The object was the essence, the very nature of the act itself. The natural law and the new law were the primary proximate measures by which the object of an action could be assessed. For an act to be morally good, its object, end, and circumstances must each be good. If the act was deficient with regard to any one of these aspects, the entire act was assessed as morally evil. Thus for an act to be supernatural it must embrace a good object, an appropriate end, and a fitting set of circumstances.

For an act to be supernatural it also needed to be elicited by a supernatural principle. The manualists did not provide elaborate distinctions with regard to categories of grace; they did not speak of grace as operant and cooperant. The simplest and least controversial manner in which to denominate this supernatural principle will be as habitual grace. Noldin/Schmitt, for instance, understood God to be exciting and helping persons toward their ultimate goal through grace.[23] Grace cooperated with the human will in that it elicited the supernatural act, i.e. it moved the will itself to conform to a good befitting the ultimate end of human nature. The will then commanded what was required for the external performance of the act, thereby maintaining human freedom and establishing the grounds for a notion of human merit.

Although the mechanics of Aristotelian and Thomistic rational psychology were essential to the understanding of the tradition on this topic, they cannot be allowed to mask the fundamental theological insight. As did their mentor Aquinas, the manualists conceived of habitual grace and the theological virtue of charity as identical; the distinction between them was rational, not real. Charity and grace were thought to orient the will to God as the ultimate end of human life and to actions in accord with that end; charity and grace made it possible for Christians to seek a life of love and service as their proximate end. An act might have its own inherent meaning for human life; it might contribute to the maintenance of the life of an individual or the species and thus possess an inherent good (*bonum honestum*). But when elicited by grace the same act became also an embodiment of love and service of God. In this regard the neo-Thomists were faithful to the fundamental insight of St. Augustine, maintained by Thomas Aquinas, Martin Luther, and John Calvin: "You arouse us to take joy in praising you, for you have made us for yourself, and our hearts are restless until they rest in you."[24]

Finally, a supernatural act must have a supernatural motive. The significance of intention with regard to the morality of an act has already been mentioned. Slater accurately portrayed the supernatural motive as one rooted in faith.[25] Grace as charity turns the will to God as its final and ultimate good; grace as faith provides a partial, though illuminating, understanding of the goal of supernatural human action. As charity turns the will to love and service of God, so faith turns the intellect to a limited understanding of the ultimate end of human nature. Again, the integrity of human nature is protected. As acts of human morality need to be guided by reason, so acts of charity need to be illumined by faith.

### (D) The Theological Virtues

The theory of morality expounded by the neo-Thomist manuals of moral theology was an ethic of virtue. This was as true for the manualists who used the ten commandments as the schema for their exposition of specific moral issues as for those who employed the cardinal virtues. The theological virtues, and charity in particular, were construed as the foundation of the religious (supernatural) and meritorious dimension of human acts. The theological virtues were central to those manuals which derived religious duties from the virtue of religion as well as those which based such duties on the first three commandments. Again, the theological virtues were the linchpin of the manuals which based moral obligation on the cardinal virtues as well as those which based moral obligation on the fourth through tenth commandments.

Each manual treated the three theological virtues of faith, hope, and charity as infused virtues.[26] The notion of infused virtues distinguished them from acquired virtues. Prudence and temperance, for instance, were considered as dispositions or habits which through diligence and perseverance persons might be able to develop. Infused virtues, however, possessed the characteristics of grace. They were considered to be gifts freely given by God which enabled their recipients to function on a supernatural level of agency. They could not be acquired as the result of any human effort. Even tendencies or dispositions which inclined persons to be open to the reception of habitual grace and the theological virtues were themselves construed as actual graces.

Yet another common feature of the theological virtues was that their formal object was God. Faith, hope, and charity, each in its own peculiar manner, were understood to be an ordering of the person to God as one's final and ultimate end.

The manner in which grace elicited acts in the will, which in turn commanded external acts, was briefly examined earlier in this chapter in relation to the concept of merit. The manualists' discussion of the theological virtues provided a more detailed elaboration of this topic. First, the gift of the virtues imposed upon their recipient the obligation of eliciting acts of faith, hope, and charity, as well as the obligation of performing external acts consistent with each of the virtues. An elicited act is one which remains within the will; in itself it does not require any external act. Thus Prümmer argued that there was an obligation to elicit interior acts of faith when God's revelation had been sufficiently proposed to one, when a dogma of faith was proposed by the church, frequently during life, and probably at the moment of death.[27] The same author also proposed that, since human nature was embodied, there were also external acts of faith incumbent upon a Christian: a positive duty to worship and to profess one's faith when questioned by public authority as well as the negative duty not to deny one's faith. Similar interior and exterior acts, elicited and commanded, were also entailed by the virtues of hope and charity.

Second, each of the theological virtues was conceived of as being lodged in a specific faculty. Faith was the theological virtue proper to the intellect; charity and hope were located in the will. The central virtue in this tradition

was clearly charity. Like his colleagues, Prümmer contended that faith was
the result of the will, under the influence of grace, commanding the assent of
the intellect.[28] The assent of the intellect in faith was construed as a commanded act; the will commands the assent of faith to that which is to be
believed. Hope was the act of the will by which the will attaches itself to God
specifically as the final end—what is desired—whereas charity was the
orientation of the will to God as goodness and love. But the primacy among
the virtues was clearly held by charity. The will turned to God as infinite
goodness, and love prompted hope, the orientation to God as the end of
human nature. Charity commanded the intellect to accept the truths which
mediate the means to beatitude. Thus acts of hope and faith were understood
as elicited or commanded acts in relation to the virtue of charity.

The theological virtues in general, and the virtue of charity in particular, provided moral theology with its religious and supernatural foundation.
When the manualists turned their attention to the requirements of the ten
commandments or the cardinal virtues their focus would be on sin, aversion
from the plan of God, and only secondarily on moral evil. Positively, a life
lived in accord with the commandments or virtues was not esteemed principally because of the moral good which was produced, but rather for the
supernatural and meritorious character of such a life. The *a priori* conditions
for such a life, this tradition strongly maintained, were that one's heart be
turned to God as the ultimate good and the final end, and that one's mind
and will be turned to revelation as the source of one's knowledge of the
means to that end. The Christian operated not on natural, but on supernatural principles.

### (E) The New Law

The manualists' treatments of the new law are included among the
indices to the theology of the genre in order to reinforce what has already
been stated under the headings of merit/grace and the theological virtues.
The common feature of these topics, as has already been suggested with
regard to merit and the virtues, was that they were only notionally distinct.
They were three different manners of comprehending the significance of
grace in relation to diverse aspects of human nature and human operations.
What the new law added to the concepts of merit/grace and the virtues was a
source of information concerning what it was that Christians were to do.

The treatise on law developed by Thomas in the *Summa Theologiae*
was more or less reproduced in each of the manuals. They each considered
the nature of law, and then the eternal, natural, divine, and human law.
Unlike Aquinas, the manualists did not discuss law within the wider theological context of divine providence and government, although Zalba alluded to
this.[29] They all understood law as a divine ordering. The ultimate norm of

morality was the eternal law, the divine plan for all of creation. Since that plan exists only in God's mind, it could not be known directly, but only through an apprehension of the manner in which it was embedded in creation. The natural law was the eternal law within the created order and particularly within human nature. As such the natural law was capable of being known by all persons. The eternal law was further clarified through the divine law revealed in the old and new covenants. Human law, to the extent that it was truly law, was a specific embodiment of eternal law as known by a reasonable legislator, was congruent to religion, convenient for the moral discipline of a community, and helpful to salvation. Each of these kinds of law embodied the basic definition of law enunciated by Thomas and repeated by each of the manualists: a law is "nothing else than an ordinance of reason for the common good, made by him who has care of the community, and promulgated." (*Summa Theologiae* I–II, 90.4) The eternal and the natural laws will be discussed more extensively in Chapter Four; only the new law, i.e. the law of the new convenant, is directly germane to the theology of the manuals.

The new law was consistently understood as first and foremost an interior event. The new law was the gift of the Holy Spirit. Sabetti/Barrett referred to the new law as the law of grace and of liberty.[30] Hürth/Abellan referred to the form of the new law as not in the first instance written, but rather handed on by preaching and impressed upon our hearts by the Holy Spirit.[31] Similar expressions ran throughout the neo-Thomist tradition. The new law was principally the gift of the Holy Spirit impressed upon the hearts of Christians and thus turning their wills to God. The new law was understood as identical to grace and the theological virtues, but viewed from a different perspective.

What the new law added to the notions of grace and the theological virtues was the notion of positive precepts: external law. This was perhaps most clearly developed by McHugh/Callan. In a set of companion statements they portrayed the tension between the inner and the outer characteristics of the law. "In both testaments," they wrote:

> ... grace and the Holy Spirit are given through faith in Christ (internal law), and doctrines, commandments, and ceremonies are prescribed (external law). ... In both testaments men are justified and saved through faith and works ... and not through the external written law or letter.[32]

The new law was consistently viewed as primarily internal, as justifying grace, as the theological virtues. But as the virtues were construed to require commanded, external acts, so the new law was interpreted as being a source of information for what Christians ought to do, how they ought to live. The sacraments, of course, were the quintessential acts derived from the new law.

Indeed as one studies the special moral theology of the manualists one begins to suspect that the primacy of the inner aspect of the new law was being obscured by the requirements of the external law. The addition of one word to the presentation of the new law by some manualists was indicative of this. Unlike Thomas, some manualists began to refer to the divine *positive* law.[33] As used here, the notion of positive law was a nineteenth century phenomenon.

The external law was a mainstay of the manualist genre which was specified in four ways. The manuals spoke of theological precepts grounded in the theological virtues, the moral precepts contained in the decalogue or the cardinal virtues which were confirmed and perfected by Christ, the precepts of the sacraments as the indispensible means of grace, and the ecclesiastical precepts of canon law. The new law as external was thus understood as providing the basis for the development and organization of special moral theology: duties related to the theological virtues, duties stemming from the decalogue or the cardinal virtues, and the duties arising from the canon law. The antecedents to the manualist genre, the medieval penitentials and the *Summae Confessorum*, the history of the decretals and canon law, had all predisposed Thomas Aquinas and then the manualists to think of moral and ethical issues in legal categories.

### (F) Sin

The neo-Thomist tradition offered two different, although compatible, definitions of sin. The first, and probably the more frequently used, asserted that "sin is a morally bad act, a privation of some obligatory good, a deflection from the order of right reason, and therefore from the law of God."[34] Similarly, Koch/Preuss stated that: "Since all temporal laws are derived from, or contained in, the *lex aeterna*, every sin involves a violation of the will of God."[35] The distinction between the divine reason and will as the criteria for the determination of sin had its own problematic implications. Was an act sinful because it was inherently disordered, unreasonable, as Thomas proposed? Or was an act evil because God so willed, as some later interpreters of Thomas would contend? Yet another definition described sin as aversion from God, the severely inordinate adherence to a creature, and the commission of a grave injury to the rational nature of human beings and the social order.[36] Here sin was clearly understood to entail a faulty orientation toward one's final and proximate ends.

Sin was presented as a problem of the will. Rather than being turned to God as one's ultimate good and end, the sinful person adhered to some creature, loved some person or thing in a manner which was inconsistent with a life of love and service. Sin was not understood as an intellectual problem or rooted in an inability to know what ought to be done, nor was sin implicit in the love of created things, nor was sin directly identified with human inclinations or passions. For these authors sin was not a philosophical but rather a theological topic. Sin was construed as the turning of the will from God and as its turning to an inordinate love of created things or persons. Sin was also never presented as simply moral evil, but rather always entailed as well the turning of the will away from God as one's ultimate good and end.

The treatment of sin by the manualists was exhaustive. It must be remembered that a primary purpose of the genre was to prepare seminarians for the administration of the sacrament of penance and that Trent had imposed the obligation of a complete confession of sins, i.e. that all sins needed to be confessed according to their species and number. Henry Davis' treatment of these matters will be presented here but essentially the same points were made in each of the manuals.

The tradition tended to speak of four general classifications of sin. Actual/habitual referred to the difference between single or occasional sins as opposed to a general disposition to commit a particular kind of sin. Personal/original pertained to the theological distinction between sins and sin, between the sins attributable to an individual and the common state of sinfulness inherited from Adam. The mortal/venial distinction referred to the gravity of sin. Mortal sin was total aversion from God which resulted in the loss of habitual grace and charity and thus the inability to perform meritorious acts. Venial sin involved the violation of the divine order in some significant manner, but did not extend to a total aversion from God. Formal and material sins were distinguished in relation to the extent to which one comprehended and was responsible for the moral evil in one's action. The foot soldier who invaded a foreign country was only materially guilty of waging an unjust war; the general who ordered such an action and knew it to be unjust and unwarranted was formally guilty of the sin.

Although venial sins were also appropriate matter for the sacrament of penance, mortal sin absolutely needed to be confessed. It was necessary to distinguish mortal sins by kind and degree. Habitual/actual was one such important distinction. Kinds of mortal sins could be further determined in relation to the virtue to which they were contrary, or the commandment they violated. The degree of sinfulness was assessed in relation to the deliberateness, intensity, and duration of the sinful act.[37]

Besides the species of sin, the number needed to be confessed also. Sins, Davis wrote, "are numerically distinct as the acts of the will."[38] If one were to read a book listed on the index of forbidden books, each time one picked up the book and read sin occurred. If one read it through in one session, one sin; if one read it over four days, then at least four sins. If several complete objects were apprehended as distinct objects of one and the same human act, then there would be several sins. If one stole money to pay for a forbidden book, one was guilty of two sins even if one never bought the book. Again, sin was comprehended in relation to the will.

The doctrine of sin is important to an assessment of the theology of the manuals for two very different reasons. First and positively, their doctrine of sin was a theological interpretation of the nature of moral evil. Sin was primarily a turning away from God as one's ultimate good and final end. Sin also involved a perversion of the moral order, an act at variance with the divine plan of governance. Second and negatively, the doctrine of sin in the manuals, the total treatment of which was the largest portion of each manual, distorted the fundamental character of their theological ethic. Their ethic was discussed above as essentially an ethic of virtue and indeed this was the case. However, their doctrine of law, particularly divine positive law deduced from the new law, and the doctrine of sin with its emphasis on the kind, species, number, and degree of sin, gave the ethic of the manualists an act-centered hue.

## II. Manualist Theology and the Distinctions Between Nature/Grace, Faith/Reason, Body/Soul, Philosophy/Theology

Liberatore, Kleutgen and the other founders of neo-Thomism may have insisted on what they considered to be the proper distinction between these pairs of theological terms because they thought that such was the mind of St. Thomas, or perhaps because they thought that such were the requirements of an adequate systematic theology. Whatever may be the truth with regard to their reasons, we can be certain of at least this much: they believed these distinctions were important in demonstrating the inadequacies of the non-Roman theologies of the traditionalists, the ontologists, and the Tübingen school, all of whom they wished to banish from the realm of theological relevancy. As their works have been discussed by Gerald McCool, both Liberatore and Kleutgen staunchly defended these related distinctions.

Liberatore's *Istituzioni di Etica e Diritto naturale* (1865) stressed an Aristotelian interpretation of human nature. The human person was "a composite of body and soul whose natural end was beatitude to be achieved through the union of his intellect and will with the truth and goodness of infinite being."[39] Although Liberatore's work remained within the realm of philosophy, the body/soul distinction was central to his enterprise. The body along with its instinctive human drives was an insufficient ground for an adequate philosophical ethic. Neither was the human mind as a self-enclosed entity able to comprehend the world in itself, nor was an ego-centered consciousness a satisfactory basis for a philosophical ethic. The necessary assumption for any true philosophical ethic was that the moral order was "an expression of God's ideas and God's creative ordering will."[40] The moral order as expressive of God's legislative will was what had been enunciated in Aquinas' metaphysical ethics grounded in God's eternal law. Moral obligation was heteronomous. Moral obligation was the result of human freedom confronting the divinely established moral order. This position must be sharply distinguished from any ethical theory which understands the moral order to correspond simply to the dictates of human reason or to be the product of human creativity.

If in the philosophical writings of Liberatore the significance of the body/soul distinction was stressed as the correct basis for an adequate theory of moral cognition, Kleutgen's theology was to emphasize the need for a correct distinction between philosophy and theology as well as between nature and grace. He understood moral theology as "an Aristotelian science which directed man to the attainment of the supernatural end of his elevated nature-union with God in the beatific vision."[41] Philosophy as directive of human action, apart from any consideration of positive and speculative theology, could never adequately comprehend the goal of human destiny nor the steps necessary to fulfill that destiny. Philosophy retained a fundamental importance within this perspective, however, because it provided the theologian with a metaphysical framework as well as a set of explanatory categories which rendered the data of theology coherent and which were illuminative of the human situation. The importance of this conception of the relationship between philosophy and theology was even more sharply stressed in Kleutgen's discussion of the nature/grace distinction.

Kleutgen's neo-Thomist theology construed sanctifying grace as an Aristotelian accident, an entitive habit inhering in the soul. As an entitive habit inhering in the soul, sanctifying grace was a stable, relatively permanent modification of human nature. The theological virtues of faith, hope, and charity were understood as operative habits inhering in the faculties of the intellect and will.[42] They enabled the intellect and will to operate on the supernatural level and enabled the acts of these two faculties to be worthy of merit. Thus the theological phenomena to be explained, sanctifying grace and the theological virtues, were depicted in Aristotelian metaphysical categories. Sanctifying grace was an accidental modification of human nature; it was not a substantial alteration of human nature. Human nature remained human nature. Sanctifying grace restored what had been lost in the fall of Adam and Eve: human nature's capacity to attain its supernatural destiny. It was the soul, not the body, which sanctifying grace altered. The theological virtues enabled Christians to perform acts congruent with their supernatural destiny. As sanctifying grace modified human nature at the level of its being, so the theological virtues modified human nature at the level of its operation. The categories of entitive and operative habits enabled Kleutgen to interpret and explain the theological data of sanctifying grace and the theological virtues. The metaphysical language explained how these gifts of God related to and gave new modes of operation to human nature. As McCool summarizes Kleutgen's position:

> The entitive habit of grace was the indispensible metaphysical ground of man's supernatural life as a child of God. The operative habits of faith, hope, and charity were rooted in the entitive habit of sanctifying grace. From these three theological virtues came man's power to persevere in his practice of the moral virtues of prudence, justice, fortitude, and temperance.[43]

The importance of these paired theological terms for the enterprise of the neo-Thomists was particularly evident in Kleutgen's assessment of the writings of the Tübingen moral theologian John Baptist Hirscher. Hirscher, a follower of Drey, developed a species of moral theology independent of the seventeenth and eighteenth century manualist sources. The idea of the Kingdom of God was central to his theological vision. He construed the Christian community as the context in which this fundamental idea strove for realization. His use of Drey's theology resulted not in a metaphysical but in a modal conception of grace in which "the supernatural order was grounded upon God's ceaseless free directing activity which was required for the realization of the Kingdom of God among men."[44] The divine ordering of the human world was not understood in relation to entitive and operative habits, but rather in relation to a conception of the manner in which divine efficient causality operated in temporal sequences of events. God was constantly acting immediately upon the system of nature, not just to sustain it, but to intervene directly in order to produce new events whose *raison d'être* was found in God's own directing providence. "The supernatural order was an organically and genetically related series of events which, as events, were part of the order of nature, but whose immediate efficient cause was the transcendent God."[45]

From Kleutgen's perspective such an interpretation of the supernatural order only produced confusion. It blurred the distinction between nature and grace so that it was difficult to identify the specific actions of God and to properly relate them to human enterprises. The positions of Drey and Hirscher conceived of divine operations in the world as independent of secondary causes. In addition the Tübingen theology lacked a central unifying framework which could guide Christians in their search for divine initiative in the contemporary world. Tübingen looked to events in the human and natural world. The neo-Thomists looked to human nature, and the soul in particular, as the locus of divine operation in the world.

It was the understanding of these pairs of theological terms held by the early neo-Thomists which influenced the positions of the late nineteenth and twentieth century manualists. Their conceptions of the discipline of moral theology, the end or goal of human existence, grace, and the theological virtues were largely an assimilation of the work of their early neo-Thomist forerunners. The developments of neo-Thomism in its second and third phases, signified by the emergence of Maritain's traditional Thomism, Gilson's historical Thomism, and Marechal's transcendental Thomism, do not appear to have altered the manner in which the authors of the manuals conceived these issues. There was one further aspect of the work of the original neo-Thomists which would significantly influence the theology of the manuals of moral theology: the concept of a unifying architectonic theological principle.

## III. The Unifying Theological Theme of the Neo-Thomists

The Aristotelian metaphysics which the neo-Thomists assimilated through their study of Aquinas provided them not only with a set of interpretative categories, but also with a metaphysical framework which related and grounded the categories in reality. In the writings of Aquinas, Kleutgen argued,

> . . . the architectonic idea was the idea of God, considered in his inner being and his exterior creative and redemptive work. St. Thomas' idea of God was the idea of the God who was related to the universe as its original source and its ultimate end.[46]

What Kleutgen was alluding to in this passage was to become a matter of central importance to the work of the neo-Thomist manualists. The notion of a metaphysical framework which would relate the various doctrines of theology and offer a worldview compatible with philosophical realism provided the basic theoretical structure for their theology. In this final section, the origin of this framework in the writings of Aquinas will be traced and then its significance for the neo-Thomist manuals indicated.

The fundamental unifying theme of Thomas Aquinas' *Summa Theologiae* as well as his *Summa Contra Gentiles* was the *exitus/reditus* schema which he adopted from Albert the Great and the Dionysian tradition. Thomas employed this unifying outline not only in his mature works, but also in his commentary on the *Sentences* of Peter Lombard.[47] The *exitus/reditus* plan was an important and consistent element in the theology of Aquinas.

The *exitus/reditus* schema considered how all things proceed out from God (*exitus*) and how all things return to God (*reditus*). According to Aquinas what proceeded most fundamentally from God was being. Being was divided into various genera which in turn were subdivided according to their specific differences. Thus human beings were understood to belong to the animal genus. What distinguished human beings from other animals was their rational nature. Thus both the *Summa Theologiae* and the *Summa Contra Gentiles* begin, after a discussion of the existence of God and his attributes, with a description of God as the cause of reality, as the ultimate efficient, formal, and final cause of all that exists, of angels and humans, organic and inorganic beings. That these beings exist, as well as the manner in which they exist, was attributable to God alone. Associated with this metaphysical framework were the theological doctrines of creation and providence. This position wedded philosophical realism to theological doctrines, i.e. it purported to provide an exhaustive explanation of the world, of reality. The *exitus* pattern was the subject of Part One of the *Summa Theologiae* and Books One and Two of the *Summa Contra Gentiles*.

The *reditus* was depicted in the Second and Third Parts of the *Summa Theologiae* and Books Three and Four of the *Summa Contra Gentiles*. The return of all things and humanity in particular to God was accomplished in two ways. First, according to this framework God had endowed his rational creatures with the end or goal of beatitude and, through their intellects and wills, with an intrinsic and natural orientation toward that end; he also instructed human beings by his law and assisted them by his grace. Second, in the Third Part of the *Summa Theologiae* and the Fourth Book of the *Summa Contra Gentiles*, Thomas examined the incarnation, the sacraments and the final things as the historically conditioned means of salvation. Thus the return pattern enabled Aquinas to present and systematically relate the theological doctrines of the supernatural end, law, grace, the incarnation and the sacraments. The *reditus* pattern and the theological doctrines associated with it intended to portray the fundamental structure, orientation, and dynamics of Christian experience in the redeemed order.

Throughout both the *exitus* and the *reditus* schemata a tight relation between theology and metaphysics was maintained. Chenu has referred to this plan as:

> . . . a magnificent means of intelligibility: in this way every thing, every being, every action, every destiny was to be placed, known, and judged according to that supreme causality, wherein their

ultimate causes will be wholly revealed in the light of God Himself.[48]

The plan provided a framework in which all of reality could be understood in relation to the Aristotelian/Thomistic notion of causality; all of reality and human existence in particular was construed from the perspective of formal, efficient, and final causality. Further, it provided a framework in which the basic doctrines of Christianity could be understood in relationship to one another. Philosophically it was an inductive system, which interpreted fundamental characteristics of the world as Thomas experienced it: contingency, change, degrees of goodness, and purposefulness. Theologically it was a deductive system, which moved from the acceptance of basic Christian affirmations to a rendering of the world as intelligible and purposeful. The Thomistic schema, however, was not simply a theoretical construct, but rather a system which purported to state the nature of reality—it was a form of realism. It was metaphysical in the classical sense; it explained the nature of and structure of reality itself. This position viewed reality as "an ontological order which furnish[ed] an admirable foundation for an epistemological order."[49] Note, however, that the ontological order grounds and is the basis of the epistemological order.

The *exitus/reditus* plan was fundamentally philosophical in its origin and orientation. In the hands of a theologian with the capacities of Aquinas, this philosophical doctrine took on a specifically theological hue. Aquinas achieved this transformation by his development of the doctrine of providence. This was a theme to which Thomas devoted considerable attention—he addressed it in four major writings. The *Expositio in Job ad Litteram* was largely devoted to interpreting the story of Job as an actual historical occurrence, i.e. literally, thus not in an allegorical or tropological manner. The events of the life of Job needed to be assessed, his argument suggested, in light of the doctrine of providence. In both of the *Summae*, the doctrine of providence was introduced as the transition between the going out of all things from God and their return to God. God was not only the cause of all, not just the Creator, but he also preserved all things in being; he was the sustainer of all as well as the ultimate cause of the operation of all. In addition, Thomas devoted two questions of the *De Veritate* to the topics of providence and predestination.

The significance of the doctrine of providence to Aquinas' theology may be the result of either the systematic value he attributed to it, or it may reflect the inherent importance of this doctrine. Certainly one reason the doctrine was so important for Thomas was because it had been denied by the Averroists. Siger of Brabant and others among the liberal arts faculty at the University of Paris, were introducing Aristotle as interpreted by Arab philosophers, Averroes in particular. Following Averroes they denied that divine providence extended to the affairs of individuals. The reasons for this involve such complex issues as the notion of a universal mind and the manner in which the celestial spheres influence human affairs, matters over which we need not delay. The important point is that, given the position of the Averoists, Thomas felt compelled to defend and maintain the *doctrina Christiana* as he had received it from the tradition. A constant theme of Thomas' exposition of the doctrine of providence was that it extended to the operations of individuals.

Thomas introduced the last section of the First Part of the *Summa Theologiae* by stating:

> After having considered the creation of things and the distinctions between them, the third issue to be considered is the government of things.[50]

In the corresponding transition in the *Summa Contra Gentiles* he wrote:

> ... there remains to be treated in this third Book His perfect authority or dignity, inasmuch as He is the End and Ruler of all things. So this will be our order of procedure: first, we shall treat of Himself, according as He is the End of all things; second, of His universal rule, according as He governs every creature; third of His particular rule, according as He governs creatures possessed of understanding.[51]

Although the topics were grouped somewhat differently in the two *Summae*, in both works a number of central theological doctrines were presented in relation to the topic of governance or providence. First, providence was presented as the manner by which God sustained his creation, but more especially the manner in which He directed creation to an end, the good. Second, the nature of the ultimate end of creation and of rational creatures in particular was enunciated. Third, Aquinas described the manner in which sub-rational beings were directed to their end by instinct, and rational beings by reason and will (the intrinsic principles of human actions). Fourth, Thomas presented the extrinsic principles of human action by which God assisted persons with His grace and instructed them by the law. These four topics were addressed in the same sequence in both *Summae*.

The unifying theme which ran throughout Aquinas' discussion of these four topics was the notion of divine governance. The discussions of beatitude, the intrinsic and extrinsic principles of human action, law and grace were each attempts to depict the manner in which God was operative in the governance of his creation, both rational and nonrational. The *Summa Theologiae* spoke of God's governance as having a twofold effect: it sustains things in the good and moves things toward the good.[52] The divine plan (*ratio*) existed first in the mind of God but also directed each individual with regard to the most minute details of his or her life. The execution of the plan, however, was accomplished through the mediation of secondary causes. Teachers, friends, or clergy could be instrumental to the living out of the plan of providence.[53] As the law and grace were construed as external means by which God influenced human acts, so he also actively governed through the intrinsic principles of intellect and will. Every power of intelligence was derived from him as the primary intelligent being. The will was moved to good because it was sufficiently and effectively moved by God—only God could fulfill the will.[54]

The *exitus/reditus* framework and the specifically theological doctrine of providence constituted the architectonic plan of the theology of Thomas Aquinas. It was this plan which Kleutgen enunciated as "the idea of God considered in his inner being and his exterior creative and redemptive work . . . [of God] who was related to the universe as its originative source and its ultimate end." There were two important implications of this theological orientation for both Thomas and the neo-Thomists. The first concerns the unity of the theological perspective and the role of moral theology within that unity. The second recognizes that this conception of theology was premised on realist claims.

The place of moral theology within the framework of Aquinas' work has been helpfully highlighted by Chenu:

> *Exitus* and *reditus* are not separate movements, which two treatments, two different treatises could study separately in a theological arrangement, but a single circuit whose unity and intelligibility rest in the natures of things, in the correspondence between form and end, according to the intelligent design of the efficient cause. In other words, theology as a science is eminently one; dogma and morality are not two parts loosely put together, one speculative, the other practical, which some exterior pressure will tie together here and there. They are the two sides of one reality, where the categories of speculative and practical, far from forming a real division, only play a part because of a constant surpassing of their technical differences.[55]

This unity within the plan of the two *Summae*, the essential interdependence between systematic theology (for Chenu, dogma) and Christian notions of morality was *de facto* destroyed by the manualists. The idea of dividing the contents of the *Summa Theologiae* into a number of philosophical and theological treatises may have been well-intentioned, it may have met a pedagogical need, but it undermined the unifying schema of the theological vision of Aquinas. Thus the process which was set in motion by William of Auxerre about 1220 to integrate the natural law within the web of theology[56] and which reached its apogee in the two *Summae* of Thomas Aquinas was destroyed by the manualists. The previous chapter indicated a number of influences which made it highly likely that counter-Reformation moral theology would have an extremely legalistic bent. When Aquinas' doctrines of law and grace were separated from the doctrine of providence, it became almost inevitable that moral theology would become a legalistic discipline verging toward positivism. Within the horizon of the doctrine of providence, and associated with the doctrine of grace, Aquinas' concept of law possessed a much more nuanced theological meaning. The manualists, on the other hand, frequently failed to demonstrate any "formal connection between the tract on the *finis* (beatitude) and the tract on the norm" of morality.[57] Again to cite Chenu:

> Morality is not a catalogue of precepts whose application is worked through innumerable cases of conscience, no more than it is a mystical flight beyond the bounds of our faculties. It is a science —practical, but a science, whose subject matter is a spiritual organism, establishing a nature in us, the principle of return to God, with all its apparatus of virtues; and the marvel of salvation is that grace, a divine life infused into our souls, will work in us as our nature, a real and permanent principle of an effective "return" to God. . . . "[58]

However deeply influenced the neo-Thomist manualists were by the writings of Kleutgen, they failed to realize, or at least were unable to assimilate the importance which he and Aquinas placed on a holistic theological viewpoint.

Finally, the implicit demand of the *exitus/reditus* plan, of the doctrine of providence, and of Kleutgen's architectonic idea was philosophical and theological realism. The schema provided a framework which claimed to interpret and render meaningful the whole of reality, especially the specifically human realm of reason, will and grace, but also the organic and inorganic world of nature and other forms of being including God, the angels and the heavenly spheres. The rise of modern science, the development of historical studies, and contemporary learning in general, would provide fundamental challenges to such claims and render many of them untenable according to the standards of current scholarship.

As Copleston has suggested with regard to Aquinas, and as Kleutgen attempted to reaffirm in the nineteenth century, the moral law was situated by this tradition in a metaphysical setting.[59] The moral order was not construed as a set of dictates of practical reason, nor as an agreed-upon system for promoting the greatest good for the greatest number, nor as a set of imperative statements which reflected one's preference, nor as a consequence of hearing God's command in the particularities of one's life. The moral order was constituted by a set of goods ordered to the ultimate end of human persons and to their proximate welfare. This was a theistic morality, neither Christocentric nor anthropocentric with regard to the origin of moral duties. The moral demand may be epistemologically independent from knowledge of God or belief in a command of God; one can know what ought to be done independently of revelation and the new law. But this morality was not "metaphysically independent,"[60] of the divine plan. What the Christian knows in the Spirit and what the pagan knows in the heart are one and the same divine plan.

## NOTES

1. Gerald McCool, S.J., "Twentieth Century Scholasticism," *Journal of Religion* 58 (1978 Supplement): S198–199.
2. Ibid., S215.
3. John P. Boyle, "The Ordinary Magisterium: Towards a History of the Concept," *Heythrop Journal* 20 (1979):380–398; 21 (1980):14–29.; T. Howland Sanks, S.J., "Co-operation, Co-option, Condemnation: Theologians and the Magisterium 1870–1978, *Chicago Studies* 18 (1979): 248–249.
4. See p. 40 above.
5. Henry Davis, *Moral and Pastoral Theology* (London: Sheed and Ward, 1935), 1:1.
6. John A. McHugh, O.P. and Charles J. Callan, O.P., *Moral Theology: A Complete Course Based on St. Thomas Aquinas and the Best Modern Authorities*, 2 vols. (New York: Joseph F. Wagner, Inc., 1929), 1:iv.
7. See H. Noldin, S.J. and A. Schmitt, S.J., *Summa Theologiae Moralis*, 2 vols., 27th ed. (Oeniponte: Sumptibus et Typis Feliciani Rauch, 1940), 1:1; Anthony Koch and Arthur Preuss, *A Handbook of Moral Theology*, 5 vols., 3rd ed. (St. Louis: B. Herder Book Co., 1925), 1:1; Marcellinus Zalba, S.J., *Theologiae Moralis Compendium: Juxta Constitutionem "Deus Scientiarum,"* 2 vols. (Matriti: Biblioteca De Autores Cristianos, 1958), 1:3; F. Hürth, S.J. and P.M. Abellan, S.J., *De Principiis, De Virtutibus et Praeceptis* (Romae: In Aedibus Pontificiae Universitatis

Gregorianae, 1948), 8. The manualist tradition stemming from St. Alphonsus Liguori does not provide a definition of the discipline; they begin immediately with Treatise I, On Human Acts, cf. Aloysio Sabetti, S.J. et Timotheo Barrett, S.J., *Compendium Theologiae Moralis*, ed., Daniele F. Creeden, S.J., 34th ed. (Neo Eboraci: Frederick Pustet Co., Inc., 1939).

 8. Davis, *Moral and Pastoral Theology*, 1:6; see also Koch/Preuss, *A Handbook of Moral Theology*, 1:26–33; McHugh/Callan, *Moral Theology*, 1:2–3; Zalba, *Theologiae Moralis Compendium*, 1:7–10; Hürth/Abellan, *De Principiis*, 12–13.

 9. Edgar Hocedez, S.J., *Le Règne de Léon XIII*, vol. 3 of *Histoire de la Théologie au XIXe Siècle* (Bruxelles: L'Édition Universelle, 1946), 326.

10. Joseph A. Komonchak, "The Ecclesial and Cultural Roles of Theology," *Proceedings of the Catholic Theological Society of America* 40 (1985):20; see also Gabriel Daly, O.S.A., *Transcendence and Immanence: A Study in Catholic Modernism* (Oxford: Clarendon Press, 1980), 9.

11. Boyle, "The Ordinary Magisterium," 14–29; Sanks, "Co-operation, Co-option, Condemnation," 248.

12. Paul Ramsey, *Basic Christian Ethics* (New York: Charles Scribner's Sons, 1950), xi.

13. Charles E. Curran, *Catholic Moral Theology in Dialogue* (Notre Dame: Fides Publishers, Inc., 1972), 24.

14. James Gustafson, *Protestant and Roman Catholic Ethics* (Chicago: The University of Chicago Press, 1978), 25.

15. Koch/Preuss, *A Handbook of Moral Theology*, 1:31; see also Dominic Prümmer, O.P., *Handbook of Moral Theology*, trans., Gerald W. Shelton, edited for American usage by Rev. John Gavin Nolan (New York: P.J. Kennedy and Sons, 1957), 3; McHugh/Callan, *Moral Theology*, 1:4–5; Hürth/Abellan, *De Principiis*, 13.

16. Hürth/Abellan, *De Principiis*, 13.

17. McHugh/Callan, *Moral Theology*, 1:5.

18. Koch/Preuss, *A Handbook of Moral Theology*, 1:5.

19. Prümmer, *Handbook of Moral Theology*, 6; see also A. Konings, C.SS.R., *Theologia Moralis*, 3rd edition (New York: Benziger Fratres, 1878), 50; McHugh/Callan, *Moral Theology*, 1:2; Noldin/Schmitt, *Summa Theologia Moralis*, 1:17–20; Zalba, *Theologiae Moralis Compendium*, 1:21–23.

20. Davis, *Moral and Pastoral Theology*, 1:7–8.

21. Benedictus Merkelbach, O.P., *Summa Theologiae Moralis*, 2 vols., 8th ed. (Paris: Desclee de Brouwer et Cie, 1946), 1:24.

22. Thomas Slater, S.J., *A Manual of Moral Theology*, 2 vols., 3rd ed. (New

York: Benziger Bros., 1908), 1:54; see also Davis, *Moral and Pastoral Theology*, 1:46; McHugh/Callan, *Moral Theology*, 1:38; Noldin/Schmitt, *Summa Theologiae Moralis*, 1:104; Zalba, *Theologiae Moralis Compendium*, 1:28.

23. Noldin/Schmitt, *Summa Theologiae Moralis*, 1:104.

24. St. Augustine, *The Confessions*, trans., John K. Ryan (Garden City: Image Books, 1960), 43.

25. Slater, *A Manual of Moral Theology*, 1:54.

26. Hürth/Abellan, *De Principiis*, 230–235; see also Sabetti/ Barrett, *Compendium*, 154–196; Slater, *A Manual of Moral Theology*, 1:165; Prümmer, *Handbook of Moral Theology*, 80–95; McHugh/Callan, *Moral Theology*, 1:47; Davis, *Moral and Pastoral Theology*, 1:256–310.

27. Prümmer, *Handbook of Moral Theology*, 84–85.

28. Ibid., 81.

29. Zalba, *Theologiae Moralis Compendium*, 1:196.

30. Sabetti/Barrett, *Compendium*, 103.

31. Hürth/Abellan, *De Principiis*, 43.

32. McHugh/Callan, *Moral Theology*, 1:117.

33. Zalba, *Theologiae Moralis Compendium*, 1:196; see also Davis, *Moral and Pastoral Theology*, 1:132.

34. Davis, *Moral and Pastoral Theology*, 1:203; Slater, *A Manual of Moral Theology*, 1:132.

35. Koch/Preuss, *Handbook of Moral Theology*, 2:2.

36. Prümmer, *Handbook of Moral Theology*, 68.

37. Davis, *Moral and Pastoral Theology*, 1:207 and 1:220.

38. Ibid., 1:226–227.

39. Gerald McCool, *Catholic Theology In The Nineteenth Century* (New York: The Seabury Press, 1977), 159.

40. Ibid., 161.

41. Ibid., 9.

42. Ibid., 191.

43. Ibid., 197.

44. Ibid., 192.

45. Ibid., 193.

46. Ibid., 196.

47. James A. Weisheipl, O.P., *Thomas D'Aquino: His Life, Thought and Works* (New York: Doubleday and Company, 1974), 70–71.

48. M.-D. Chenu, "The Plan of St. Thomas' Summa Theologiae," *Cross Currents* 2 (1952):70–71.

49. Ibid., 74.

50. *Summa Theologiae*, I-II, Introduction to Qs 103–109.

51. *Summa Contra Gentiles*, III, 1.101.

52. *Summa Theologiae*, I-II, 103.4; *Summa Contra Gentiles*, III, 2 and 3.
53. *Summa Theologiae*, I-II, 103.6; *Summa Contra Gentiles*, III, 77.
54. *Summa Theologiae*, I-II, 104.3; *Summa Contra Gentiles*, III, 66 and 67.
55. Chenu, "The Plan," 75.
56. Dom Odon Lottin, *Problèmes de Moralité*, vol. 2 of *Psychologie et Morale aux XIe et XIIe Siècles* (Louvain: Abbaye du Mont César, 1948), 123.
57. Vincent MacNamara, "Religion and Morality II," *Irish Theological Quarterly* 44 (1977):180.
58. Chenu, "The Plan," 75.
59. Frederick Copleston, *Aquinas* (Harmondsworth, Middlesex: Penguin, 1955), 220.
60. Vincent MacNamara, *Faith and Ethics: Recent Roman Catholicism* (Dublin: Gill and MacMillan, 1985), 189.

*4.*

# The Moral Theory of the Neo-Thomist
# Manuals of Moral Theology

The purpose of this chapter is to continue and to nuance the interpretation of the neo-thomist manuals of moral theology initiated in the previous chapter. What will occupy our attention in the pages to follow is the theory of morality which can be found embedded in the texts of this theological genre. The theology and moral theory of these books constitute their theoretical components. The nexus between these two elements must be understood in terms of the relationship between theology and philosophy as this was construed by the neo-Thomists, i.e. philosophy provided the theologian with a metaphysical framework as well as a set of explanatory categories which rendered the data of theology coherent and which were illuminative of the human situation. Although most of the topics to be discussed below are principally philosophical in nature, one must repeatedly recall that as employed by the manualists they were in the service of theology.

The neo-Thomist manuals discussed five topics which can be used as indices to their moral theory: 1) the nature of morality and moral obligation; 2) the human act; 3) conscience; 4) the law, and especially natural law; and 5) the determinants of morality. As the previous chapter utilized McCool's interpretation of the early neo-Thomists to highlight the theology of the manualists, so this chapter will employ twentieth century neo-scholastics such as Dom Odon Lottin, Etienne Gilson, and Jacques Maritain with regard to their theory of morality.

## I. The Nature of Morality and Moral Obligation

To understand the fundamental conception of morality which runs throughout the neo-Thomist manuals is to comprehend the basic goal of this chapter. Although this section will provide the substantive position of the manualists on this topic, each of the other indices will provide a refinement and further specification of this general theme.

The manualists displayed a virtual unanimity of opinion with regard to the nature of morality. McHugh/Callan succinctly stated that "morality is the agreement or disagreement of a human act with the norms that regulate human conduct with reference to man's last end."[1] Similarly, Sabetti/Barrett wrote:

> The essence of morality consists primarily in the condition of the relation of the human act to the eternal law which is the divine plan, the will of God ordering the natural order to be preserved and condemning its perturbation. . . . The secondary essence of morality consists in the relation of human acts to right reason.[2]

The same fundamental notion was expressed by Zalba. Morality was conceived by him as a quality of human acts which rendered them worthy of praise or blame and which consisted in the proceeding of an act "from free will and reason adverting to the rule of morality."[3]

The theory of morality which permeated the writings of the neo-Thomist manuals was inherently dipolar; it was constituted by the relationship between human acts as volitional, cognitive acts and the norm or standard of morality. Morality itself was neither a human act nor the standard but the relationship between them. Morality was conceived in a dipolar manner in that it consisted of a subjective pole, the human act as the product of the will and reason, and an objective pole, the norm or standard of morality. The subjective pole of morality will be developed further in subsequent discussions of the human act and conscience, the objective pole in regard to the law. The specificity of morality *qua* morality, the pivotal aspect of the relationship itself, will be examined in the context of the determinants of morality: object, end, and circumstance.

The teleological character of the manualist moral theory was an aspect given special prominence in the writings of Hürth/Abellan and Francis O'Connell. For the former the *imago dei* constituted the link between the divine and the human; it was the norm according to which the human assimilation of the divine ought to take place.

> Morality in a less full sense, that is, as attending only to the nature of good and evil, is understood as an act deliberately placed in relation to a norm; in the full sense, that is, as also attending to what is licit and illicit, morality is the relation of such an act to the norm of morality inasmuch as it is subject to the will of God.[4]

There are two important features of this statement which ought to be noted. First, the "full sense" of morality directs the attention of the moral agent beyond worldly, humanistic conceptions of the norm of morality as simply "the nature of moral good and evil." These authors continued in their discussion of morality to explicitly reject the moral standards of the Utilitarians and the Hedonists as well as Kantian autonomy. The full sense of morality, they argued, can only be assessed in relation to the will and/or plan (*ratio*) of God. The issue for them was not primarily moral good or evil, but rather whether human acts were to be deemed sinful or meritorious.

O'Connell proposed that morality meant "a transcendental relation of a human act, either of agreement or disagreement, to a norm or rule of goodness and evil, based on man's nature in its entirety."[5] O'Connell's interpretation of morality as a transcendental relation must be construed as yet a further rejection of any purely or even primarily human norm as adequate to the demands of Christian morality. In relating one's self to a human good (*bonum honestum*), one was in the same act relating one's self to God as the ultimate good.

Although the transcendental and ultimate referent of this theory of morality was consistently its central feature, there were also proximate and material moral goods and evils. As will become clearer in the subsequent discussion of the law and the determinates of morality, some human acts were described as intrinsically evil (*malum per se*) and others as true instances of the human good (*bonum honestum*). The neo-Thomists were aware that persons lived in a world in which specifically human needs had to be addressed; they were aware as well of the need to discern the manner in which human life could be richly lived. Their moral theory was not a rejection of such proximate and immediate concerns, but rather an expression of their conviction that such human flourishing could only occur in a world order devised by divine reason and will. The neo-scholastic Dom Odon Lottin expressed a similar conviction in his interpretation of Aquinas:

> The moral value of every intermediate end is regulated by the final last end. Then moral action is morally good in the measure it approaches the last end.[6]

Moral obligation as portrayed by the manualists arose primarily as a function of the law. For Henry Davis, "obligation arises from the law, which determines a certain standard of action, according to which we must act."[7] Similarly, Koch/Preuss stated that the objective norm of morality is "the rule by which man must regulate his conduct . . . [it] is the will of God manifested through nature and revelation."[8] Moral obligation within this tradition was never construed as primarily a human phenomenon, but rather as a dimension of human experience which originates in divine governance and initiative for the manner in which human life was to be lived, that is, in a manner conducive to the final end of human beings.

Although rejecting any autonomous notion of moral obligation, the neo-Thomist manualists attempted to stress that moral obligation was not an alienating experience. Noldin/Schmitt made this point quite clearly. After stating that the moral order was established by God as the road by which persons are led to the final end and the means by whose observation persons arrive at their end, they went on to affirm that:

> . . . since order in general is the relation of one thing to another, to construct the moral order the first things to be considered are the relations by which one man is referred to another; there are three such relations in human nature: the religious relation, the individual relation, and the social relation. Man is referred to God as his first principle and final end; he is referred to himself, he is led by many diverse inclinations and potencies which constitute his nature so that the inferior are referred to the superior and especially the superior to the inferior; man, however, is referred to other creatures, both rational and irrational. Human nature is so ordered that the part is ordered to the whole to constitute society with other men, and thus he is justly instructed in the use of material things, inasmuch as their use is consistent with his final end. Thus the moral order is by nature an order toward the end, since the entire nature of man with all his relations is thus ordered to God as his final end.[9]

Noldin/Schmitt maintained the relational character of morality as discussed above; they made reference to the moral agent's ultimate and final relationship to God as well as his or her proximate relation to human goods. Noldin/Schmitt remained consistent with the tradition in their arguments for the primacy of the divine ordering. What the above quote clarifies, and where these authors were again representative of the tradition, is that the ordering of human actions by divine governance was interpreted not as an alienating element, but rather a fulfilling and enriching dimension of moral obligation. The path along which moral obligation sought to compel human acts was one which would only lead to the flowering of human purposefulness. O'Connell made the same point quite elliptically: moral acts ought to be "in accordance with human nature and the purposes for which that nature was made."[10] This conception of morality and moral obligation fostered by the neo-Thomist manuals provided Bruno Schüller with the innovative approach to Christian morality which he initiated in *Gesetz und Freiheit*.[11]

## II. The Human Act

Significant portions of the neo-thomists' considerations of the human act were devoted to obstacles or impediments to specifically human activity. They were concerned to determine the manner and extent to which fear, coercion, and ignorance could diminish or destroy the distinctly human dimension of morality. Such notions were important for the determination of the culpability to be assigned to sins presented in the confessional. These constraints, however, need not be a central concern for the limited purpose of this investigation. Rather the purpose here must be to determine those characteristics of the human act which directly pertain to morality. The will was understood to be the primary source of the moral act; a correlative role was assigned to the intellect. Another dimension of the human act frequently addressed by these authors was the significance of natural inclinations to specific goods.

The moral dimension of human acts according to the neo-Thomist manualist tradition was understood as a product of the will. Zalba stated this forcefully:

Only the internal, deliberate act of the will is by its very nature formally capable of morality; it alone has of its very nature the meaning of morality. . . . External acts contribute nothing towards increasing or diminishing the formal goodness and evilness of an act since it is determined by the interior act. . . ."[12]

The previous chapter's presentations of merit/grace and the virtue of charity have already indicated the primary role attributed to the will in this tradition. The theological virtue of charity was construed as lodged in the will and fundamentally ordering human persons to God as infinite goodness and love. Charity was also understood as capable of eliciting further internal and external acts. As important and significant as such acts were, they were secondary and subsidiary to charity and the will. The will informed by charity constituted the most decisive characteristic of the subjective pole of morality.

The primacy accorded the will and charity by these authors certainly did not exclude the importance of external works; this will become evident in the examination of the virtue of charity as an element in the social ethic of this tradition. In fact the point of the manualists was that the will and charity were at times required to command external acts. What this notion of primacy of the will attempted to account for was that one could sin without the placing of an external act; it also provided a basis for the stress on intention or motivation (the end) as an aspect of a meritorious act. Gilson's philosophical interpretation of St. Thomas led him to an analogous conclusion: "We must conclude that human acts are formally specified by the end toward which the interior act of the will tends, and they are materially specified at the most by the objects to which the exterior act is referred."[13]

The role of reason in the neo-Thomist conception of morality was not the function attributed to reason by most modern ethical theories. The neo-Thomists would never have conceived reason's function as the determination of the logical consistency between ethical statements, nor as an autonomous source of moral norms. When Prümmer, for instance, referred to human reason as the proximate objective standard of morality,[14] he was simply alluding to the rational capacity of human nature to perceive in some manner the divine order or plan, the eternal law, and not to a capacity of human reason to constitute for itself the norm of morality or dictates of practical reason.

The faculty psychology of the neo-Thomists conceived of the intellect and will as distinct but related cognitive faculties. Reason was the intellectual faculty oriented to the true, the will a volitional faculty oriented to the good. The will was considered dependent upon the intellect in that it perceived true, actual instances of the good. Reason could direct the act of the will because both faculties could relate to the same material object; reason could comprehend it inasmuch as it was true, the will inasmuch as it was good. Thus the will was to be guided and instructed by reason in its quest of the good. The will, however, remained free; it could choose what was only apparently good. The will was the faculty which ultimately ordered individual persons to the proximate and ultimate goods of their lives. Reason as a component in neo-Thomist moral theory will be looked at again in the context of the natural law; however, its function within this system can be further refined in relation to the basic human drives which contribute élan to this conception of morality.

The meaning of human appetites, affections, passions or natural inclinations, as they were variously referred to by these authors, and their place in neo-Thomist moral theory were controversial issues. Once again this is a topic which will be examined further in relationship to the natural law positions developed by these authors as well as in the context of their applied moral theory. There the question will be whether the natural law is to be thought of as right reason or as right reason guided by the natural inclinations of human nature. An exploration of how the appetites and affections were construed in regard to the human act will provide only an initial investigation of this topic.

Davis viewed concupiscence as inclinations "of any sensitive appetite towards sensible goods or away from sensible evil as apprehended by imagination."[15] So conceived the inclinations were considered in a pre-rational and pre-moral manner, as orientations of the concupiscent dimension of human nature to what *prima facie*, and apart from any sort of reflection, appeared as a sensible good or evil. As developed within this genre, these inclinations were never construed in relationship to psychoanalytic categories; they were never thought of as expressions of the id, ego, or superego. The instinct to withdraw one's hand from fire, or more complexly, the immediate attractiveness of a sumptuous meal apart from a consideration of one's need for food and whether such a feast exceeded the bounds of temperance, reflect the purely sensitive function accorded these appetites. As purely sensitive orientations, and thus apart from rational reflection and/or an act of the will, such orientations were thought of as pre-moral. Thus in and of themselves orientations such as the sexual inclination were neither good nor evil in a moral sense. Although the inclinations could distract right reason or incline the will to be improperly ordered, Davis could also allude to their central import for human well-being. They not only were instruments of self-preservation, he argued, but they also constituted the capacities of human nature for change, growth, evolution and improvement of the individual.[16] In a similar vein, Koch/Preuss suggested that the inclinations are neither evil nor unworthy of human nature, rather they "precede, incite, and elicit the decision of the will, and are frequently the very requisites of free will actions,"[17] and thus were capable of becoming concurrent causes in the production of moral good. This aspect of the neo-Thomist moral theory was to be developed later by contemporary natural law theorists John Finnis[18] and Germain Grisez.[19]

## III. Conscience

The importance of the treatise on conscience in the manuals of moral theology in general and the neo-Thomist manuals in particular cannot be overemphasized. Conscience was construed as the subjective norm of morality; it referred to the intellectual capacity of individuals to perceive what the moral law required of them. This is the aspect of the neo-Thomists' consideration of conscience which will be investigated in the paragraphs below. A cognate topic which was also considered in the treatise on conscience was the issue of probabilism or the dispute over the systems of morality, as it was also called. Since the latter question was for the most part resolved by the time of the neo-Thomist manuals, it will be examined only briefly.

"Conscience," Prümmer wrote, " is the subjective standard of morality."[20] In the same vein, Davis stated that conscience is "the subjective, proximate standard of morality";[21] Hürth/Abellan similarly asserted that "the essence of conscience consists in the ultimate practical judgment of morality."[22] Once again it needs to be emphasized that these references to a subjective standard of morality ought not be construed as suggesting a form of autonomy, nor should one assume that self-interest or any other self-referential moral standard was being proposed by these authors. McHugh/Callan emphasized quite clearly that conscience ought not to be considered as autonomous, i.e. as independent of external law and authority. The standard of morality, they wrote, "is not each one's wish or opinion, but God as the Last End and the external natural and positive law as the means to that end."[23]

Noldin/Schmitt offered their readers a concise, positive definition of conscience. Conscience is "a property of the intellect which with great ease and clarity knows the most universal principles of morality or the supreme principles of the natural law" and is thus capable of forming "a practical judgment concerning the morality of a proximate judgement."[24] Conscience was understood as the ability of practical reason—the use of intelligence with regard to an act—to move from the abstract, theoretical notions of the natural law, or from general principles of faith,[25] to a concrete determination of what was to be done here and now. To give this much money to this poor person for this reason and in relationship to these circumstances is a morally good act; such concrete determinations of what ought to done in the practical dimensions of life belonged to the sphere of operation accorded to conscience.

Conscience could be exercised with regard to a proposed action or to one that had taken place; it was the proximate, subjective norm of morality. Informed by the general principles of natural law and/or the general principles of faith, a sensitive conscience could yield the best practical decision a person could make with regard to what ought to be done. A person was obliged to act upon the dictate of conscience even if such a practical judgement did not conform to the actual requirements of the objective moral law.

Perhaps an example can clarify this point. If it can be conceded for the sake of discussion that a person who has contracted AIDS has a moral obligation at least to inform potential sexual partners of this fact, then the following example may be illuminative. Several years ago Bertha had extensive surgery that required multiple transfusions; unbeknownst to her, she has become an AIDS carrier. Last spring she met Titus, to whom she is now married. From the perspective of the neo-Thomist manuals, she now has a moral obligation to be sexually active with her spouse and, when he makes a sexual request, her conscience may frequently conclude that she ought to respond affirmatively. Objectively, i.e. from the perspective of the moral law itself, she is acting in a morally inappropriate manner; she needs at least to inform her spouse concerning her condition. Nevertheless, given her ignorance of her ailment, she must follow her conscience and ought to be sexually active with him. If she eventually learns what has occurred, neither she nor anyone else could suggest that she acted in a morally inappropriate manner. Note that the central point of the example and of the tradition's emphasis on one's obligation to follow even an erroneous conscience is that it was impossible for this woman to turn her will to what was morally evil. Her will chose only the good of intimacy with her spouse, not the evil of deception.

The notion of conscience as developed within the tradition was not concerned with the development of universalizable moral norms nor with the justification of the general principles of morality. Conscience was not the virtue of the philosophical or theological ethicist, but rather the virtue of the moral agent, by which he or she could arrive at practical moral decisions concerning what ought to be done in light of the natural law and the principles of faith.

The debate over probabilism or the systems of morality was directly concerned with the relationship between obligatory moral norms and decisions of conscience. Zalba briefly indicated to his readers the two manners in which the moral systems question was posed:

> For some the moral system is the complex of moral principles by which one moves from speculative doubt to a practically certain conscience; for others, it is the doctrine concerning the method of, or way of moving from a remote, speculative, doubtful judgment concerning the obligation of a law, which cannot be directly removed, to a virtually certain practical judgment of conscience concerning a true good.[26]

There were many methods introduced, particularly in the seventeenth and eighteenth centuries, as means of solving these conflicts. The extremes were laxism—in lieu of a certain conscience, one could do as one wished—and rigorism, which required that human freedom yield to the requirements of law, even if those requirements were in legitimate doubt. The middle positions ranged from the proposal that one could legitimately follow either of two probable opinions, to the requirement that one ought to conform to the more probable opinion, to the position of St. Alphonsus that the conscience can act in accordance with either of two equiprobable opinions.

The details of this arduous debate and the involvement of the papacy in its resolution cannot be allowed to conceal the contemporary relevance of this topic. The controversy arose largely in response to the rigorous interpretations of the moral demands of Christianity arising from Jansenism. The Jansenists, who rejected the theology of Aquinas and the scholastics in favor of that of St. Augustine, proposed a rigorist interpretation of the moral

demands of Christian life. The crux of the issue became the point at which
the will of the Christian must yield to the demands of specific interpretations
of the divine law. The opinions ranged from rigorism to laxism with the
various forms of probabilism in between. Although the mechanics of this
debate have become archaic, the issue has once again become important. As
the American Catholic community has come to reflect the divisions within
American Protestantism, i.e. between inclusivist and exclusivist positions,
between those who find anonymous Christianity and empathy with one's
culture a meaningful way to be Christian and those who seek to acquire a
Christian identity clearly distinguishable from that of the wider society,
there may once again be a need to address the issues at the center of the
debate over probabilism. More specifically, how can the American Catholic
community deal with the plurality of convictions and practices among its
members regarding abortion, contraception, divorce, and other controversial
ethical issues?

## IV. The Law

The role of the moral law within the framework of the neo-Thomist
manuals of moral theology was partially addressed in Chapter Three's consideration of the new law as an element in their theology. The present
examination of this theme will focus on what this tradition meant by "law"
as well as the manner in which the notion of the eternal, natural, and divine
laws functioned in relationship to the moral theory of the genre. In its own
distinct manner, each of these types of law represented a manner of eluci-
dating the objective norm of morality, the standard with reference to which
human acts ought to conform.

Most of the manualists began their examination of law by referring to
Thomas Aquinas' definition (*Summa Theologia* I–II, 90.4): law is an ordinance of reason for the common good, made by one who has care of the
community and promulgated.[27] Although the link was generally not made
explicit by the manualists, their use of this definition would seem to imply
that they intended to maintain continuity with the thought of Aquinas, i.e.
that the law was the means by which divine governance and providence
operated with regard to rational beings. Thomas' definition of law, however,
drew heavily upon the decretalist tradition; Isadore and the decretalists were
cited frequently by Aquinas throughout question 90, especially in the responses and the answers to the objections.

The continued use of legal categories to describe moral phenomena
would eventually become a major issue for the manualist genre, especially in
relation to specific moral questions. The legal categories of St. Thomas could
sustain their relevance only so long as providence implied governance and

anthropomorphized God as a monarch. Only in relation to such a conception of God, which in fact was latent in most of these manuals, could Konings write with regard to God as supreme and universal lawgiver that:

> . . . all others receive power directly or indirectly from him. God is the ultimate and essential norm of whatever order and He alone enjoys dominion in rational creatures of which He is the principal and final end.[28]

Such a passage conflates metaphysical concepts of God as the principal and final end of human persons and the notion of God as the ultimate norm of morality—concepts generally shared by the Thomist and neo-Thomist traditions—with the use of terms such as "power" and "dominion" which were not generally ascribed to God in this manner. This mixing together of terms was a result of commingling metaphysical language with anthropomorphic concepts of God.

The continued use of legal language also contributed to statements which could be construed as suggesting legal voluntarism or positivism. How, for instance, should the following statement of Koch/Preuss be understood?

> The objective norm of morality, i.e. the rule by which men must regulate their conduct, is the will of God manifested through nature and revelation . . . [law is] another name for the divine will recognized as the standard of human conduct.[29]

The tradition usually referred to divine reason, or divine reason and will, as the norm of morality. Although the origin of this controversy lies in the writings of Suarez and Scotus, nevertheless, positions which allude only to the divine will as the norm of morality open the door to legal positivism; the law is what the monarch says it is apart from its inherent reasonableness. Thomas' definition explicitly referred to law as a dictate of reason.

In an even more positivist vein, Zalba defined law in its proper sense as:

> . . . the rule of morality prescribed by a legislator, either an individual or the most powerful member of a community, determining what ought to be done or omitted in relation to a good as determined by a particular or common nature.[30]

In a footnote Zalba immediately commented that, although this definition did not apply to the eternal law, which exists only in the mind of God, it did apply to the "statutes ordained by God as the author of nature and revelation," as well as to ecclesiastical and civil statutes. Thus the moral law ought to be able to be perceived with the same clarity with which one can read the statutes in a civil code or canon law. These evolving notions of law and the manner in which God was understood as the source of the moral law would have a bearing upon these authors' interpretations of the eternal and especially the natural and divine laws.

Davis and other manualists remained close to the metaphysical notion of eternal law. "The eternal law," wrote Davis:

> ... is first in the order of being and causality ... the whole community of the universe is governed by Divine reason ... the very idea of the government of things in God, the ruler of the universe, has the nature of law.[31]

Such a conception of the eternal law appears to maintain the relation between providence and morality. The eternal law thus understood refers to the "whole community of the universe," not just to the sphere of human morality. As Prümmer stated, it "embraces the physical and moral orders."[32] For Koch/Preuss the eternal law was "the source and measure of all law, physical, spiritual, ethical."[33] The eternal law was interpreted as the divine ordering of creation, of both rational and non-rational creatures. Noldin/Schmitt[34] and McHugh/Callan[35] stressed that the ordering of the eternal law was an orientation of rational beings not just to their proximate end, but to their final end.

Although Zalba used Augustine's rather than Aquinas' definition of the eternal law, he nevertheless seems to have been influenced by Aquinas' theory. In his explanation of the eternal law he wrote of it as the divine plan and the will of God inasmuch as it is:

> a divine practical statement or an efficacious concept or ordination as directive to a proper end, through a simultaneous act of reason and will which imprints on irrational creatures an inclination to the necessary end, and in rational creatures imposes moral obligations with regard to [their] essential relations to God, self, and others.[36]

Although the overall tenor of this explanation was similar to those of Zalba's colleagues, his theory immediately assigned specific moral obligations to rational beings and did so using categories usually associated with the moral requirements of the natural law and the virtue of charity.

The manualists of moral theology concurred that the eternal law was the ultimate, objective norm of human morality. The eternal law was identical to the divine being and thus was not directly and immediately available for human investigation; it could never be known directly and in itself. Therefore, the natural law as well as the divine law took on special importance; they were the proximate, objective norms of morality which could be known through reason and revelation. It must be borne in mind that as the natural law and the new law become the central topics of discussion their relationship to the eternal law was not disjunctive; they were not thought of as three distinct, unrelated kinds of law. The primacy rested with the eternal law; the natural law and the divine law were participations in and manifestations of the eternal law. There was one law, the eternal law: God's governance and providence with regard to his creation. The natural law constituted humankind's ability, partially and in a limited manner, to perceive the eternal law through reason; divine law enabled one to comprehend the eternal law less imperfectly as a consequence of revelation and faith.

There were two distinct positions taken by the neo-Thomist manualists with regard to the natural law. The one emphasized natural law as right reason; the second associated the natural law with human nature as endowed with reason and natural inclinations. The subsequent discussion of the natural law will attempt to highlight these two distinct interpretations of the natural law, indicate the legalistic language employed by several of these authors, and relate their theories of natural law to those of several neo-scholastic philosophers.

Konings was among those who espoused right reason as the fundamental aspect of the natural law. "The one rule of human morality," he wrote,

> ... is right reason, to which the human act ought to conform. Right reason is distinguished in two ways: uncreated, which exists in the divine mind, i.e. the eternal law; created, a light impressed by God on a rational creature.[37]

Although this author does not use the term "natural law," his language and meaning were expressive of the basic tenets of those representatives of the tradition who interpreted natural law as "right reason." In a similar vein, Slater defined the natural law as "derived from the eternal law of God and as nothing else than the rule of action suited to human nature as such."[38] Further on in his text he stated:

> The rule of conduct which right reason manifests to us, and which conscience, the voice of God, commands us to follow, constitutes the natural law which is a participation in human reason of the eternal law of God, willing that right order should be observed, forbidding it to be disturbed.[39]

The significant difference between these two definitions was that the former portrayed natural law as simply "right reason" whereas the latter spoke of "the rule of action suited to human nature as such." Slater did not appear to attribute to any aspect of human nature a role in the realization of the norm of morality other than the function of reason as such. Thus "nature" simply functioned as a sobriquet for "right reason." Koch/Preuss similarly argued that "the moral law of nature is understood as the sum total of those ethical precepts which God had implanted in the rational nature of man . . . written in their hearts . . . [and] promulgated by reason."[40] Prümmer represented the same elements of the tradition when he wrote that the natural law "contains only those precepts which are derived from the very nature of man . . . [and] grasped by the natural light of man's reason without the aid of divine and human authority."[41]

Henry Davis was among the advocates of that strain of the tradition which defined natural law in relationship to human nature as a composite of both reason and natural inclinations. He spoke of it as:

> . . . a share of the Eternal Reason, whereby it has a natural inclination to its proper act and end; and this participation of the Eternal law in the rational creature is called the Natural Law.[42]

Two pages further on in his text, he referred explicitly to the natural law and the natural appetites common to all persons. "The Divine Wisdom," he proposed, "must wish reasonable creatures to be directed towards their ultimate end conformably to the nature proper to them. . . . "[43] McHugh/ Callan took essentially the same approach to the natural law as did Davis.[44] Zalba contended that the natural law was "a divine ordination of a rational creature toward its final end necessarily expressed in its nature and commanded by the natural light of reason."[45] He then went on to explain that by human nature he meant nature in its complete constitution, i.e. in its social relations, in its transcendent end, and even in its essential inclinations.

These authors were consistent among themselves in at least two regards. First and most obviously, they all understood the natural law in relation to the eternal law. The natural law was, at least in part, a mode of knowing the eternal law. It was never an arbitrary creation of human intelligence nor could it be simply reduced to a type of naturalistic ethics. The primary and ultimate ordering of the natural law was to the final end of persons. The natural law also ordered human life to moral and physical goods within the terrestrial sphere as proximate and secondary goods. To understand the moral theory of these authors, however, requires that both the primary and secondary ordering of human life be acknowledged and that the primacy of the one be maintained in relation to the other.

Second, the neo-Thomist manualists understood human reason as having an especially significant role in the natural law. On the one hand, reason was a sharing, a participation in the eternal law. It was a capacity which enabled persons to know what they ought to do. Reason in this context was understood as the formal cause of morality; it determined the specific acts which were in accord with the eternal law. The will was the efficient cause in which a person set his or her will upon the good as perceived in a specific act. To return to a theme of Chapter Three for a moment, this was also the reason that the ethic of the manualists was essentially an ethic of virtue. The presumption was that charity had turned the will to God as infinite goodness and love. Within this context of the primacy of charity and will, the function of the natural law and reason was to aid the moral agent in assessing correctly proximate material moral goods. The theological and moral virtues were considered to provide more than sufficient guidance in the vast majority of instances. It was not expected that there was a need for an explicit appeal to the natural law each time an agent acted. The natural law as an exercise of reason had two functions within the tradition: to assist persons in the forming of their conscience in instances of true moral uncertainty and as a meta-ethic to be used by theologians in justifying and clarifying the moral implications of the virtues.

The role of natural inclinations was an issue which divided the positions of the neo-Thomist moral theologians. The one group identified the natural law with right reason. They construed the distinctive, and thus defining, aspect of human nature to be reason, which then became identified with the proximate norm of morality. The second group concurred that reason was indeed the distinctive hallmark of human nature, but added that reason itself was inclined by nature to certain specifiable goods: minimally the goods of existence, procreation and education of children for the benefit of the species, the need to live in society and to know about God. The theologians who adopted this particular approach tended to relate natural law and its precepts to objects and thus duties to God, self, and neighbor.[46] Whereas the first group derived the requirements of natural law from right reason alone as a participation in the eternal law, the second contended that right reason ought to be exercised in relation to the pre-moral dispositions embedded in human nature as spontaneous sensitive inclinations to the proximate and ultimate ends of human existence. Further, this second group also tended to understand the natural law in terms of fundamental human relationships to God, self, neighbor, and world, rather than in simple terms of human essence. Although both of these positions were clearly articulated by the neo-Thomist moral theologians, this difference does not seem to have led them to different conclusions with regard to specific moral issues.

A final comment with regard to the natural law theory depicted in this genre is in order to indicate once again its tendency toward legalism. Thomas Aquinas spoke of principles of practical reason (I–II, 94.4) as well as of precepts of natural law (I–II, 94.2), but in both instances he seems to have meant "the principles of practical inquiry, which are also the limits of practical argument—a set of underivable principles for practical reason."[47] Even in their general consideration of natural law, apart from any consideration of substantive issues, the manualists interpreted the precepts of natural law as entailing specific moral requirements. Thus McHugh/Callan spoke of moral precepts deduced from the very nature of man.[48] These authors shared the conviction that the natural law entailed the knowledge of a moral order metaphysically constituted in the ordering of human nature, whether that nature was conceived of as right reason or as natural inclinations known by right reason. Just as a correct assessment of the notion of a human person led to the conclusion that it was an individual, subsistent being with a rational nature, so a correct investigation of morality would lead to the perception of an objective moral order to which human acts ought to conform. Thus Noldin/Schmitt spoke of the objective moral order "established by God consisting in operations which, considered in the relations of men to God, self, and neighbor, necessarily ought to be done or omitted."[49]

Brief reference has already been made to the writings of John Finnis and Germain Grisez as modern representatives of the Thomistic tradition who have attempted to articulate Thomas' natural law theory in the contemporary philosophical setting. Both authors have stressed an interpretation of the precepts of the natural law as starting points for the reasoning process as well as the role of the natural inclinations as leading to positive and negative moral duties. Two earlier expositors of Aquinas' natural law theory also provided alternative constructive arguments: Vernon Bourke and Jacques Maritain.

Bourke argued that right reason was the central theme in Thomas' ethics and that his understanding of natural law was empirical and intellectualist.[50] Bourke rejected any approach to the ethical theory of Aquinas which was premised on an intuitive and voluntarist interpretation or any approach which began with a definition of man's nature and then deduced laws from that nature as expressions of human duties. Bourke argued that the concept of "right" (*jus*) is prior to and more fundamental to Aquinas' ethics than "law" (*lex*). "Right" implies, he proposed, a just thing to be done in a relationship between persons, a relationship of fair dealing between persons. "Law," then, becomes the oral or written expression of what is generally right in such relations. According to Bourke, Aquinas did maintain that the natural law was an imperfect knowledge of the eternal law, but also that good and evil in general, and moral good and moral evil in particular, can be known by reasoning about ordinary human experience. Bourke's interpretation of Aquinas remained consistent with the realist epistemology of the neo-Thomists as well as their distinction between the objective and subjective poles of morality. He also maintained, however, that "Thomas's stress on a prudent consideration of the purpose and predictable results of each voluntary action has something in common with utilitarianism and naturalistic pragmatism."[51]

Yet another interpretation of Aquinas's natural law theory which was sharply at variance with that of the neo-Thomist manualists can be found in the writings of Jacques Maritain. Maritain contended that there were two elements in Aquinas' natural law theory: the ontological and the gnoseological. The ontological component of the natural law consisted of the nature of man: "An ontologic structure which is a locus of intelligible necessities, man possesses ends which necessarily correspond to his essential constitution and which are the same for all."[52] Thus Maritain believed that there existed an order or disposition of necessities and ends to which the wills of persons ought to be directed.

To this point, Maritain's position appears similar to the position of those manualists who depicted an objective moral order based on reason and fundamental human inclinations. Maritain's position, however, was clearly distinguished from theirs when he addressed the gnoseological element in the natural law, i.e. how it is known. He did not speak in this context of precepts or rules, but rather of knowledge through inclination. Such knowledge, he argued:

> . . . is not clear knowledge through concepts and conceptual judgments; it is obscure, unsystematic, vital knowledge by connaturality or congeniality, in which the intellect, in order to bear judgment, consults and listens to the inner melody that the vibrating strings of abiding tendencies make present in the subject.[53]

The "abiding tendencies" referred to the natural inclinations. Maritain's position with regard to knowledge by connaturality had been more completely presented in *The Range of Reason* where he argued that:

> . . . man being an historical animal, these essential inclinations of human nature either developed or were released in the course of time; as a result, man's knowledge of the Natural Law progressively developed, and continues to develop. And the very history of moral conscience has divided the truly essential inclinations of human nature from the accidental, warped or perverted ones.[54]

The distinctive aspects of Maritain's position were, first, his proposal that moral knowledge remained at the level of vital knowledge by connaturality, rather than the strong prescriptive tendencies of the manualists; and second, that moral knowledge required an historical process by which the "truly essential inclinations of human nature" could become known. The historical element in this ethical theory enabled a provocative thinker such as Maritain to speak about "The Historic Possibilities of the Realization of a New Christendom."[55] However, such historic possibilities as well as the historical side of this ethic pertained only to an adequate comprehension of those inclinations with which human nature has been endowed. The moral order itself was considered static; what fundamentally changed was the adequacy of human perception of that order.

The divine law referred to the ordinances set forth in the Old and New Testaments. The new law, as opposed to the old law, had been given to Christians in the revelation of Jesus Christ and in the gift of his abiding Spirit. The new law as a facet of the moral theory of the neo-Thomists was distinguishable from its theological role. Whereas the latter emphasized the habitual grace and charity dimensions of the new law as a turning of the Christian's will to God, the former stressed specific external acts which ought to conform to the requirements of the precepts. In this regard, the new law became the basis of a body of precepts related to the natural law, the decalogue and the love commandments of the New Testament. Although only the external aspects of the new law will be developed here, this limited presentation must not be allowed to overshadow what has already been stated with regard to the inner nature of the new law in Chapter Three.

The manualists shared a common conviction that the new law was divine positive law:

> . . . added by God to the natural law in order to direct the actions of man to his supernatural end, to assist him to a better observance of the natural law, and to perfect that which is wanting in human law.[56]

The new law was generally construed as imposing no moral duties not already required by the natural law. The positive character of this law was based on the conviction that the inner workings of the new law needed to be given external expression. This became a key feature of the new law for these authors and provided the justification for their expositions of special moral theology as well as their considerations of the sacraments and canon law. The precepts of the new law, argued Davis and others, were theological in regard to faith, hope and charity (each of which required external acts); they were moral as contained in the decalogue and confirmed and perfected by Christ; they were also the basis of the requirements associated with the sacraments and canon law. Thus, although given very limited treatment by the manualists, the new law provided the theoretical justification for the entire applied moral theory of the manualists. The new law must be understood as the central and organizing element of this moral theory. Apart from the new law, the moral theologians had no justification for their treatment of the theological virtues, the sacraments or canon law. Apart from the new law, their treatment of the decalogue and/or the cardinal virtues could not be related to the ultimate destiny of humanity and to good acts as meritorious.

## V. The Determinants of Morality

The determinants or fonts of morality were the immediate bases which specified the objective morality of the human act and ultimately decided its moral goodness or evil.[57] Following St. Thomas the manualists evaluated the morality of human acts in relation to their object, end, and circumstances. Each of these characteristics pertained to the objective pole of their moral theory. As the human act and conscience formed the subjective pole of this theory, so the law and the determinants of morality formed its objective pole.

The object of the human act pertained to the nature of the act itself. Sabetti/Barrett spoke of the object as that "around which the act immediately turns and as that in which proximately and in itself the will of the agent terminates . . . objective goodness or badness."[58] Similarly Prümmer wrote that the object of the act was "that to which the action tends of its very nature primarily and necessarily."[59] The object of the human act was conceived in relation to the moral rather than the physical order, because it was being considered explicitly as an object of moral choice. Indeed the same act could be discussed as a purely physical act, or as a pre-moral act, but when viewed as a determinant of morality it was necessarily viewed from the perspective of morality. As Slater enunciated this notion, the object was that which "the will primarily and directly intends."[60]

The object as a determinant of morality provided the main context in which the manualists discussed some acts as intrinsically evil, acts such as the direct destruction of the life of an innocent person, masturbation, and homosexual acts. Neither the circumstances nor an agent's intention could alter the intrinsically evil nature of such acts. By their nature such acts were mortally sinful. The law, either natural or divine, was the standard by which the objective character of acts was to be determined. Davis based the immorality of intrinsically evil acts on the fact that they were "contrary to rational nature."[61] For Noldin/Schmitt the objective moral character of the act was "the relation existing between such an act and the moral order which owes its existence to a command or prohibition of the lawgiver."[62]

Human acts could be construed as morally good, morally evil, or indifferent. The pre-moral character of indifferent acts remained totally abstract, their moral evaluation could only be determined in relation to their concrete ends and circumstances. To walk, in and of itself was morally indifferent, but to walk to commit a crime was itself an immoral act. Intrinsically evil acts could never be altered by their end or circumstances to become morally good. A morally good act could become evil if done for the wrong reason or under inappropriate circumstances. To give money to the poor was a morally good act, but to do so in order to be praised rendered the act evil.

The end as a determinant of morality is a theme that has already been discussed. The ultimate end of the human act ought always to be the glory of God. In all that he does, Prümmer wrote, "man must put before himself some good motive which is related to God at least implicitly. . . . [He] may not act for pleasure alone."[63] Sabetti/Barrett expressed the crux of the issue when they stated that "the end is the reason why something is done, the *finis operantis* [the end or purpose of the person performing the act]."[64] As the examples above indicate, the end provided a further specification of the morality of an act; it rendered good acts better and indifferent acts good or evil. A good intention, however, could not alter the morality of an intrinsically evil act.

The circumstances provided yet further modifications and specifications of the moral act. They are "conditions which are accidental to the substantial act which can and do render acts comformable or not to right reason."[65] The circumstances extended to the Aristotelian categories: who, what, where, with whose help, why, how, and when. To kill an innocent person was sinful; to kill a priest (who) in a church (where) with the help of a deacon (with whose help), to obtain his prebend (why), during Mass on Sunday (when) would each be considered further specifications of the intrinsic evil of the act and render it yet more heinous and sinful.

The relationship between the object, end, and circumstances of the moral act gave rise to the dictum: *bonum ex integra causa; malum ex quodam defectu*, i.e. the good arises from integral causality, evil from some defect of the causes. For an act to be morally good it must be good with respect to its object, end and circumstances. If there were an evil aspect to any one of these the act in its entirety was assessed as evil.

## NOTES

1. John A. McHugh, O.P. and Charles J. Callan, O.P., *Moral Theology: A Complete Course Based on St. Thomas Aquinas and The Best Modern Authorities*, 2 vols. (New York: Joseph F. Wagner, Inc., 1929), 1:23.
2. Aloysio Sabetti, S.J. and Timotheo Barrett, S.J., *Compendium Theologiae Moralis*, ed., Daniele F. Creeden, S.J., 34th ed. (Neo Eboraci: Frederick Pustet Co., Inc., 1939), 27.

3. Marcellinus Zalba, S.J., *Theologiae Moralis Compendium: Juxta Constitutionem "Deus Scientiarum,"* 2 vols. (Marietti: Biblioteca De Autores Cristianos, 1958), 1:107.

4. F. Hürth, S.J. and P.M. Abellan, S.J., *De Principiis, De Virtutibus et Praeceptis* (Romae: In Aedibus Pontificiae Universitatis Gregorianae, 1948), 184.

5. Francis J. O'Connell, C.SS.R, *Outlines of Moral Theology* (Milwaukee: Bruce Publishing Company, 1953), 18.

6. Dom Odon Lottin, "L'Ordre Moral and l'Ordre Logique," *Annales de l'Institut Supérieur de Philosophie* 5 (1924):363.

7. Henry Davis, *Moral and Pastoral Theology,* 3 vols. (London: Sheed and Ward, 1935), 1:12.

8. Anthony Koch and Arthur Preuss, *A Handbook of Moral Theology,* 5 vols., 3rd ed. (St. Louis: B. Herder Book Co., 1935), 1:119.

9. H. Noldin, S.J. and A. Schmitt, S.J., *Summa Theologiae Moralis,* 3 vols., 27th ed. (Oeniponte: Sumptis and Typis Feliciani Rauch, 1940), 1:39–40.

10. O'Connell, *Outlines,* 18.

11. Bruno Schüller, *Gesetz Und Freiheit: Eine Moraltheologie Untersuchung* (Dusseldorf: Patmos Verlag, 1966).

12. Zalba, *Theologiae Moralis Compendium,* 1:117.

13. Etienne Gilson, *The Christian Philosophy of St. Thomas Aquinas,* trans. L.K. Shook, C.S.B. (New York: Random House, 1956), 260.

14. Dominic Prümmer, O.P., *Handbook of Moral Theology,* trans. Rev. Gerald W. Shelton, ed. for Amer. usage by Rev. John Gavin Nolan (New York: P.J. Kennedy and Sons, 1957), 8.

15. Davis, *Moral and Pastoral Theology,* 1:20.

16. Ibid., 1:21.

17. Koch/Preuss, *A Handbook of Moral Theology,* 1:106.

18. John Finnis, *Natural Law and Natural Rights* (Oxford: Clarendon Law Series, 1980).

19. Germain Grisez and Russell Shaw, *Beyond the New Morality* (Notre Dame: University of Notre Dame Press, 1974); see also Germain Grisez, *Christian Moral Principles,* vol. 1 of *The Way of the Lord Jesus* (Chicago: Franciscan Herald Press, 1983), 117–130.

20. Prümmer, *Handbook of Moral Theology,* 58.

21. Davis, *Moral and Pastoral Theology,* 1:36–37.

22. Hürth/Abellan, *De Principiis,* 120.

23. McHugh/Callan, *Moral Theology,* 1:199.

24. Noldin/Schmitt, *Summa Theologiae Moralis,* 1:208–209.

25. Prümmer, *Handbook of Moral Theology,* 58.

26. Zalba, *Theologiae Moralis Compendium,* 1:381.

27. Noldin/Schmitt, *Summa Theologiae Moralis*, 1:114; see also Sabetti/ Barrett, *Compendium*, 74; Prümmer, *Handbook of Moral Theology*, 27; McHugh/Callan, *Moral Theology*, 1:90; Thomas Slater, S.J., *A Manual of Moral Theology*, 2 vols., 3rd ed. (New York: Benziger Bros., 1908), 1:47; Davis, *Moral and Pastoral Theology*, 1:117.

28. A. Konings,C.SS.R, *Theologia Moralis*, 3rd ed. (New York: Benziger Fratres, 1878), 50.

29. Koch/Preuss, *A Handbook of Moral Theology*, 1:119–120.

30. Zalba, *Theologiae Moralis Compendium*, 1:173.

31. Davis, *Moral and Pastoral Theology*, 1:123.

32. Prümmer, *Handbook of Moral Theology*, 29.

33. Koch/Preuss, *A Handbook of Moral Theology*, 1:120.

34. Noldin/Schmitt, *Summa Theologiae Moralis*, 1:118.

35. McHugh/Callan, *Moral Theology*, 1:94.

36. Zalba, *Theologiae Moralis Compendium*, 1:180.

37. Konings, *Theologia Moralis*, 10.

38. Slater, *A Manual of Moral Theology*, 1:92.

39. Ibid., 1:116.

40. Koch/Preuss, *A Handbook of Moral Theology*, 1:122.

41. Prümmer, *Handbook of Moral Theology*, 29.

42. Davis, *Moral and Pastoral Theology*, 1:124.

43. Ibid., 1:126.

44. McHugh/Callan, *Moral Theology*, 1:96.

45. Zalba, *Theologiae Moralis Compendium*, 1:182.

46. McHugh/Callan, *Moral Theology*, 1:96; Davis, *Moral and Pastoral Theology*, 1:126; see also Zalba, *Theologiae Moralis Compendium*, 1:182–183.

47. Germain Grisez, "The First Principle of Practical Reason," *Aquinas: A Collection of Critical Essays*, ed., Anthony Kenny (Garden City: Anchor Books, 1969), 349.

48. McHugh/Callan, *Moral Theology*, 1:95.

49. Noldin/Schmitt, *Summa Theologiae Moralis*, 1:120.

50. Vernon Bourke, "Is Thomas Aquinas A Natural Law Ethicist?" *The Monist* 58 (1974):52–53; see also Vernon Bourke, *Graeco-Roman to Early Modern Ethics*, vol. 1 of *History of Ethics* (Garden City: Image Books, 1970), 142–146.

51. Bourke, *Graeco-Roman Ethics*, 146.

52. Jacques Maritain, *Man and the State* (Chicago: University of Chicago Press, 1951), 86.

53. Ibid., 91–92.

54. Jacques Maritain, *Range of Reason* (New York: Charles Scribner's Sons, 1942), 27.

55. Jacques Maritain, *Integral Humanism*, trans. Joseph Evans (Notre Dame: University of Notre Dame Press, 1968), 211–255.

56. McHugh/Callan, *Moral Theology*, 1:110–111; see also Davis, *Moral and Pastoral Theology*, 1:132; Zalba, *Theologiae Moralis Compendium*, 1:196.

57. Zalba, *Theologiae Moralis Compendium*, 1:122.

58. Sabetti/Barrett, *Compendium*, 29.

59. Prümmer, *Handbook of Moral Theology*, 21.

60. Slater, *A Manual of Moral Theology*, 1:45; see also Zalba, *Theologia Moralis Compendium*, 1:127.

61. Davis, *Moral and Pastoral Theology*, 1:55.

62. Noldin/Schmitt, *Summa Theologiae Moralis*, 1:266–67.

63. Prümmer, *Handbook of Moral Theology*, 23–24.

64. Sabetti/Barrett, *Compendium*, 30.

65. Davis, *Moral and Pastoral Theology*, 1:60–61.

# 5.

# The Casuistry of the Neo-Thomist Manuals of Moral Theology

Casuistry is generally understood to be the art or science by which general moral norms are applied and interpreted in relation to specific moral actions. Chapter One discussed the origin of casuistry in Roman Catholic pastoral theology as a product of the medieval penitentials and especially the *Summae Confessorum*. The limited objective of the present chapter will be to provide several instances of the manner in which the manualists applied their general moral theory in relationship to the decalogue and/or the theological and cardinal virtues. The principles of totality and double effect as understood by St. Thomas and the manualists will be examined in the first part of the chapter. These two principles provided the manualists with major tools for interpreting complex moral phenomena and a means by which specific moral rules might be applied to them. As was indicated in Chapter Two some manuals organized their presentation of special moral theology in relation to the ten commandments, whereas others did so in relation to the theological and cardinal virtues. Still others discussed special moral theology in a manner which blended both of these approaches. The second part of the chapter will examine aspects of the neo-Thomists' treatment of justice, charity, and temperance. Although the second part of this chapter takes its structure from an exploration of the virtues, an alternate structure which was employed by some of the manualists was based on the decalogue. In the latter form, this chapter would discuss the topics as related to the 5th, 7th, 8th, and 10th commandments as corresponding to the virtue of justice; the 1st, 2nd, 3rd, 4th and, in some instances the 5th, commandments as corresponding to charity; the 6th and 9th commandments as corresponding to the virtue of temperance. The manner in which an individual theologian organized his special moral theology does not seem to have influenced his understanding of the duties imposed by the specific virtues or commandments.

# I. The Principles of Double Effect and Totality

## (A) The Principle of Double Effect

The principles of double effect and totality were both articulated by St. Thomas and later assimilated into the manualist tradition. For Aquinas the principle of double effect outlined the moral requirements which justified the use of force in self-defense by private individuals (*Summa Theologiae* II–II, 64.7); the principle of totality was used to legitimate the use of force in capital punishment and the loss of an arm or leg in the case of amputation for medical reasons (*Summa Theologiae* II–II, 64.2 and 3). The manualists extended their application of the principle of double effect beyond the question of legitimate self-defense to include, at least for some of them, topics such as just war, the permissibility of the indirect killing of innocent persons, and material cooperation in the sin of another. The principle of totality was also extended in its application with regard to medical developments, principally as a refinement of one's obligation to prolong one's life. There were important intermediary figures in the transmission of the tradition between Thomas and the neo-Thomist manualists. The sixteenth and seventeenth century commentators on the writings of St. Thomas—Cajetan, de Lugo, Suarez, and Vasquez—contributed to the refinement of the principle of double effect and the just war theory. These intermediary figures played a significant role in transposing the natural law arguments of Aquinas into the language of rights and law which permeates the manuals.

If the discussion of these two principles could be limited to their use by Aquinas and the manualists, one would be dealing with principles which possess a relatively limited scope of application. However, since the early 1970s a growing number of contemporary moral theologians have argued that these two principles are in fact one, and have further proposed that, in the words of Peter Knauer, they constitute "the criterion for every moral judgment."[1] The "Proportionalist debate," as this heated controversy has been named, will be a topic of discussion in Chapter Twelve. The purpose here must be limited to introducing some of the historical background of the current debate.

For St. Thomas the principle of double effect and the principle of totality were natural law arguments governed by the principle of right reason. Thomas presented the principle of double effect in relation to the question of self-defense, not just war.[2] He began the article by stating that there are acts which have two effects, one intended and the other not; the key, however, consisted in the claim that the *morality* of an act was determined by what was intended. An act which intends to save one's own life does not intend an illicit goal, e.g. the death or physical harm of an unjust attacker, but simply intends to preserve one's self in existence, an act in accord with a primary precept of the natural law. What Thomas' theory did preclude was the use of greater force than necessary to repulse the aggressor. The justification for the employment of sufficient force, and only sufficient force, in response to the unjust aggressor was a dictum enunciated by Cicero, adopted by St. Augustine, and assimilated into the decretalist tradition: it is permissible to repel force with force provided it goes no further than due defense requires. To respond with greater force than necessary or to intend to kill an aggressor was understood to render the act of self-defense morally culpable. The phrase that will become pivotal to the development of this principle requires that the act which constitutes self-defense must "be proportionate to the end intended," i.e. self-preservation.

According to St. Thomas, legitimate self-defense was limited to a proper intention of preserving one's life; it could not intend the death of the aggressor. Further, there was in natural law theory a positive duty to defend one's life against an aggressor; one had a natural law duty to conserve one's life. The repelling of injuries and the repulsion of force, as Frederick Russell interprets the decretalists, were considered natural law rights. The punishment of injuries already received was part of the *jus gentium* and could properly be imposed only by those with civil authority.[3] Finally, legitimate self-defense was considered by St. Thomas within the context of the virtue of justice. It specifically sought to maintain a just relation between persons— communicative justice—in a situation where there was no time for the imposition of legitimate civil authority.

What was occurring in these passages was of considerable moment. The decretalist tradition represented the manner in which moral issues were assessed largely in legal categories. What Thomas was attempting to accomplish in this discussion was not just to provide a rationale for self-defense, but also to transform the legalistic categories of the decretalist tradition into specifically moral terminology and reasoning. His focus was on the intention of the will and what the will was led to by right reason: to intend to preserve one's self in existence. The first precept of the natural law required that "whatever is a means of preserving human life, and of warding off its obstacles belongs to the natural law" (*Summa Theologiae* I–II, 94.2). The natural law specified the object of the act: the warding off of a menace to one's self. As Joseph Mangan observed in his study of the history of the principle of double effect, "before the time of St. Thomas there is no indication of a definitely formulated principle of the double effect,"[4] meaning by that a formulation in the terminology of ethics.

Mangan's helpful study illuminates the manner in which the principle of double effect was further refined in the writings of Cajetan and the nineteenth century Jesuit manualist Joannes Gury, until it received its modern formulation in the neo-Thomist and neo-scholastic manuals:

A person may licitly perform an action that he foresees will produce a good and a bad effect provided that four conditions are
verified at one and the same time: 1) that the action in itself from
its very object be good or at least indifferent; 2) that the good
effect and not the evil effect be intended; 3) that the good effect be
not produced by means of the evil effect; 4) that there be a proportionately grave reason for permitting the evil effect.[5]

Although some manualists express the principle in terms of three rather
than four conditions, this does not imply a significant difference between
them with regard to their understanding of the principle, but rather, some
merely blended the first and second condition into one. Some referred to such
acts as "voluntary in cause" or as the "indirect voluntary" meaning that the
cause of the act was intended, but that the evil effect, although foreseen,
was not intended.

The discussion of the principle of double effect as found in the writings
of the neo-Thomist manuals had become much more stereotyped and generalized since its exposition in the *Summa Theologiae*. It was generalized in
that its potential scope extended to any act which might have two effects
inextricably intertwined, one of which was good and the other evil; it was no
longer restricted to the context of a proportioned response to the unjust
violence of another. The principle of double effect had become stereotyped in
that, although the four conditions reflected Thomas' discussion of the principle, they had now been set into a relatively standard formulation and generalized in a manner which extended the principle's scope of application. The
neo-Thomist theologians usually failed to make any reference to the natural
law basis of the principle of double effect. They presented the principle
without the justification of the principle. Thus they were able to extend the
application of the principle to topics which could not be addressed in relation
to one's duty to protect and prolong one's own life.

The neo-Thomist manualists extended the scope of the principle of
double effect to five distinct moral issues: just war, the indirect killing of
innocent persons, material cooperation in the sin of another, the treatment of
ectopic pregnancies, and the excision of a cancerous, pregnant womb. In
contrast to the principle's development in the *Summa Theologiae*, there was
a tendency in the manuals for its application to become elliptical. The details
of its use were not always clearly indicated, and the natural law justification
of specific actions frequently yielded to legalistic interpretations.

The issue of just war was a significant topic for many of these theologians. The emergence of the nation-state, colonialism and its association
with a zeal for religious conversion, as well as the realities of modern, global
warfare were all issues which affected their treatment of just war. The

precise issues which are important in this context, however, are their discussion of the justice of both offensive and defensive wars and the reasons they provide for their conclusions.

Davis, Noldin/Schmitt, Zalba, McHugh/Callan, and Slater each addressed the topics of offensive and defensive war.[6] Offensive war was justified by these authors as based on the right to avenge an injury or the claim to enforce a right; defensive war was grounded in the right to self-defense against unjust aggression. Whether they addressed the issue of war from the perspective of charity (McHugh/Callan) or from that of justice (all the others), they each applied both *jus gentium* (the right to avenge an injury) and *jus naturale* (the right to prolong one's life) in their arguments. With regard to the latter right they generally make the argument that if an individual has a right to self-defense, so a similar right must be attributed to the state. Although they do not elaborate at much length any of the four conditions of the principle of double effect, they do stress the necessity of sufficient or proportionate reason. McHugh/Callan proposed that "the injury must be so grave that it outweighs the risks and losses of war."[7] Slater suggested that such reasons might include the retaking of a captured country, the avenging of a grave insult or injury to the state, freedom for the oppressed, and insuring the free preaching of the gospel.[8]

The weakness of these positions emerges from their statements concerning avenging injury and repelling force without an adequate moral argument to sustain them. Whereas Thomas had permitted the use of self-defensive force only to protect one's self from bodily harm, now the principle of sufficient or proportionate reason extended to the morality of using such force for goals only indirectly associated with a country's welfare. The application of the principle had taken on a self-evident character. Proportionate reason was being employed without a critical eye being kept on the basic good to be safeguarded: the protection of one's life from an unjust aggressor. It is difficult to imagine that the readers of the manuals, principally seminarians, would have been able to infer the natural law arguments which supported such positions.

The moral argument for the legitimacy of personal self-defense was treated in a similar manner. Noldin/Schmitt retained the phrase "*servato tamen moderamine inculpatae tutelae,*"[9] (that self-defense is limited only to the use of sufficient force), but they did not adequately present the natural law argument which justified this dictum. The principle had taken on the force of a rule. Zalba, McHugh/Callan, Slater, and Davis each emphasized the need for moderation in the exercise of force as well as the importance of sufficient or proportionate reason.[10] Among the sufficient reasons proffered were: public safety, private safety from death or loss of limb, the protection of property and chastity.

The question of the indirect killing of persons extended to several classes: one's self, non-combatants in warfare, and the abortion of fetuses in ectopic pregnancies. Each of these issues was addressed in relation to the principle of double effect. The indirect killing of one's self as well as of non-combatants had the usual requirement that such deaths be allowed only for proportionate reasons, be those reasons social and/or personal. Koch/Preuss stipulated the salvation of souls, the safeguarding of life or other equivalent goods as instances of such proportionate reasons.[11]

The question of ectopic pregnancies and thus the moral acceptability of indirect abortions deeply troubled these authors. Although all who treat the question allowed an indirect abortion in such an instance, the issue of proportionality became difficult for them. Davis permits the procedure "if the excision is necessary and the only means, and if all precautions are taken to safeguard, as far as possible, the lives of both mother and fetus."[12] Noldin/Schmitt and McHugh/Callan concur with Davis where there exists a proportionately grave reason.[13] The cause of their uneasiness was, I believe, that they were aware that the traditional arena of application of the principle of double effect was being altered in this context. The question had now become one of life versus life; gone was any sense of an unjust attack. Although this was also the case with the indirect killing of one's self and of innocent non-combatants, the realities of the human condition had always been such that persons jeopardized their lives for noble causes and that non-combatants died in war. The issue of indirect abortion raised the poignant question of life versus life, or possible life, apart from any aggression. McHugh/Callan posed the issue explicitly as one of temporal life versus temporal life.[14] Slater affirmed that indirect abortion was a licit "means to save [the mother's] life, even if what is a remedy for her causes the death of the fetus."[15]

The issue of one's material cooperation in the sin of another was another occasion for the application of the principle of double effect. What the manualists permitted was material cooperation, not formal cooperation. In certain instances, one could assist in the serious sin of another as long as one did not consent to the evil or directly cause the evil. A nurse might be required to assist in a direct abortion or sterilization, intrinsically evil acts, but he or she must not consent to the malice of the procedure nor directly cause the evil. The nurse's material cooperation would be limited to handing surgical instruments to the surgeon or caring for the client before or after surgery. What made such cooperation morally tolerable was the presence of a sufficient or proportionate reason. McHugh/Callan provided their readers with a positive and negative list of proportionate reasons. The graver the sin, the greater the reason for cooperation must be; the nearer the cooperation was to the act of sin, the greater the reason; the more the sin depended upon cooperation, the greater the reason; the more certain the evil, the greater the reason; the more obligation one might be under to avoid sin (e.g. as a priest or religious), the greater the reason for such cooperation must be. Such reasons might be the gain or loss of a great good, the public safety of the church or the state, the prevention of the loss of life or property.[16] As in the case of ectopic pregnancies, the principle of double effect was being extended to a new area of application. Although one can understand the pressure and coercion to which a nurse might be exposed, such coercion must at best be considered analogous to an unjust attack and a threat to one's life. Even more importantly, the principle now implied not an attempt to repulse an evil, but cooperation in an evil act for the sake of a good other than the preservation of one's own life. Clearly the principle of double effect had gone through considerable development between its articulation in the *Summa Theologiae* and its interpretation in the neo-Thomist manuals.

### (B) The Principle of Totality

In the same question in which Thomas gave initial formulation to the principle of double effect, he also laid out the parameters of what has become known as the principle of totality. The issue which gave rise to this principle was the justification for capital punishment (*Summa Theologiae* II–II, 64. 2 and 3). Whereas in the case of self-defense Thomas allowed individuals to employ sufficient force to protect their lives, the moral exercise of capital punishment was limited to appropriate civil authorities. Capital punishment, since it involved a positive harm to a member of the community, needed to be judicially determined in relation to the welfare of the common good. Second, and again unlike the morality involved in self-defense, the death of the criminal involved the direct killing of another person. The essential question was the justification of such a radical action. Thomas gave two closely related reasons. The first drew upon the analogy of amputation and argued that if one part of the body requires amputation for the welfare of the whole, then it was morally permissible to amputate. Thomas simply drew upon a moral dictum which was present in the literature of casuistry at least since the time of the Raymundina: for just cause, and not for the sake of imposing indignity, a part of the body could be removed for the sake of the whole.[17] Thomas further justified the analogy between amputation and capital punishment by asserting that the individual, the citizen, was related to society as a part to the whole. What was implied here was the organic notion of the state, a whole composed of parts whose perfection lies in the common good.

There were two natural law principles operative in Thomas' consideration of the principle of totality. First, as in the case of self-defense, the community had an obligation to continue itself in existence, a precept of the natural law. Second, right reason also led to the conclusion that the whole is greater than any of its parts. This self-evident principle, which Thomas employed frequently, was implicitly transmuted from the realm of logic into the realm of morality; "greater" now implying the greater moral worth of the whole in comparison to the moral worth of any of its parts. These natural law arguments were not explicit in Thomas' text, however they appear to sustain the sense of the text. Right reason was as imperative in this context as in self-defense.

The neo-Thomists addressed the question of capital punishment as well as that of mutilation and, each in its own way, both questions turned out to stimulate very interesting discussions. With regard to capital punishment, Davis stated that "God has given to the State the right over life and death, as He has given to every man the right to self-defence against unjust aggression."[18] Davis made no pretense at arguing this point in relation to the principle of totality, but rather he simply argued the point in relation to proportionate reason. Peace and the security of life and property justified capital punishment. Similarly Zalba argued that "it is permitted to public authority to kill directly malefactors because of a crime proportionately grave and certainly proved in the proper manner."[19] Although he did not develop his position to any length, Slater stayed closer to Thomas in asserting that "the state has the powers which are necessary to serve its end, the temporal happiness of citizens."[20]

In their examination of the question of mutilation, the neo-Thomist manuals retained the analogy of part to whole and endorsed the principle that a part of the body could be removed for the preservation of the whole. Zalba also required, however, that the removal of a part be an indirect act, that is, not intended in itself, and that it be done for a proportionate reason.[21] An interesting application of the principle of totality was made, and I believe correctly, by McHugh/Callan. They affirm that the principle implied an obligation to use ordinary means to prolong life, that the treatment of a part ought not be allowed to undermine the welfare of the person as a whole.[22]

The distinction between ordinary and extraordinary means of prolonging life became a significant issue in Catholic medical ethics in the late 1940s. On the basis of the virtue of charity a person was construed to have an obligation to himself to protect and prolong life. In his famous *Medico-Moral Problems*, Gerald Kelly developed this duty in relation to the natural law duty to avoid evil and to pursue good. He then proposed that "there are reasonable and proportionate limits to one's duty of doing good."[23] Ordinary means to prolong life, he continued, ought to be considered reasonable and proportionate; extraordinary means go beyond the requirements of reason and proportionality. Such means included excessive pain, expense, or inconvenience. Once again, it is obvious how far the concept of proportionate reason has been removed from its original use as a justification of self-defense and capital punishment. Proportionality and sufficient reason have here become the criteria by which one can determine that the obligation to prolong one's life has ceased. The proposal of McHugh/Callan would suggest that to require the use of extraordinary means might entail an inappropriate injury to the person as a whole. To impose or even expect the use of extraordinary means to prolong the lives of some chronically or critically ill persons may inappropriately deprive them of their wholeness. It could sacrifice spiritual and personal goods for the sake of life, a good subordinate to the spiritual and human goods of a person.

## II. Applications of the Decalogue and/or the Virtues

As we have already seen, the manuals of moral theology articulated their concrete moral teaching, usually called special moral theology, in relationship to the decalogue or to the theological (faith, hope, and charity) and cardinal (prudence, justice, temperance, and fortitude) virtues. Either of these frameworks provided the manualists with abundant opportunities to portray the concrete moral requirements of Christianity. The followers of St. Alphonsus Liguori generally presented their special moral theology in relationship to the decalogue. The Dominicans and many Jesuits used the schema of the virtues. Others combined the two approaches, presenting first the theological virtues and then turning their attention to the decalogue. Whatever the framework, the neo-Thomist manuals provided their students with an exhaustive treatment of the moral requirements incumbent upon members of the Christian community.

An examination of three topics addressed in the manuals can provide an adequate example of the manner in which these authors applied their theology and moral theory to specific moral issues. Their teaching concerning justice, charity, and temperance will be examined below. Each of these topics encompassed a large number of subtopics, not all of which can be discussed here. Their treatment of justice, for instance, ranged from an elaboration of one's duty towards the life of innocent persons to an examination of the moral obligation of restitution, the binding force of civil contracts, and topics associated with lying (justice concerning internal goods). All that can be attempted here will be a summary of the key aspects of their discussion of justice, charity, and temperance, and to highlight this with several specific examples.

### (A) The Virtue of Justice

The neo-Thomist manuals of moral theology contained long and detailed discussions of the virtue of justice and its application to specific issues. This section will set forth a presentation of the theory of the virtue found in these texts and then the manner in which they discussed ownership, theft, and restitution. Ownership of private property was construed as the right in accord with the virtue of justice, theft as the vice opposed to the virtue, and restitution as the essential means of restoring the damage inflicted by theft.

## (1) The Theory of the Virtue of Justice

To understand the neo-Thomist treatises on justice it is important to realize that they were not talking about a philosophical theory. It is not that the manualists would necessarily be confused by John Rawls' *A Theory of Justice*,[24] or Michael Walzer's *Spheres of Justice*,[25] but rather they would find such considerations of justice incomplete. Although they would share Rawls' concern for a universal theory of justice and Walzer's emphasis on the concrete possibilities for justice latent within a particular society, they would find both authors deficient with regard to their fundamental conceptions of justice. The first and most basic characteristic of justice for the neo-Thomist manualists was that it was a virtue inhering in the will and inclining persons to give to others what was due them, "the moral virtue by which we are inclined to the justice of giving to each his due."[26]

The manner in which the theological virtues were considered by the tradition to be lodged in the intellect (faith) and will (hope and charity) had a counterpart with regard to the cardinal or moral virtues. Prudence was considered the moral virtue of the intellect; temperance and fortitude the moral virtues of the concupiscible (the desire for objects as sensible) and irascible (the desire for objects as difficult to obtain) appetites; justice the virtue of the will. The manualists had an elaborate conception of justice derived from the Aristotelian/Thomistic tradition. The point of their theory, however, was to portray the manner and the objects toward which the will of a just person ought to be oriented.

A second important characteristic of the virtue of justice according to these authors was that it was based on the distinction between persons.[27] This was implicit in the definition of justice as what was due or owed to another. This characteristic of justice had particular importance to the manualists, however, because it provided a significant way of distinguishing justice from charity, which was understood as based on the union of humanity by common origin and destiny as well as God's love for all persons and their love of God. In other words the object of justice was construed as natural honesty and uprightness, as opposed to charity, which had God as its object; the one was a natural virtue, the other was supernatural.

A third feature of the manualists' treatment of justice was that the basis of what was owed to each person was grounded in human nature and expressed in terms of rights. Davis defined a "right" subjectively as "the inviolable moral power to have, do, or exact something"; objectively considered, a right was "the object of this moral power, the thing about which this power is exercised."[28] Thus, subjectively a right was a claim; objectively a right referred to the object claimed. Rights were neither the product of social consensus nor of the magnanimity of a monarch, but rather an inherent moral power of persons. The proximate ground of rights, Zalba argued, was "human nature, the dignity and incommunicable inviolability of the existing person, and thus of his right to be and act with respect to other persons as equals to himself, and to whom he should never be subordinated as a mere means."[29] Koch/Preuss defined justice strictly in terms of human nature and thus spoke of respect as what is owed to the persons of our fellow human beings.[30] The ultimate basis of rights, the basis of "every obligation and office," wrote Zalba, "is derived ultimately from God; He himself is the ultimate source of every right."[31] According to Davis rights are "the expression of natural, inviolable and necessary tendencies without the fulfillment of which life would be impossible . . . they are expressions of Divine wisdom and will."[32] Rights were the product of the nature with which God had endowed his rational creatures and were claims to what was necessary for human existence: the maintenance of one's own life as well as that of others, the propagation and rearing of children, the goods coincidental to the social and religious lives of persons.

The manualists developed their examination of justice in relation to the traditional distinction of communicative or personal justice between persons as individuals, legal justice as the duties of individuals to the state, and distributive justice as the duties of the state to individuals. Communicative justice included topics such as the right of an individual to life, contracts, ownership, restitution, and in some instances truthfulness. Legal justice dealt with the obligation to obey just laws, the paying of taxes, and the duty to bear arms in defense of one's country. Distributive justice addressed the allocation of goods to individuals within a society and was increasingly influenced after 1891 by the social teachings of Leo XIII and Pius XI.

*(2) Ownership*

Noldin/Schmitt proposed a very extensive notion of ownership or "dominion," in the technical language of the manuals. Dominion was "the power of disposing of a person or a thing."[33] This sweeping concept of dominion provided the authorization for jurisdiction as well as the ownership of specific goods. Koch/Preuss' more restrictive definition of dominion as "the permanent and exclusive right of retaining, controlling, and disposing of an object in one's own interest and according to one's own interest"[34] was closer to the customary definition of the manualists.[35]

Dominion or ownership was generally construed as a right to certain specifiable goods which could be used, consumed, or alienated in relation to the interests of their possessor.

The goods over which ownership could be exercised were of various sorts. Zalba considered internal goods such as the soul, human potencies, the senses and members of the body, external goods such as property and money, and mixed goods such as fame and honor as legitimate categories of goods which pertained to dominion.[36] Similarly, Davis spoke of the life and bodily members of a person as things over which one exercised qualified ownership—one could use them but not dispose of them. External things, however, were subject to the complete ownership of a person.[37] Since there was a considerable range of goods over which a person could exercise dominion, there could be an equally wide range of acts which might impugn one's just claims. Murder, violence against another person, calumny, and libel, as well as theft, robbery, and fraud were each vices opposed to dominion or ownership.

The legitimation of the claim to dominion was established by a series of natural law arguments. For Davis the right to private property could be substantiated in three related manners. First, "to say that he shall have no complete dominion over anything is opposed to man's very life and his human dignity."[38] This contention was simply a reassertion of the natural law requirement that whatever is a means of preserving human life and warding off obstacles to it belongs to the natural law. Davis did not consider a person's claim to external goods to be limited to those goods necessary for the support of mere life, to the mere protection of biological life; he included human dignity as an element which the right to property intends to protect. Second, he contended that in no other way could a father reasonably provide food for his family than by having lucrative property which he could in turn hand on to this family. Davis' appeal at this point was to the second precept of the natural law—the duty to procreate and to educate children. Finally, he proposed that ownership fostered peace between people and encouraged greater care of the goods of the earth. Here the allusion was to the third precept's requirement that persons live in society. Zalba asserted a similar natural law basis for ownership: "Man needs many external goods in order to be able to attain the end established for him by God according to his nature."[39] Slater expressed the identical position:

> God has imposed on [man] the obligation of maintaining himself and those who are dependent upon him, and he has a consequent right to make his own whatever is necessary and useful for the purpose, if it has not already been appropriated by someone else.[40]

Three further characteristics of the manuals' discussions of property need to be mentioned briefly: the subject of the right of ownership, title to ownership, and the claims of the poor. The right to ownership was considered characteristic of persons who have moral faculties, i.e., rational beings.[41] This right was generally understood to extend to the insane and to unborn children; they too needed what was necessary for the pursuit of their final end.

The manualists consistently referred to occupation, accession, prescription, and contract as the sources and validations of an individual's claim to specific external goods.[42] The more contemporary manuals, such as Zalba and Davis, gave increasing emphasis to labor as a basis for a claim to external goods. The details and complexities of these titles are not essential to the purposes of this chapter. What is important is that they functioned as intermediaries between rights and just claims. The fact that one needed food or land did not give one a right to the monarch's fields or to his deer. Something other than rights was the basis of a claim to a specific good. The specification of these titles was once again the product of the decretalist and canonical traditions.

Third, although the manualist tradition strongly emphasized the right to private property, it also placed important limitations upon it. As did civil law, the manuals acknowledged the right of the state to restrict and even usurp private property for the sake of the common good. They would not object to appropriate uses of eminent domain, zoning ordinances, building codes or the imposition of legitimate taxes. The common good was the single most important curb on the manualist notion of ownership. The other restriction was that in situations of extreme need, where there was a real and immediate danger of loss of life or another significant good, one's right of ownership yielded to the demands of the person in need. The need had to be extreme, not grave or common. That one was hungry did not justify poaching; imminent danger of starvation did. In times of famine when a whole population might be in danger of starvation, poaching would not be morally acceptable; starvation under such conditions would be a common danger shared by all or most of a population. In extreme need, Noldin/Schmitt asserted, "one must morally do what is necessary to save one's life."[43] Note that they did not assert that one *may* take what does not belong to oneself in such situations, but that one *must*. Davis clearly indicated the natural law basis of such a claim:

> In such need, the goods of the earth are common property; rights to exclusive private ownership lapse; there is, in fact, an obligation to preserve life, which is a higher good than property.[44]

Perhaps even more strongly, Slater stated that:

> . . . material things were created for the preservation of human life and no rights of ownership can prevail against the higher claim of one who is in extreme necessity.[45]

Such claims against private property were severely restricted by the manualists. The poor ought to beg and the wealthy ought to give alms to prevent situations of extreme need from arising. The poor may not exercise such a claim against someone equally destitute. In extreme need, however, the poor possessed a claim in justice against the private property of a person of means.

### (3) Theft

Each of the manualists used the same definition of theft, which Slater acknowledged to have been part of the decretalist tradition. "Theft is the secret taking away of the property of another against his reasonable will."[46] Theft was one of the vices and sins contrary to the virtue of justice and, in some instances at least, against charity as well. The common teaching of the manualists was that thievery was "grave by nature though accidentally slight," i.e. in some instances, although minor damage was done to the rights of another, their rights remained substantially intact.[47] Specifically, theft was a violation of communicative justice. The gravity of the sin needed to be assessed in relation to the damage done to another. This was done in several manners. In general, to steal a day's wage or what was necessary to support an average family for a day was considered to cause serious damage. To steal the same amount from a wealthy person was thought to cause less harm and thus to be only a venial sin. The seriousness of thievery was assessed, in part, in relation to the damage done to specific persons. However the manualists also set an absolute sum which always constituted grave matter and thus mortal sin. The amount varied in relation to the value of different currencies. By contemporary American standards it would probably be approximately $100. Regardless of the wealth of the person from whom money was stolen, a theft of $100 would always be considered serious sin. The reason for this was that thievery always violated the social order; it damaged society by making persons insecure in their possessions. The establishment of such an absolute sum was essential in order to protect the security and harmony of the social order, so that persons could live in society in peace and tranquility. The seriousness of this sin, therefore, was determined in relation to the private and public damage done. While conceding that in some cases thievery might be only venially sinful, the manualists all shared the haunting concern of Koch/Preuss that thievery was in itself a mortal sin "inspired by immoral motives and uncontrolled passion" and that "it grossly violates the justice and charity which each man owes to his neighbor."[48]

### (4) The Duty of Restitution

The manualists imposed the duty of restitution with regard to numerous kinds of damage inflicted upon the property of persons: possession in good faith (one believes that one has clear title to property when in fact that title is encumbered), possession in bad faith (the thief's possession of stolen goods), injury to the property of another, damage to the name or reputation of another, and cooperation in the evil of another (scandal). The complexities associated with the amount, manner and time of restitution are peripheral to the present concerns; the concept of restitution, however, is important.

The central concern of restitution was the reparation of the violated rights of others and the reconstructing of the natural order of justice.[49] The obligation of restitution was based in the natural law. This meant that restitution was essential for security and peace within a community, an appeal to the third precept of the natural law. However, the manualists also contended that it was in the very nature of property that it seek its owner (*res clamat domino*), benefit its owner (*res fructificat domino*) and perish at the expense of its owner (*res perit domino*). The grounds of restitution were once again vestiges of the decretalist tradition and portray the fundamental underlying conception of justice within the tradition: there is a moral order to be protected, preserved and, when violated, restored.

### (B) The Virtue of Charity

The neo-Thomist conception of charity as a theological virtue was discussed in Chapter Three, and its relation to the virtue of justice in the preceding section of the current chapter. The virtue of charity, however, also entailed specific duties to God, self, and neighbor. Thus there was a wide spectrum of moral issues which could be raised in regard to it. There was the general obligation to keep one's will turned to God as the ultimate good and, more concretely, the need to pray and to make acts of good intention. There were duties to protect one's life and the welfare of the body. With regard to one's neighbor there were occasions when the giving of alms was necessary, when fraternal correction was called for, as well as the duty to avoid scandal and cooperation in the evil of others. The present discussion will focus on the order of charity itself and the specific issue of almsgiving.

### (1) The Order of Charity

The moral requirements of charity toward one's neighbor were more extensive and demanding than was the case with justice. Justice dealt with the order between persons as distinct members of society; charity was concerned with the unity between persons in the creative and redemptive orders, with the spiritual bond between persons arising from their origin in one creator and their shared destiny in a common good and end. The virtue of charity might not seem immediately capable of generating neat, precise moral requirements as was the case with justice. How does one set priorities between the welfare of one's self and the welfare of others? Does charity imply that I ought to do all that could be done to foster the welfare of my neighbor? Should I risk my life to save the soul of another, to save the life of another, to protect the property of another? The manualists' elaboration of the order of charity intended to prioritize the objects of one's love and to establish a balance between the welfare of the self and the welfare of the other so that realistic moral requirements could be demarcated.

Slater prefaced his comments regarding the order of loves by stating that one:

> ... must look at the claims which others have on our charity; [charity] must appreciate things at their true value, otherwise in wishing to confer a favor it will do harm to the object of love; it must assist others wisely according to their necessity, otherwise it will foster hypocrisy and produce professional and able-bodied beggars.[50]

Although this quotation set perhaps too suspicious a tone for a discussion of the order of love, it accurately portrayed the reason for seeking an order. Love ought to be effective and not so diverse and unfocused as to lose its potential for actual accomplishments. Charity was not construed as sentimentality nor as undisciplined romanticism. The order of charity discussed the priority according to which persons ought to be loved as well as the objects to be loved or desired on their behalf.

With regard to persons, the order of love required that God was to be loved above all else, then ourselves, and finally the neighbor as one's self.[51] This was further refined with regard to love of neighbor so that one ought to love persons in relation to their proximity to God and to one's self, or in relation to the extent of their claim upon one. The priority on love of God was obvious; he was the ultimate end and good of human life. Love of self was set prior to love of neighbor because the former was the norm of the manner in which the neighbor was to be loved (Mt. 22.39). The notions of proximity and claim parallel each other. Persons closer to God have a greater claim to our love because they share more fully in the source of charity, divine love. The discussions of proximity and greater claim in relation to the self were reminiscent of Thomas' questioning whether one should love one's children more than one's parents, one's father more than one's mother, or one's parents more than one's spouse. The manualists did not repeat Thomas' biological and "degree of excellence" arguments in this regard; they were content to acknowledge that there was a need to prioritize one's love of neighbor.

The manuals also described a priority with regard to the objects which one desired for one's self and others. One's own spiritual welfare was the most important object of love; then came the spiritual welfare of one's neighbor. The bodily welfare of one's self had precedence over the bodily welfare of another. External goods for one's self and others were the last among the priorities of love. These objects were understood to be set in a hierarchy so that the lower could be sacrificed for the sake of the higher. Prümmer listed a set of four rules which clearly outlined this priority.

> First rule: In another's extreme spiritual necessity, we are obliged to help him even at grave risk to our own bodily life, provided that there is serious hope of saving him and no serious public harm results.
>
> Second rule: Except when another is in extreme spiritual necessity, there is no strict obligation of helping him at the risk of serious bodily harm.
>
> Third rule: In another's grave need (spiritual or temporal) we must help him if we can do so without serious inconvenience, unless justice, piety, or our office make greater demands of us.
>
> Fourth rule: In common or slight necessity we must be prepared to suffer some slight inconvenience in helping our neighbor.[52]

Although not all of the manuals provided such a set of rules, nevertheless the substance of their positions was essentially the same. What one finds in these discussions is a prioritizing of goods: the establishment of an objective order of preferential love. Spiritual goods were construed as more important than bodily goods, bodily goods more important than external goods. The order of loves was relevant to the manualists' discussion of scandal, fraternal correction, the toleration of cooperation in the sin of another, and almsgiving.

## (2) Almsgiving

The obligation to give alms was considered one of the precepts, one of the moral obligations, inherent to the virtue of charity. Almsgiving was generally established on the basis of both natural law and divine law. The most frequent natural law argument appealed to the giving of alms as a means of sustaining the peace and order of society.[53] It was also argued that almsgiving was part of the nature of real love,[54] that anyone who experienced true need would so wish to be treated,[55] and that such acts maintained the temporal order's purpose of benefiting all.[56] The divine law basis of the requirement was articulated by reference to appropriate passages from the Old and New Testaments. It is interesting to note that even in their consideration of a theological virtue the manualists stressed the natural law as the foundation of a moral duty along with the divine law. The divine law, at least in this instance, was not considered to have imposed a moral duty in addition to what was already required by the natural law.

The duty of almsgiving was analogous to the duty imposed by the virtue of justice to share one's surplus goods with persons in extreme need. The obligation was conditioned both by the resources of the potential donor and the need of the recipient.[57] The condition of the recipient was once again divided into extreme, grave, and common necessity. The resources of the donor were divided into what was needed for the support of himself and his family, what was essential to the maintenance of his state or way of life, and what was superfluous to the two prior needs. The manualists concurred that there was a serious obligation to give something to the poor from one's superfluous goods. This was a general obligation which could be fulfilled in numerous ways. A person might fulfill this duty by giving to the poor directly or by contributing to institutions. There was no obligation to give to a particular poor person in common or grave need. In extreme need, the poor could make legitimate demands upon the superfluous goods of another. This topic clearly parallels the manualists' consideration of the claims of the poor with regard to justice. What is distinctive in this context is the emphasis placed on the obligation of the wealthy to care for the poor. Davis refers to the affluent as "trustees of the poor,"[58] whereas the discussion of justice stressed the legitimacy of the claims of the poor. A strong sense of *noblesse oblige* ran through these texts in a manner that at times seems to demean the poor; however, there was also a strong conviction that there were limits to the ravages of poverty which the affluent ought not to tolerate.

### (C) Temperance/The Sixth and Ninth Commandments

The manualists' consideration of the virtue of temperance and the requirements of the sixth and ninth commandments contained their teaching on sexual morality. No other portion of the manuals has continued to receive more public and scholarly scrutiny. *Humanae Vitae*'s (1968) condemnation of all types of artificial means of birth control, as well as the more recent statements of the Vatican on homosexuality, human reproduction, divorce, and abortion have each contributed to keeping these issues in the forefront of public attention. The purpose of this section cannot be an exhaustive treatment of any of these topics as such, but rather simply to provide several instances of the casuistry, the applied moral reasoning, of the manualists with regard to human sexuality. This can be most efficiently accomplished through an examination of impurity (*luxuria*) as the vice opposed to the virtue of chastity, the classification of sexual sins, and the appropriate use of sex in marriage.

### (1) The Vice of Impurity

The virtue of temperance was understood to control sensual desire for goods as pleasurable (the concupiscible appetite); thus it included the norms of moderation with regard to food and drink as well as sexuality. The relationship between the sensual desire associated with food and drink and the sensual desire associated with sexual acts was a significant element in the ethic of some of the manualists. "The means of conserving the individual is nutrition," wrote Noldin/Schmitt, "the means of conserving and propagating the species is the commingling of the sexes in legitimate matrimony."[59] The delights of taste and venereal pleasure were associated with appetites or drives toward the maintenance of the lives of individuals and the encouragement of the propagation of the species respectively; they were instinctual drives which led to the fulfillment of the primary and secondary principles of the natural law—the maintenance of life and the propagation of the species. In the same vein Slater wrote:

> As nature has taken care that the individual should take the food and drink necessary for his personal support by giving him the spur of appetite for nourishment and pleasure in taking it, so the same great Mother has taken care of the race by joining venereal pleasure to the act of procreating children.[60]

This analogy between sensual pleasures and their human goods or ends (the object of an act) constituted the basic moral rule in the area of sexuality. Slater continued, "This pleasure is lawful when indulged in between married people and according to the laws of marriage. In all other cases it is unlawful, and is forbidden by the Sixth and Ninth Commandments."[61]

Davis and others made the same point, but did so by means of a definition of impurity (*luxuria*), the vice opposed to chastity. "Impurity is, then, defined as the inordinate appetite for or use of venereal movements, that is, inordinate in respect to the good of the species."[62] Impurity constituted the general species of sin opposed to the virtue of chastity or the sixth and ninth commandments. Note that impurity is defined in relation to harms to the species, not in relation to harms to individual men and women.

### (2) The Classification of Sexual Sins

Impurity was subdivided into complete or incomplete acts. Davis stated a distinction which runs throughout the manuals:

> Impurity has for its object, as already suggested, venereal pleasure, which may be complete in men by the seminal ejaculation, and in women by the diffusion of vaginal glandular secretions . . .

or it may be incomplete when it does not reach that degree, but still is present in the sexual organs, incipient when the organs are preparing to proceed to the orgasm, full and vehement, when they are about to exert the orgasm.[63]

Complete acts of impurity were further subdivided into acts in accord with nature and acts contrary to nature. The acts in accord with nature were fornication, adultery, rape, and incest. Such acts were deemed a harm to the species because they could lead to children who would not be properly reared. Onanism (as either a form of birth control or simply as masturbation), sodomy, and bestiality were acts against nature. Such acts harmed the species because they were incapable of begetting children. Incomplete acts of impurity were such things as looks, touches, dancing, and the reading of lewd books with the direct intention of venereal pleasure.

The common teaching of the manualists was that all directly voluntary acts intending venereal pleasure, apart from those which occurred within marriage, were grave mortal sins.[64] Unlike intentional violations of justice or charity, directly voluntary sins of impurity did not admit of smallness of matter; they were never simply venial sins. Why were these sins taken with such utter seriousness by these authors? The reasons for this can be seen in the arguments they presented in support of the evils associated with impurity. Whereas sins against justice and charity were at least in part assessed in relation to the harm done to other individuals, sexual sins were always evaluated in relation to the social and moral orders, the values of procreation and the proper rearing of children. Venial sins against charity and justice were possible because in some instances they left the moral order largely intact and unthreatened. To steal from the wealthy left the order of justice substantially undamaged. Fornication, adultery and homosexuality were always viewed as direct and immediate dangers to the social and moral orders themselves. They posed dangers to the human species as such.

### (3)  The Use of Sexuality Within Marriage

Any directly intended venereal pleasure outside of marriage was considered to be intrinsically immoral, contrary to nature's purpose,[65] against the dictate of reason,[66] or a perversion of an order ordained by God and nature.[67] Such pleasure, "should be experienced in, and should attract to, that mutual act between man and wife, designed by nature for the propagation of the race, whether or not the effect ensue."[68] No other purpose for this pleasure could be rationally assigned, and therefore no use of it outside marriage could be considered rational. More specifically, only marriage could provide a stable, healthy environment for the rearing of children. Although fornication and adultery might contribute to the continuance of the race, they could not provide an appropriate setting for the nurturing of young human life. Although an individual might be wealthy and stable enough to provide a good home, nevertheless such actions were intrinsic disorders which would lead to the neglect of children on a large scale.[69] A second evil consequence of permitting venereal pleasure outside of marriage would be that there would be little inducement for men and women to undertake the burdens of married life. One of the basic and perfect (i.e. capable of securing its own ends) institutions of society was considered to be threatened.[70] The second precept of the natural law was thought to be immediately and directly jeopardized by the seeking of venereal pleasure outside of marriage.

The positive element in such arguments was the seriousness with which the manualists addressed issues of sexuality and especially the social dimension of human sexuality. However, they utterly failed to grasp its interpersonal aspects, nor did they sufficiently perceive its human and Christian dimensions. McHugh/Callan wrote that:

> . . . sex pleasure has been ordained by God as an inducement to perform an act which is both disgusting in itself and burdensome in its consequences. . . .[71]

Their discussion of coitus within marriage was burdened with the notions of the conjugal debt, the duties arising from the marriage contract, and the proper insemination of the female. Whereas Davis viewed intercourse within marriage from the perspective of justice, not charity or intimacy, McHugh/Callan viewed it as a biological event for the sake of propagation; love and intimacy were of marginal moral significance in the manualists' assessment of the act. Such analyses would eventually give rise to the charges of biologism and physicalism.[72]

With these general moral rules in place the neo-Thomist manualists could readily assess specific sexual sins. The sins against nature were inherently immoral because they possessed no possibility of procreation. Sexual sins in accord with nature, fornication, adultery, rape, and incest, were inherently immoral because they could not properly provide for possible offspring and in some instances also constituted violations of justice.

The casuistry of the neo-Thomist manuals of moral theology provided very specific resolutions to complex moral issues. The genre's scope of interest ranged from the morality of warfare to the nature of ownership and its duties to the licitness of specific sexual acts. The casuistry of the manuals attempted to provide seminarians with both a method for resolving questions of conscience and specific answers to all the questions which they might confront as ministers of the sacrament of penance. Indeed it was the morality mediated through the neo-Thomist manuals in particular which shaped the moral life of Roman Catholics for almost a century. Although neo-Thomism held the center stage of Catholic theology, it was not the only player upon the stage. Throughout the one hundred years of its dominance neo-Thomism interacted with modernism, neo-scholasticism, the theology of the Catholic faculty at Tübingen, and the *nouvelle théologie* of the 1940s and 1950s. The next four chapters will delineate the major positions of these alternatives to neo-Thomism.

## NOTES

1. Peter Knauer, "The Hermeneutical Function of the Principle of Double Effect," *Natural Law Forum* 12 (1967):133.
2. Thomas' presentation of the just war theory can be found in the *Summa Theologiae* II-II, 40.1. He argued that for a war to be just it must be waged by a legitimate ruler, for a just cause, and with a proper intention. The just cause which he cited was that given by St. Augustine: a war may be waged to punish injuries inflicted. This was the most consistent legitimation for just war which can be found in the Decretals. [See F.H. Russell, *The Just War In the Middle Ages* (Cambridge: Cambridge University Press, 1975), esp. Chs. 4 and 5.] The right intention, that good be promoted and evil avoided, excluded any self-aggrandizement or the infliction of suffering beyond what was required to reestablish the order between persons which had been destroyed by the unjust aggressor. Note the manner in which Thomas used a principle of the natural law to define the proper intentionality of one waging a just war. What is most striking about Thomas' presentation of the just war theory is that he situates the discussion within the virtue of charity, not justice. Thus he primarily understood the malice of an unjust war to be the violation of the virtue of charity and specifically a violation of peace, i.e. the harmony of one's own desires into an ordered unity as well as a union between one's own desires and those of another person. The punishment of injuries intended only to reestablish the proper relation between persons, especially rulers.
3. Russell, *The Just War*, 131–132.
4. Joseph T. Mangan, S.J., "An Historical Analysis of the Principle of Double Effect," *Theological Studies* 10 (1949):42.
5. Ibid., 43; see also Thomas Slater, *A Manual of Moral Theology*, 2 vols., 3rd ed. (New York: Benziger Brothers, 1908), 1:6–8; Henry Davis, *Moral and Pastoral Theology*, 3 vols. (London: Sheed and Ward, 1935), 1:13; H. Noldin, S.J. et A. Schmitt, S.J., *Summa Theologiae Moralis*, 3 vols., 27th ed. (Oeniponte: Sumptis et Typis Feliciani Rauch, 1940),

1:51; Gerald Kelly, *Medico-Moral Problems* (St. Louis: The Catholic Hospital Association of the United States and Canada, 1958), 12–14.

6. Davis, *Moral and Pastoral Theology*, 2:120–123.; see also Noldin/ Schmitt, *Summa Theologiae Moralis*, 2:337–40; Marcellinius Zalba, S.J., *Theologiae Moralis Compendium: Juxta Constitutionem "Deus Scientiarum,"* 2 vols. (Marietti: Biblioteca De Auctores Cristianos, 1958), 1:892–902; John A. McHugh, O.P. and Charles J. Callan, O.P., *Moral Theology: A Complete Course Based on St. Thomas Aquinas and the Best Modern Authorities*, 2 vols. (New York: Joseph F. Wagner, Inc., 1929), 1:545–563; Slater, *A Manual of Moral Theology*, 1:319–23.

7. McHugh/Callan, *Moral Theology*, 1:549.

8. Slater, *A Manual of Moral Theology*, 1:320.

9. Noldin/Schmitt, *Summa Theologiae Moralis*, 2:318.

10. Zalba, *Theologiae Moralis Compendium*, 1:869; see also McHugh/Callan, *Moral Theology*, 1:547; Slater, *A Manual of Moral Theology*, 1:508; Davis, *Moral and Pastoral Theology*, 2:125.

11. Anthony Koch and Arthur Preuss, *A Handbook of Moral Theology*, 5 vols., 3rd ed. (St. Louis: B. Herder Book Co., 1925), 3:95.

12. Davis, *Moral and Pastoral Theology*, 2:147.

13. Noldin/Schmitt, *Summa Theologia Moralis*, 2:325; see also McHugh/Callan, *Moral Theology*, 2:115.

14. McHugh/Callan, *Moral Theology*, 1:115.

15. Slater, *A Manual of Moral Theology*, 1:313.

16. McHugh/Callan, *Moral Theology*, 1:610.

17. *Summa Sti. Raymundi De Barcinonensis*, (Hants: Gregg Press Limited, republished 1967), 156.

18. Davis, *Moral and Pastoral Theology*, 2:123.

19. Zalba, *Theologiae Moralis Compendium*, 1:866.

20. Slater, *A Manual of Moral Theology*, 1:305.

21. Zalba, *Theologiae Moralis Compendium*, 1:852.

22. McHugh/Callan, *Moral Theology*, 1:640.

23. Kelly, *Medico-Moral*, 131.

24. John Rawls, *A Theory of Justice* (Cambridge: Belknap Press, 1971).

25. Michael Walzer, *Spheres of Justice* (New York: Basic Books, Inc., 1983).

26. Zalba, *Theologiae Moralis Compendium*, 1:906; see also Dominic Prümmer, *A Handbook of Moral Theology*, trans., Rev. Gerald W. Shelton, edited for American usage by Rev. John Gavin Nolan (New York: P. J. Kennedy and Sons, 1957), 117; Slater, *A Manual of Moral Theology*, 1:222; Davis, *Moral and Pastoral Theology*, 1:261; Koch/Preuss, *A Handbook of Moral Theology*, 5:10.

27. Prümmer, *Handbook of Moral Theology*, 117; see also Zalba, *Theologiae Moralis Compendium*, 1:931.
28. Davis, *Moral and Pastoral Theology*, 1:261.
29. Zalba, *Theologiae Moralis Compendium*, 1:908.
30. Koch/Preuss, *A Handbook of Moral Theology*, 5:10
31. Zalba, *Theologiae Moralis Compendium*, 1:907; see also Davis, *Moral and Pastoral Theology*, 2:261.
32. Davis, *Moral and Pastoral Theology*, 2:261.
33. Noldin/Schmitt, *Summa Theologiae Moralis*, 2:342.
34. Koch/Preuss, *A Handbook of Moral Theology*, 5:225.
35. Zalba, *Theologiae Moralis Compendium*, 1:934; see also Slater, *A Manual of Moral Theology*, 1:226; Davis, *Moral and Pastoral Theology*, 2:230.
36. Zalba, *Theologiae Moralis Compendium*, 1:943.
37. Davis, *Moral and Pastoral Theology*, 2:232.
38. Ibid., 2:236.
39. Zalba, *Theologiae Moralis Compendium*, 1:948.
40. Slater, *A Manual of Moral Theology*, 1:228.
41. Ibid., 1:230; see also Zalba, *Theologiae Moralis Compendium*, 1:955; Noldin/Schmitt, *Summa Theologiae Moralis*, 2:353; Davis, *Moral and Pastoral Theology*, 2:242.
42. Davis, *Moral and Pastoral Theology*, 2:153–261 and 2:323–379; see also Noldin/Schmitt, *Summa Theologiae Moralis*, 2:369–380; Slater, *A Manual of Moral Theology*, 1:242–246; Zalba, *Theologiae Moralis Compendium*, 1:978–1008.
43. Noldin/Schmitt, *Summa Theologiae Moralis*, 2:401.
44. Davis, *Moral and Pastoral Theology*, 2:280.
45. Slater, *A Manual of Moral Theology*, 1:252.
46. Ibid., 1:251; see also Noldin/Schmitt, *Summa Theologiae Moralis*, 2:393; Zalba, *Theologiae Moralis Compendium*, 1:1318; Davis, *Moral and Pastoral Theology*, 2:268; Koch/Preuss, *A Handbook of Moral Theology*, 5:354.
47. Davis, *Moral and Pastoral Theology*, 2:269; see also Zalba, *Theologiae Moralis Compendium*, 1:1320; Slater, *A Manual of Moral Theology*, 1:253; Koch/Preuss, *A Handbook of Moral Theology*, 5:350.
48. Koch/Preuss, *A Handbook of Moral Theology*, 5:351.
49. Davis, *Moral and Pastoral Theology*, 2:284; see also Slater, *A Manual of Moral Theology*, 1:255; Koch/Preuss, *A Handbook of Moral Theology*, 5:375; Zalba, *Theologiae Moralis Compendium*, 1:1254.
50. Slater, *A Manual of Moral Theology*, 1:117.
51. Prümmer, *Handbook of Moral Theology*, 98; see also Davis, *Moral and*

*Pastoral Theology*, 1:319; McHugh/Callan, *Moral Theology*, 1:462; Noldin/Schmitt, *Summa Theologiae Moralis*, 2:79. Slater, *A Manual of Moral Theology*, 1:117; Zalba, *Theologiae Moralis Compendium*, 1:78.

52. Prümmer, *Handbook of Moral Theology*, 99.
53. Zalba, *Theologiae Moralis Compendium*, 2:88; see also Prümmer, *Handbook of Moral Theology*, 100; McHugh/Callan, *Moral Theology*, 1:485.
54. Davis, *Moral and Pastoral Theology*, 1:323; see also Zalba, *Theologiae Moralis Compendium*, 2:88.
55. McHugh/Callan, *Moral Theology*, 2:485.
56. Noldin/Schmitt, *Summa Theologiae Moralis*, 2:93; see also Zalba, *Theologiae Moralis Compendium*, 2:88.
57. Davis, *Moral and Pastoral Theology*, 1:323–327; see also Slater, *A Manual of Moral Theology*, 1:123–124; Noldin/Schmitt, *Summa Theologiae Moralis*, 2:92–94; Prümmer, *Handbook of Moral Theology*, 100; McHugh/Callan, *Moral Theology*, 1:485–489; Zalba, *Theologiae Moralis Compendium*, 2:87–99.
58. Davis, *Moral and Pastoral Theology*, 1:323.
59. H. Noldin, S.J. and A. Schmitt, S.J., *De Sexto Praecepto et De Usu Matrimonii* (Oeniponte: Sumptibus et Typis Feliciani Rauch, 1940), 6.
60. Slater, *A Manual of Moral Theology*, 1:209.
61. Ibid.
62. Davis, *Moral and Pastoral Theology*, 2:177; see also Prümmer, *Handbook of Moral Theology*, 230; Noldin/Schmitt, *Summa Theologiae Moralis*, 2:6.
63. Davis, *Moral and Pastoral Theology*, 2:177.
64. Ibid.; see also Prümmer, *Handbook of Moral Theology*, 230; McHugh/Callan, *Moral Theology*, 2:509; Noldin/Schmitt, *Summa Theologiae Moralis*, 2:12.
65. Davis, *Moral and Pastoral Theology*, 2:177.
66. McHugh/Callan, *Moral Theology*, 2:508.
67. Noldin/Schmitt, *Summa Theologiae Moralis*, 2:11–12.
68. Davis, *Moral and Pastoral Theology*, 2:177–178.
69. Ibid., 2:178; see also Noldin/Schmitt, *Summa Theologiae Moralis*, 2:12.
70. Davis, *Moral and Pastoral Theology*, 2:179; see also Noldin/Schmitt, *Summa Theologiae Moralis*, 2:12.
71. McHugh/Callan, *Moral Theology*, 2:508.
72. Charles Curran, "Natural Law and Contemporary Moral Theology" and "Sexuality and Sin: A Current Appraisal" in *Contemporary Problems In Moral Theology* (Notre Dame: Fides Publishers, Inc., 1970).

# 6.

# The Tradition in
# Crisis and Transition

Leo XIII's encyclical "Aeterni Patris" (1879) strove "to restore the golden wisdom of St. Thomas, and to spread it far and wide in the defense and beauty of the Catholic faith. . . ."[1] As a consequence of this papal initiative, neo-Thomism emerged as the dominant strand of Roman Catholic theology. Throughout the remaining years of the nineteenth century and approximately the first half of the twentieth century, neo-Thomism retained its hegemony among the systems of Catholic theology as well as its close association with the papacy. The neo-Thomist manuals of moral and dogmatic theology were the prevalent texts in the seminaries of Europe and the United States.

Catholic theology, however, as Bernard Reardon has clearly documented, "has rarely been the monolithic system which either its defenders or its critics frequently wish to portray."[2] Despite both its dominance in Catholic theological circles and its papal encouragement, neo-Thomist theology had significant competitors for its position of preeminence throughout the almost one hundred years of its existence. The modernist movement at the turn of the century and the theologians of the *nouvelle théologie* at the end of World War II are the best known such competitors. The Tübingen moral theology of Hirscher, which Kleutgen strove so ardently to supplant, continued to find expression in the writings of Fritz Tillmann and would later influence the work of Bernard Häring. The writings of two Belgian priests, Thomas Bouquillon and Dom Odon Lottin, provided manuals of moral theology based on Aquinas which were significantly different from the neo-Thomist manuals. The emergence of transcendental Thomism in the writings of Karl Rahner, Bernard Lonergan and others, as well as the development of theological paradigms less directly based in the thought of Aquinas, were to create the current milieu in Catholic theology, a milieu best characterized as one of pluralism. Despite the predominance of neo-Thomist theology during

123

this period, the existence and contributions of these alternative theologies ought not to be dismissed. What is new in the pluralism of post-Vatican II Catholic theology is not its existence, but its recognition and its degree.

This chapter will assess two developments in European Catholic theology from 1890 to World War I: modernism and Thomas Bouquillon's *Theologia Moralis Fundamentalis* (1890). Although there seems to be no evidence that modernism directly influenced moral theologians or produced its own literature in the area of moral theology, the modernists did define a theological orientation that was to become important. Thomas Bouquillon's *Theologia Moralis Fundamentalis* offered a significant alternative to the neo-Thomist manuals of the period.

## I. The Modernists

The Modernists, writes Alec Vidler:

... were a number of individual Roman Catholics who in one way or another came to realize that the received teaching of their Church was out of harmony with contemporary thought and who decided to do what they could to promote a reform of the Church's teaching.[3]

Vidler's definition asserts several key characteristics of modernism. First, it was not a coordinated, integrated movement. Although Maurice Blondel's philosophy of action influenced several of its French principals, modernism possessed no central figurehead or founder. Nor were its central figures, Alfred Loisy, Lucien Laberthonniere and George Tyrrell, a group formed around a common cause, rather they were individuals in whose work some common concerns can be detected. The "received tradition" against which the modernists were reacting was the neo-Thomist theology which had consciously defined its position as a clear and decisive alternative to contemporary European intellectual developments throughout the nineteenth century. It was precisely those intellectual developments which the modernists intended to engage. The modernists attempted to challenge neo-Thomism by reexamining the New Testament in the light of modern scholarship and then relating their discoveries in a manner which would illumine contemporary human experience.[4]

### (A) Lucien Laberthonniere
Lucien Laberthonniere represented the philosophical side of the modernist controversy. He was deeply influenced by Maurice Blondel's philosophy of action, as well as by the works of Leon Ollie-Laprune and Eduard Le

Roy. An exploration of four aspects of his writings must suffice for the limited purposes of this essay: his doctrine of immanence, the role of dogma, his rejection of the Aristotelian-Thomistic tradition, and the function of the papal teaching office.

Laberthonniere's doctrine of immanence was derived from Blondel's concept of "action." Immanence was set out in opposition to intellectualism; it denied that truth could be reached solely through an intellectual process. Vidler asserts that for the followers of Blondel "action:"

> . . . is used to mean not one particular kind of activity, e.g. doing as opposed to thinking, but the whole of our life with all that is given in our experience, that is to say a reality that is always in movement, always incomplete, always becoming.[5]

A philosophy of immanence asserts that experience, the reality that persons live, is itself a source of truth. What was being denied, and what was in direct opposition to neo-Thomism, was the contention that the truths by which Christians ought to live could be deduced from abstract metaphysical principles or abstract dogmatic statements. The philosophy of immanence maintained that faith should not be viewed as the acceptance of abstract formulas, but rather as something to be realized in and through the fulfillment of the inner longings of the human personality. At issue was the claim for a correlation between the needs and aspirations of the human personality and the data of revelation. This was not a doctrine of pure immanence, however. Faith and revelation could enable Christians to penetrate more deeply the transcendent exigencies of the human personality than they would be able to without divine assistance.

Given this notion of human cognition in relation to revelation, Laberthonniere was required to provide a non-traditional conception of dogma. Dogmas, he wrote:

> . . . are not simply dark and enigmatic formulas that God has promulgated in the name of His omnipotence to deaden the pride of our spirit. They have a moral and practical sense; they have a vital sense more or less accessible to us according to the degree of our spirituality on the whole.[6]

Such an understanding of the meaning of dogmas enabled Laberthonniere to modify Blondel's concept of action and to replace it with what he called a metaphysics of charity or moral dogmatism. Dogmas have a practical meaning; they show what we are and what we ought to be and how we can become what we ought to be.[7] Dogmas affect persons; they are not just intellectual propositions to which assent is to be given.

The Aristotelian-Thomistic tradition was the source, Laberthonniere contended, of the intellectualism which deprived Catholicism of the concrete, realistic meaning of revelation. The abstract notion of dogma which he thought he found in Aquinas removed from Christianity its fundamental spirit and replaced it with the alien theories of Aristotle.[8] Thomistic theology was thus conceived as the antithesis of what a metaphysics of charity construed the fundamental task of theology to be: the presentation of an image of what Christian life ought to be.

Laberthonniere also developed a unique interpretation of the papal teaching office. Indeed the papacy possessed authority, but that authority was to serve and not to dominate. "Its purpose was educative, not to suppress intellectual initiative but to develop it, not to negate but to guide and encourage personal autonomy and liberty."[9] To assert such an interpretation of the teaching office within forty years of Vatican I's decree on papal infallibility, a decree formulated to strengthen the papal stance against the intellectual as well as the political and social errors of the day, was to invite ecclesiastical criticism. The essence of Laberthonniere's claim, however, was to assert that the papal teaching office was a pastoral office and thus not directly relevant to academic theological discussions.

### (B) Alfred Loisy

Laberthonniere challenged neo-Thomism by means of an innovative philosophical system which attempted to replace the abstract theological formulations of Aquinas. Alfred Loisy sought to return to the source of Christianity through historical research and biblical exegesis. Loisy was a prolific author who published major studies of the synoptics and the fourth Gospel as well as essays on a variety of social and intellectual issues. Almost a quarter-century after the modernist controversy had ended, he wrote an interesting book on the relationship between religion and morality.[10] The work which most directly linked Loisy to the modernist movement was *The Gospel and the Church*,[11] a brilliant reply from the Catholic tradition to Adolf Harnack's 1899–1900 Berlin lectures entitled *What Is Christianity?*[12]

Modern biblical exegesis and historical work on the sources of the gospels were beginning to develop among French theologians in the latter part of the nineteenth century. This scholarship, however, immediately began to confront traditional notions of inspiration. Scriptural passages which had been used to support theological doctrines such as the divine institution of the seven sacraments and the Petrine office had usually been interpreted literally, i.e. in a manner consistent with the dogmatic teaching of the church and neo-Thomism. Loisy's rigorous scientific method sharply distinguished his work from that of many of his more traditional contemporaries. He viewed the scriptures as a collection of human documents which contained truths conditioned by the time, place, and circumstances of their origin. His project intended to determine what these documents asserted and then to propose revisions in the dogma of the church so as to render it consistent with the findings of exegesis.[13] Loisy, like Laberthonniere, hoped to secure a significant modification of traditional Catholic orthodoxy.

Adolf Harnack, Loisy's Protestant antagonist, had identified the essence of Christianity with an awareness of God the Father and his kingdom along with the centrality of the love commandment. According to Harnack, these elements constituted the abiding essence, the kernel of Christianity. The dogmatic and institutional developments of Christianity were construed as accretions to Christianity which simply distorted its true nature. The task of theology was to peel away these appendages so that the true nature of Christianity could become manifest. Loisy's critique of Harnack was most convincing in its simplicity. He denied that there was an essence or kernel that constituted the timeless nature of Christianity. According to Loisy, the New Testament documents from which Harnack purported to draw his portrayal of Christianity were themselves evolving, historical documents, the products of the primitive history of Christianity.[14]

The goal Loisy set for himself in writing *The Gospel and the Church* was to analyze and define the bonds which unite the gospel and the church in history. The second and third sections of his book outline the inadequacies of Harnack's interpretation of the essence of Christianity. The fourth, fifth, and sixth parts, which deal with the church, dogma, and worship, are the most important for the purposes of this study. They reveal not only the historical connections between the gospel and the church, but also Loisy's profound respect for a living tradition.

For Harnack, the social and legal structure of the church was a significant distortion of the gospel. What was initiated by Jesus was the kingdom of God, not the institutional church. Part of Harnack's claim in this regard was that the kingdom was a purely inner, spiritual kingdom. Loisy's rebuttal was two-pronged. First, the kingdom was addressed to the whole person, body and soul. Second, although the gospel "contains no formal declaration for or against the constitution of human society in the world,"[15] neither does it preclude the formation of institutions for specific purposes. The origin of the church lies among the followers of Jesus who persevered after the resurrection and who set out to "form a circumscribed group, perfectly distinct, a very centralized, even a hierarchical fraternity."[16] Thus the positive thrust of Loisy's argument was the location of the origin of the institutional church in the responses of the followers of Jesus to the historical circumstances in which they found themselves. The institutional church is consistent with Christianity because both are evolving, historical entities. "There is no institution," Loisy wrote:

> ... on earth or in history whose status and value may not be questioned if the principle is established that nothing may exist except in its original form. Such a principle is contrary to the law of life which is movement and a continual effort of adaptation to conditions always new and perpetually changing.[17]

On the one hand, Loisy's response to Harnack was an important and perhaps telling reply, and indeed it was potentially an important contribution to a theology based on scripture and tradition. On the other hand, and as could not go unnoticed in a church so recently concerned with ecclesiology, Loisy did not find in Matthew 16:18 ("You are Peter and on this rock I will build my Church") the sole and sufficient theological warrant for the existence of the Roman Catholic Church.

Loisy's contentions with regard to the development of dogma and Christian rituals, especially the sacraments, parallel his argument for the historical development of the papacy. Reflection on Christian beliefs and practices and the formation of these reflections into doctrinal statements were practices consistent with Christianity.

> It is only by starting from a scholastic conception, abstract and unreal, of revelation and dogma that a conclusion is reached condemnatory of all the fruit of Christian reflection upon the object of Christianity.[18]

Like Laberthonniere, Loisy viewed the dogmatic theology of Aquinas and the neo-Thomists as unrelated to life; it failed to animate a life of vibrant Christian religiosity. A theology which could stimulate and sustain such a life would be consistent with Christianity. Although Loisy's concern for a vital Christianity was an important element in his response to Harnack, the implied rejection of the dominant theology which his approach required would not go unnoticed by his Catholic readers.

Loisy also contended that the development of Catholic ritual and the identification of the seven sacraments were the products of the historical development of Christianity. Their origin was not to be sought in explicit words of institution spoken by Jesus and recorded in the New Testament. Rather the sacraments were means of Christian ritual which began to develop in the apostolic church and which continued to be clarified further at least into the thirteenth century. The church, dogma and ritual were each legitimate ways in which Christianity had maintained itself and identified itself over the course of time. "Principles are the soul of religion," he stated, "but principles without religious institutions and doctrines are, in sober truth, a soul without a body, something which has neither reality nor consistency in the realm of the present life."[19]

### (C) George Tyrrell

George Tyrrell was neither a noted philosopher nor an academic theologian, nor was he a biblical scholar. He was, however, a gifted expositor of the theological and scriptural developments occurring within modernism. In his 1908 Lenten Pastoral Letter supporting Pius X's condemnation of modernism, Cardinal Mercier wrote:

> The most penetrating observer of the present modernist movement—the one most alive to its tendencies, who has best divined its spirit, and is perhaps more deeply imbued with it than any other, is the English priest Tyrrell.[20]

At least with regard to Tyrrell, the Cardinal was correct. Tyrrell had absorbed the writings of French authors such as Laberthonniere and Loisy and translated them into journal articles for the educated Catholic laity of England. He wrote with a passion and conviction that gave his writings a strong flavor of the author's emotions and beliefs.

He shared with Laberthonniere and Loisy the conviction that doctrines must be relevant to the life of the faithful. In *Oil and Wine*, he wrote that:

> . . . life is the test of religious truths; the true words are "the words of eternal life"—the life, not merely of intellectual truth, not merely of ethical purity of conduct, interior and exterior, but of our felt and experienced relationship to the incomprehensible realities of the world to come—the life, in other words, of faith and hope and divine love.[21]

For Tyrrell the value of dogmatic statements does not rest on their consistency with one another nor in their affirmation of some abstract truth. The value of theological statements consists in their capacity to initiate and sustain, to nurture and develop the concrete relationship between human persons and God. "Doctrines are but explanations of the source and end of the attraction, and of the means by which the end is to be realized . . . Hence every explanation of the other world is both analogical and inadequate . . . "[22] Like his French counterparts, Tyrrell was staunchly opposed to the abstract dogmatism of neo-Thomism. In an even more strident vein, he replied to Cardinal Mercier's Lenten Pastoral:

By regimental drill, by governmental coercion, you may form a political party, you may drive the multitudes to Mass and the Sacraments, you may teach them the same formulas, you may scare them into obedience, you may make them wheels in a machine, but you will never make them living members of a living organism; you will never wake their intelligent interest or enlist their profoundest enthusiasm.[23]

There is also a theology of immanence present in Tyrrell's writings. According to Tyrrell, life gives rise to theology; it is natural for religious persons to reflect upon and give expression to their religious vitality. Doctrines cannot be deduced from either metaphysical statements or scriptural quotations. Theological statements so arrived at are no more than empty words.

. . . [T]he demonstrated truths of religion are not more than this to a man until he see their bearing upon his life, or upon certain elements of his life, which they promise to foster and develop; until they offer to him the mastery of a spiritual world whose wealth he desires to appropriate. If the life to which they point be to him in every way uncongenial, strange, and violent, their hold on his intellect will be purely external; he will be puzzled, not convinced.[24]

Theology thus ought to develop from the religious experience of Christians, not from the external authority of a revealed body of truths.

### (D) The European Side of Americanism

An interesting sidelight to modernism is its relationship to the "phantom heresy" of Americanism. Americanism as a phenomenon of late 19th-century American religious history will be examined in some detail in a subsequent chapter. One aspect of Americanism at least paralleled, if it did not indeed influence, the modernists. In 1897 Abbé Felix Klein of the Institut Catholique in Paris translated into French the biography of Isaac Hecker, including Archbishop John Ireland's introduction. Klein prepared as well his own introduction to highlight aspects of Hecker's thought for French readers. The publication of Klein's work was to cause a storm of controversy which Klein would recount more than fifty years later in *Americanism: A Phantom Heresy.*[25]

Cardinal Mercier's Lenten Pastoral Letter viewed modernism as a body of doctrines which "have pushed their shoots as far as the United States."[26] It is impossible to determine precisely what the Cardinal had in mind when he penned this phrase, but he may have been reflecting on the controversy in France stemming from the publication of Hecker's biography. This book widened the gap between French progressives and conservatives. As Klein was later to state:

> Progressives looked at the young, vigorous body of Catholics overseas with envious admiration, and urged France to learn some practical lessons from America; on the other hand, French conservatives regarded with great suspicion a country so strongly Protestant and Masonic, so deeply committed to secular education and so determined to end European control of the Western hemisphere.[27]

What did the progressives find so enticing in American Catholicism, and what did the conservatives fear from the same front?

Klein's introduction emphasized Hecker's acceptance of the modern world and the manner in which it fostered the material and spiritual betterment of humankind. He understood Hecker to have seen custom as "an excuse for backwardness and decadence" and thus to have insisted on the necessity "to cultivate the spirit of initiative and to modify our system of education."[28] The new, the innovative, was not seen by Hecker as necessarily evil, but rather as a potential source for yet further human development. While maintaining the doctrine of original sin, Hecker sharply contrasted the Catholic interpretation of the doctrine to that of Luther and Calvin. According to Hecker, Catholicism maintained that human nature was not totally corrupted; it remained capable of some good even after the sin of Adam. Catholicism was "wonderfully calculated and adapted to call forth, sustain, and perfect the tastes, propensities, and peculiarities of human nature."[29]

A third feature of Hecker's thought which would become controversial focused on the role of the Holy Spirit in the guidance of individuals. Hecker's theology was presented as acknowledging the external role of the Holy Spirit guiding and directing the members of the church through the papal teaching office and the sacraments. Since the external role of the Holy Spirit had been clearly acknowledged at the First Vatican Council, it was now possible to speak of a new era which could "give more attention to the invisible divine activity."[30] To many such an emphasis on the "invisible divine activity" would seem to be similar to the modernists' theory of immanence. It seemed to portend a rise of subjectivism in Catholic theology similar to what the magisterium had found objectionable in the writings of Luther and Kant.

An important French critic of Americanism, A.-J. DeLattre, picked up on precisely these points. He accused Hecker of diminishing the significance of the passive virtues of uniformity, discipline and obedience and replacing them with a stress on the active virtues of initiative and personal effort.[31] He feared the consequences of a doctrine which stressed the immediate direction of the Holy Spirit in the lives of individuals. Would the Holy Spirit lead this generation in ways inconsistent with the direction provided to previous generations? America's prodigious industrial, agricultural, commercial, and financial activity had nothing to do with Christian virtue. They were activities of the purely human order.[32] Hecker, DeLattre was convinced, had succumbed to American individualism, which was nothing more than an individual egoism which rendered persons indifferent to the interests and needs of their neighbors.[33]

Of course Americanism was not the source of modernism; it was neither the seed of nor the intellectual inspiration for modernism. Modernism's origins lay in progressive French Catholic movements earlier in the century and in the development of critical historical and biblical scholarship in Germany. Late nineteenth century American Catholicism, with its openness to much in American culture and, in the instance of Hecker, its innovative theology, offered French progressives an alternative view of the Catholic way of life.

Leo XIII's letter of 1899 to the American bishops, *Testem Benevolentiae*, attempted to eradicate Americanism, i.e. anything that "would give rise to the suspicion that there are among you some who conceive and would have the church in America to be different from what it is in the rest of the world."[34] Leo's letter makes explicit reference to Klein's publication of the life of Hecker, to the role of the Holy Spirit in the guidance of individuals, and to the distinction between the active and passive virtues.

### (E) *The Condemnation of Modernism*

Pius X's decree *Lamentabile*, followed by his encyclical *Pascendi Dominum Gregis*, both published in 1907, brought an end to Catholic modernism. Although Laberthonniere and Loisy continued to publish (Tyrrell died in 1909), their contributions were no longer considered within the ambit of Catholic theology. In 1910, by order of a *motu proprio*, *Sacrorum Antistitum*, candidates for the priesthood and professors of theology and philosophy teaching in seminaries or pontifical institutions were required to take the oath against modernism at the beginning of each academic year. It is interesting to note that Catholic professors in German universities were not required to take the oath. The oath began:

I———firmly embrace and accept each and every definition that
has been set forth and declared by the unerring teaching authority
of the Church, especially those principal truths which are directly
opposed to the errors of the day.

The oath concluded:

> I declare that I am completely opposed to the error of the modern-
> ists who hold that there is nothing divine in sacred tradition . . . the
> purpose of this is, then, not that dogma may be tailored according
> to what seems better and more suited to the culture of each age;
> rather, that the absolute and immutable truth preached by the
> apostles from the beginning may never be believed to be different,
> may never be understood in any other way.[35]

Professors who could not subscribe to the oath were to be removed from or
denied teaching positions.

Papal authority assured the continued dominance of neo-Thomism well
into the twentieth century. Vigilance committees were to be established in
each diocese to ensure that Catholic teaching was consistent with the requirements of *Pascendi*. The papacy was "thus able to control the whole
Church more effectively than ever before" and was committed to strict
traditionalism in theology and to the utmost resistance to innovation.[36] This
first attempt to critique neo-Thomism from within the Catholic tradition was
brought to a sudden halt. Why was this the case? There were at least four
reasons.

First, modernism would necessarily appear to neo-Thomists to be an
attack upon the papal teaching office. Laberthonniere's proposal that the
teaching office was to be educative and in service to the church stood in
sharp contrast to the monarchial understanding of the papacy which had
returned to dominance in the second half of the nineteenth century. The
basic characteristic of the theology of papal teaching in this period emphasized its authoritative character. Laberthonniere's view was simply too
sharply at variance from the dominant neo-Thomist understanding of the
role of the papacy.

Second, according to the theology of the neo-Thomists, God basically
acted in the world in two manners. In the first place, through habitual and
cooperating grace, the Holy Spirit directed the wills and intellects of Christians to instances of the good which both served human life in the present
and also served as means to beatitude. Such were the inner workings of the
new law and grace. But in addition, in his work of creation God had created
an objective order of goods which participated in the eternal plan and thus
were truly good. Apart from the miraculous, God functioned in the world
through the order of goods established in creation. The notions of divine
immanence which began to develop in modernism were in sharp opposition to
the neo-Thomist conception of divine activity. As Kleutgen had objected to
the modal theories of grace in Tübingen theology, so his intellectual descen-

dants disagreed with the theories of modernism. Immanence suggested that God might be acting in a less controlled, less predictable manner.

Third, neo-Thomism developed its systematic theology in relationship to Aristotelian metaphysics. Their theological universe was tightly woven together; it was a comprehensive interpretation of Christian reality. Modernism introduced the notion of history, the notion of change and development. For Loisy and Laberthonniere, Harnack's kernel of Christianity and neo-Thomism's systematic theology were ultimately one and the same. Both attempted to provide timeless, definitive interpretations of the nature of Christianity. Both failed because they did not grasp the fundamentally historical nature of Christianity. According to the modernists God continued to be an active force in the ordering of both the objective and subjective poles of Christian morality.

Finally, the entire project of modernism was fundamentally opposed to the project of neo-Thomism. The former strove to engage the culture and scholarship of the nineteenth century; the latter sought to develop a clear alternative to both contemporary culture and scholarship. Laberthonniere was a student of non-Thomistic philosophy. Loisy was a student of non-scholastic literary methods. Given these basically different understandings of what theology should be about, it is no wonder that modernism and neo-Thomism would clash. Thomas Bouquillon, however, offered something of a middle course between modernism and neo-Thomism.

## II. Thomas Bouquillon: A Thomistic Alternative

Thomas Bouquillon was a priest of the diocese of Bruges who came to the United States in 1889 to become a member of the original faculty of the Catholic University of America. He had received his S.T.D. degree from the Gregorian in Rome and had taught from 1867 to 1877 at the seminary in Bruges and then for eight years at the Institut Catholique in Lille. He was an important influence on both William Joseph Kerby, the founder of the Sociology department at the Catholic University as well as of the National Conference of Catholic Charities, and John A. Ryan, the most eloquent American Catholic spokesperson on social justice during the first half of the twentieth century.[37] Bouquillon's writings provide an important and illuminating context in which to read Ryan's works.

Bouquillon's contribution to the development of American Catholicism will be assessed in a later chapter. The focus here must be limited to his *Theologia Moralis Fundamentalis*.[38] This work was completed before his arrival in the United States. However, it clearly portrays his particular interests and approaches to moral theology. His manual can be characterized by its conception of the relationship of moral theology to the social sciences and its insistence on a moral theology based in dogmatic theology. It is helpful in reading Bouquillon's manual to keep in mind his 1899 essay "Moral Theology At The End Of The Nineteenth Century,"[39] which vividly portrays what he considered to be amiss in the majority of manuals of the period.

Moral theology, Bouquillon contended:

> ... [had] failed to put itself in touch with new currents of thought; failed to anticipate problems of life and to win consideration for the solutions which it offers. Modern civilization has forced to the foreground serious problems which properly belong to the domain of Moral Theology, but the world has not asked that science for guidance in meeting them. Even the clergy seem to be satisfied with the narrow professional side, for when important questions arise, such as those of wages, property in land, education, they as a rule seek solutions not in a profound study of the principles of moral theology, but elsewhere.[40]

In Bouquillon's opinion, moral theology had become a marginal discipline. Separated from the important questions of the day, its focus was limited to assisting priests in the hearing of confessions. The manualists destroyed the organic unity of moral theology and dogmatic theology: the vision of Augustine and Aquinas had been lost.[41] The manuals were becoming too large and tended to address only questions proper to pastoral, ascetical, and liturgical theology. The manuals utterly failed to consider the profound and disturbing questions arising from the emerging social order. What, then, was his solution?

First, Bouquillon argued that moral theology must be understood as a science. "Moral theology," he wrote, "is the science supported by revelation of the laws and means by which man, elevated to the supernatural order, is directed and assisted in order that he might live in accord with the divine order and arrive at salvation."[42] The principles of this science were "those moral truths which are necessary to the solution of particular moral questions and which dominate the entire matter of morality so that if they were not known it would be impossible to proceed to a safe explanation of things ... "[43] Moral theology was a science in that it was the way of knowing the necessary means to reaching humankind's final end. The ambit of moral theology included the ultimate end of humanity, the means to the end, the rules to the end, the acts to the end, and the accession of the end.

> This moral order in the present economy of salvation is not merely natural but supernatural, and can be defined as the disposition of man elevated to divine sonship toward God the Father and his

return to God through supernatural means and according to supernatural relations.[44]

The scientific nature of moral theology was refined yet further in Bouquillon's 1899 essay. "The separation of moral theology from the other sciences does violence to it and to them. No university center can be complete without it."[45] The companion sciences to which moral theology must be intimately related, he argued, were ethics, sociology, politics, economics and law. Each of these disciplines addresses the free activity of human beings and the laws which govern them. Whereas each of the social sciences is "confined to particular spheres of human action and its direction to proximate contingent goods," moral theology is concerned with "all human activity, which it directs to man's supreme destiny—the absolute good."[46] Moral theology must be related to the social sciences because they deal with proximate means, which are in fact the means to salvation itself.

The element common to both moral theology and the social sciences was law. *Theologia Moralis Fundamentalis* addressed all of the usual topics associated with the treatise on law, but did so in a unique manner. Bouquillon's treatment of the definition of law, the natural law, and the law of grace followed the usual pattern. When he turned to civil law, however, he rejected the purely penal theory, that is, that civil law is not morally binding and subjects its violators to civil penalties only; he insisted that civil law bears a moral obligation upon those subject to it.[47] Public laws pertaining to a just wage imposed a moral obligation upon employers; they were subject to the judgment of God as well as that of civil courts. He also developed the concept of domestic law by which members of a family "are directed to physical, intellectual, moral and religious goods" by the economic authority of the head of a household.[48] His treatment of ecclesiastical law was extensive; however, it dealt exclusively with the jurisprudence of canon law. He did not consider any particular canons, nor the canon law of the sacraments.

In all of their free activities human agents are directed by law. Civil law, the economic order, etc. were directive to some proximate end, but they "ought to conform to the ultimate end" of human beings.[49] The task of moral theology was to insure that the social sciences and the leaders of the newly emerging social and political orders attended not only to the proximate ends of the citizenry, but to their final end as well. Moral theology had to be present in the university where social science research was conducted in order to become familiar with its findings and to assess them from a theological perspective.

The relationship of moral theology to the social sciences articulated by Bouquillon was one of the striking characteristics of his work. A second hallmark was the close relationship he maintained between moral theology and dogmatic theology. Even the casual reader of Bouquillon cannot avoid noticing the variety of theologians he cites. Kleutgen, Scheeban, Franzelin, Palmeri—the leading dogmatic theologians of his day—are mentioned throughout his treatment of theological questions. Bouquillon's treatment of specifically theological topics was not simply *pro forma* nor was it a simple repetition of what predecessors had written. Bouquillon's theology was innovative and insightful.

All of creation, but human beings in particular, was created to give glory to God. The theological context of moral theology was to be explicitly theocentric, in fact more so than that of the neo-Thomists. The formal glorification of God as the end of human life insured that no created being was to be served before God.[50] "As the glory of God is the primary end of man, so it is also the principle norm of his operations; beatitude, however, as the secondary end, is only a subordinate end of his [man's] operations and impulsive principles."[51] The primary orientation of life was not conceived as a human good; even union with God became secondary to giving glory to God.

The theological theme of giving glory to God was not relevant solely in terms of the final end of human beings, nor solely to their explicitly religious life of prayer and worship. The exclusive destiny of human beings was considered to be "the most firm basis of dignity, independence, of true liberty and judgment for life and its necessities. . . . [T]heories which are opposed to Catholic dogmatic theology's position on the end of man, lead to the destruction of personal individuality, and [give rise to] the state or omnipotent community which modern pseudo-political practice tries to construct."[52] Bouquillon's dogmatic theology legitimated the relationship between moral theology and the social sciences. Union with God as the destiny of human nature was understood to be the basis of human dignity and freedom; the role of the state was to foster these rich dimensions of human personhood.

Bouquillon clearly needs to be understood as a Thomist. His affection for and admiration of the writings of Aquinas is readily apparent. Certainly he had read and was influenced by the neo-Thomists. He makes the same sharp distinctions between faith and reason, nature and grace which permeate the neo-Thomist manuals. But he selects from them as he selects from other sources. Bouquillon was not a neo-Thomist. *Theologia Moralis Fundamentalis* demarcated an original theological position which drew upon a wide array of resources. His understanding of the role of moral theology as an essential discipline within higher education distinguished his position from that of the neo-Thomists. His insistence upon the relationship between the social sciences and moral theology as well as his distinctive interpretation of the relationship between moral and civil laws would be among his contributions to the nascent American Catholic theology. Bouquillon was an original and insightful theologian of whom it was said that he "is the most erudite man in the Catholic world today."[53] The neo-Thomists dominated the theological conversation, but there were other voices, Bouquillon's among them.

## NOTES

1. "Aeterni Patris" in *One Hundred Years of Thomism*, ed. Victor B. Brezik, C.S.B. (Houston: Center for Thomistic Studies, 1981), 195.
2. Bernard Reardon, *Liberalism and Tradition* (New York: Cambridge University Press, 1975), viii.
3. Alec Vidler, *The Modernist Movement in the Roman Church* (Cambridge: Cambridge University Press, 1934), 8.
4. T. M. Schoof, *A Survey of Catholic Theology, 1800–1970* (Paramus: Paulist Press, 1970), 48.
5. Vidler, *Modernist Movement*, 187.
6. Lucien Laberthonniere, *Essais de philosophie religieuse*, 272, cited in Claude Tresmontant, *La crise moderniste* (Paris: Editions du Seuil, 1979), 204.
7. Alec Vidler, *A Variety of Catholic Modernists* (Cambridge: Cambridge University Press, 1970), 83.
8. Ibid., 85–86.
9. From Laberthonniere's *La notion chrétienne de l'autorité*, cited in Vidler, *A Variety*, 86.
10. Alfred Loisy, *La Morale Humaine* (Paris: Emile Nourry, Editeur, 1928).
11. Alfred Loisy, *The Gospel and the Church*, trans. Christopher Home (London: Isbister and Company, Limited, 1903).
12. Adolf Harnack, *What Is Christianity?*, trans. Thomas Bailey Saunders (New York: Harper and Row, Publishers, 1957).
13. Vidler, *Modernist Movement*, 84–85.
14. Loisy, *The Gospel*, 23–36.
15. Ibid., 82.
16. Ibid., 146.
17. Ibid., 166.
18. Ibid., 212.
19. Ibid., 236.
20. George Tyrrell, *Medievalism: A Reply To Cardinal Mercier* (London: Longmans, Green, and Co., 1908), 9.
21. George Tyrrell, *Oil and Wine* (Longmans, Green, and Co., 1907), 7.
22. Ibid., 3–4.

23. Tyrrell, *Medievalism*, 32.
24. George Tyrrell, *Lex Orandi or Prayer and Creed* (London: Longmans, Green, and Co., 1903), vii-viii.
25. Abbé Felix Klein, *Americanism: A Phantom Heresy* (Atchison: Aquin Book Shop, 1951).
26. Tyrrell, *Medievalism*, 6.
27. Klein, *Americanism*, 51.
28. Ibid., 9.
29. Ibid., 10.
30. Ibid., 12.
31. A.-J. De Lattre, S.J., *Un Catholicisme Américain* (Namur: Auguste Godenne, 1898), 7.
32. Ibid., 10–11.
33. Ibid., 12.
34. Reprinted in Klein, *Americanism*, 322.
35. *The Church Teaches*, by the Jesuit Fathers of St. Mary's Kansas (St. Louis: B. Herder Book Com., 1965), #88–90.
36. Vidler, *Modernist Movement*, 220.
37. C. Joseph Nuesse, "Thomas Joseph Bouquillon (1840–1902), Moral Theologian and Precursor of the Social Sciences in the Catholic University of America," *The Catholic Historical Review* 72 (1986): 601–606.
38. Thomas Bouquillon, *Theologia Moralis Fundamentalis*, 2nd ed. (Bruges: Beyaert-Storie, 1890).
39. Thomas Bouquillon, "Moral Theology At The End Of The Nineteenth Century," *Catholic University Bulletin* 5 (1899).
40. Ibid., 246.
41. Ibid., 258.
42. Bouquillon, *Theologia Moralis*, 4.
43. Ibid., 141.
44. Ibid., 143.
45. Bouquillon, "Moral Theology," 249.
46. Ibid., 254.
47. Bouquillon, *Theologia Moralis*, 423.
48. Ibid., 445.
49. Ibid., 6.
50. Ibid., 148.
51. Ibid., 152.
52. Ibid., 148.
53. An unnamed Belgian ecclesiastic cited in Nuesse, "Thomas Joseph Bouquillon," 602.

# 7.

# European Catholic Theology
# from World War II to Vatican II

The horrors of World War I brought an end to liberal Protestant theology in Europe. Protestant Christianity found it impossible to remain at ease with civilizations capable of producing the enormous destruction of life and property which occurred during the war. If such were the accomplishments of modernity, Christianity must be about something else, something distinctive. The voices of dialectical theology—Karl Barth, Emile Brunner, Rudolf Bultmann, and others—began to look not so much to the order of creation or to any human institution to decipher the will of God, but rather to scripture as the revelation of the will of God.

There was no corresponding development in Catholic theology; neo-Thomism continued to be the prevalent voice in Catholic theology. There were at least two reasons why this was the case. First, Catholic theology had never really gone through a phase of liberalism such as was true of Protestant theology. Although modernism sought to engage the cultural and intellectual developments of the age, it never identified its theology with the conviction of the inevitable progress of humankind, nor did it identify its views of Christianity with the historical conditions of any contemporary society. Nor had modernism ever been a particularly large movement within Catholicism. There simply was no liberal theology within Catholicism to react against. Second, and at least as importantly, *Lamentabile* and *Pascendi* were still of recent memory. Given the repressive theological climate engendered by those documents, it was not likely that any innovative theological school would emerge.

Between World War I and World War II the most creative Catholic theological scholarship was historical. It was during this period that Etienne Gilson, Martin Grabmann and others produced their remarkable historical studies. What characterized the work of these intellectual historians was, as Bernard Lonergan has commented with regard to his own early studies, the

140

"attempt to reach up to the mind of Aquinas."[1] Critical editions of the writings of Aquinas, Bonaventure, and other medieval theologians were produced as well as numerous translations into a variety of languages. Although the findings of these historians did not alter the neo-Thomist manuals of moral theology, the program of Leo XIII's *Aeterni Patris*, the foundational document of neo-Thomism, did charge theologians to augment and perfect the old with the new.[2] The study of the past would eventually give rise to a view of what the "new" might be.

World War II was to have an impact on European Catholic theology that was not totally unlike that which World War I had on Protestant Christianity. Existentialism and Communism posed threats to Catholicism in France and Germany. Both movements struggled to capture the hearts and minds of Catholics in these countries. Some theologians, first in France, then in Germany, became convinced that neo-Thomism was a type, a genre of Catholic theology, which could not meet these challenges. The dominant strain of Catholic theology was under attack both from within and without the church. What emerged was, first, the *nouvelle théologie* in France, and then the transcendental Thomism of Karl Rahner and Bernard Lonergan. Both the *nouvelle théologie* and transcendental Thomism will be examined in this chapter.

## I. The *Nouvelle Théologie*

In a significant article which appeared in the first issue of *Études* published after World War II, the French Jesuit Jean Daniélou wrote:

> The theologian ought also to situate values within the total vision of Christian man and, as a result, more clearly demonstrate the primacy of the new creation which is operative among mankind through grace and which expands itself in the theological virtues, principles of familiarity with God and supernatural charity with all persons.[3]

This article, which articulated a program for Catholic theology in the post-war years, argued for the necessity of returning to the sources of theology: scripture, the Fathers, and the medieval authors. It further suggested that Catholic theology needed to address the issues arising from contemporary philosophy and particularly the significance of history. The point of these proposals was to insure that theology became engaged with the life of Christian people. The task of theology, as defined by Daniélou, was to meet the needs of souls, to be led by the spirit of the apostolate, and to be totally engaged in the work of building up the body of Christ. Theology and action, reminiscent of the proposals of the modernists, ought not to be separated.[4]

Daniélou was suggesting a radical reorientation of Catholic theology. The contention that contemporary philosophy was significant for the theological enterprise and was something from which Catholic theology might profit, was a striking departure from the presuppositions of neo-Thomism. To argue that an historical study of the development of Christian doctrines could facilitate a more adequate interpretation of their contemporary meaning was to recall the dangers of modernism. Daniélou was proposing that Catholic theology tread a new path. That path became known as the *nouvelle théologie* (the new theology).

As significant as Daniélou's article was, it was not unrelated to similar discussions which preceded it. As far back as 1929, the moral theologian Arthur Vermeersch had complained about the apparent inability of the manualists to keep abreast of contemporary events, both philosophical and social. He chided his confreres for their excessive negativity and encouraged a more serious consideration of the role of the theological virtues in the Christian moral life.[5] In 1940 Gustav Thils proposed a radical reshaping of moral theology. He attacked the manualists for failing to make Christ the center of morality, for overlooking the role of the sacraments in the moral life, and for concentrating on the object of moral action itself and not setting it within the context of the personal values present within the complete action.[6] Thils' book was not solely critical; it also developed a constructive proposal. Moral theology, he wrote:

> . . . ought to become more fully Christian in all its perspectives and universal in its extension to all that is human, ontological in its ultimate foundation and sacramental in its concrete base and, finally, theological in the soul which vivifies it.[7]

Thils' moral theology was transformationist and personalist. Its Christocentrism extended not just to the duty to model one's life on Christ but also to the sacraments as the means which open the Christian community to the principles of imitation and which encourage the assimilation of the grace of Christ. The believer takes on the life of Christ, which becomes the principle of Christian action. Thils was also keenly aware of the impact of culture and society on theology. "Man masters more and more of the universe by his knowledge, uniting the cosmos in one regard and encircling it in himself; he becomes more and more each day the king of creation."[8] Thils viewed the task of the Christian as one of unifying and spiritualizing the world. The world was to be made and remade in the image of Christ. This was not neo-Thomist theology.

Jacques Leclerq's *L'Enseignement de la Morale Chrétienne* (1949) described the teaching of the manualists as spiritless and deprived of the dynamics of Christian life. The neo-Thomist manuals, in his estimation:

> ... form a majestic assemblage, presented in a conventional language foreign to our vocabulary, treating of strange questions which, to the extent they concern us, can be admired like an ancient palace which one might visit as an historical monument, but without ever wanting to live there.[9]

Leclerq's constructive position was fundamentally Christocentric. Christ gave to his followers a way of life, a moral attitude, which transforms humankind and manifests itself in exterior life and action. Christians ought to revise all their scales of values, to upset everything; nothing in their spirit nor in their life ought to remain the same. The task of the Christian was neither to stand in awe of nature, nor to destroy it, but rather to realize that humankind is the highest created value and is destined to accomplish the meaning and purpose of creation by transforming itself.

These quotations from Daniélou and Leclerq could mislead one into thinking that moral theology was the principal concern of *the nouvelle théologie*. But this was clearly not the case. The theologians associated with the *nouvelle théologie* were principally historians and exegetes. However, their return to the Fathers and medieval theologians was intended to demonstrate that the ahistorical methodology of the neo-Thomists was not in accord with the teaching of the Fathers nor with that of Thomas Aquinas and other medieval theologians. Over time the meaning of doctrines had changed, and neo-Thomism itself had provided one such change. *The nouvelle théologie*, however, also had a second major purpose; it strove to articulate a pastoral theology adequate to the needs of the post-war church.

Unlike modernism, *the nouvelle théologie* can be associated with two specific schools. One was the Dominican house of studies, *Le Saulchoir*, in which Marie-Dominique Chenu and Yves Congar were the principal figures. Henri de Lubac and Jean Daniélou provided much of the inspiration for the Jesuit seminary at Fourviere; their colleagues included Yves de Montcheuil and Pierre Teilhard de Chardin. The name given to this movement was first sarcastically applied to it by Reginald Garrigou-Lagrange in a 1946 essay entitled, "*La nouvelle théologie, où-va-t-elle?*" (The New Theology, Where is it Going?)[10] The wave of the *nouvelle théologie* was to break upon European Catholicism in the post-war years. Yet many of its major works were written before the war. Each school produced a monograph series. The Jesuits edited *Sources Chrétiennes*, the Dominicans, *Unam Sanctam*. Both schools were involved in exegetical work on the Fathers of the Church as well as medieval philosophy and theology. The endeavors of each school were inspired by the work of immediate predecessors; the Dominicans by Ambroise Gardiel (*Le Donne révéle et la théologie, La Structure de l'âme et l'expérience mystique*), the Jesuits by Pierre Rousselot's *L'intellectualisme de Saint Thomas* and Joseph Maréchal's *Le point de départ de la metaphysique*. Both schools produced important works in the late 1930s, but only after the war did they significantly attract the attention of Roman theologians and papal authorities. The publication of Pius XII's *Humani Generis* in 1950 brought the movement to an end. The crux of the issues raised by the *nouvelle théologie* can be sufficiently identified, for the purposes of this study, by an examination of some of the works of Chenu and de Lubac.[11]

### (A) Marie-Dominique Chenu

If there existed a programmatic outline of the *nouvelle théologie* it was Chenu's *Une école de théologie: le Saulchoir*.[12] Chenu began this essay by locating the mission of the *Saulchoir* within the context of Dominican spirituality and the tradition of Dominican theology. He carefully outlined the nature of St. Thomas' theological work and acknowledged the significance of Ambroise Gardeil as the founding father and inspiration of the *Saulchoir*. He then addressed the theology and philosophy appropriate to this school as well as the importance of medieval studies.

Theology, Chenu contended, ought to be neither speculative nor positive; rather theology is the product of "the essential relation between religious conceptions and scientific conceptions of the gift of faith."[13] The central element for theology was understood as the experience of faith, *fides qua*. Faith, "the incarnation of the divine truth in the very tissue of our spirit," was inserted as a power in our spirit.[14] Faith was thus presented as an absolute referrer of persons to God; faith was viewed as transcendental, not categorical.

The categorical aspect of faith was the product of revelation being inserted in time, "written and presented in historical facts and texts."[15] The task of theology was to get at the reality of the mystery of God which had been given in human words. "If faith is absolute and escapes history, then the pure faith is in the infused light and not the dogma."[16] Not even scripture, Chenu continued, ought to be conceived of as "a sort of external proof of one or another dogma or the truth of the tradition."[17] The test of dogmatic formulations was the permanent Christian conscience of the church, "the presence of the Spirit in the social body of the church, divine and human in Christ."[18] The Catholic tradition constituted the embodiment of this permanent Christian conscience as the "principle of organic continuity of which the magisterium is the infallible instrument."[19] Thus a "theology worthy of the name is a spirituality which discovers rational instruments adequate to its religious experience."[20]

Chenu's emphasis on the transcendental character of the faith present within the church as the norm and criteria for explicit categorical formulations of faith would necessarily be rejected by neo-Thomists. It offered a different understanding of the relationship between faith and reason. His conception of dogmas as fragile expressions of a more ultimate faith and his suggestion that not even Scripture provided an external proof of dogmatic formulas were significant departures from the dominant theology of the day. Although Chenu carefully explained that this faith was primarily a characteristic of the church, his position would be viewed by many as too subjective. In a manner reminiscent of Loisy's position, Chenu's theology challenged the validity of the objective norms of Catholic faith: scripture and dogma.

If Chenu's conception of theology was an oblique attack on neo-Thomism, his presentation of the role of philosophy was a frontal assault. The perennial philosophy, as it was currently practiced, focused on abstraction as the proper measure of the intelligible.

Philosophy takes an exclusively deductive characteristic in the "system," a regimentation of definitions and conclusions where the irrational is suspect or neglected as though it were unintelligible.[20a]

The neo-Thomists failed to grasp St. Thomas' distinction between *ratio* and *intellectus*. The result had been a series of propositions presented as abiding truths. What had been lost was the quest, the drive to understand, the sense that understanding reveals rather than conceals the possibility of further and deeper insights. For Chenu, the failure of contemporary Catholic philosophy to understand St. Thomas' theory of *intellectus* resulted in an objective positivism which "destroys curiosity, [a positivism in which] dispute is replaced by scholastic exercises which are only a parody of dialectic."[21]

Positively, Chenu presented philosophy as "the history of the human spirit in search of first truths."[22] It was a basic form of humanism. No question was ever to be considered closed. Philosophy "implies a personal engagement, a reconsideration of ancient problems as always real and investigated with a sympathetic passion."[23] The fundamental characteristic of philosophy was its drive for further understanding (*intellectus*). A system of philosophy with its logical machinery has spiritual values only in the organic principles which guide it; "there it finds its stability and its capacity for progress, its perennialness and its suppleness."[24]

To the neo-Thomists Chenu's philosophy, like his theology, would seem to lack the objectivity and timelessness which they considered so important. His emphasis on *intellectus* would be seen as stressing the subjective side of human understanding. How could a rule of faith be established on the basis of a conception of philosophy which required in principle an openness to further study and reformulation? Would not such an openness constitute the basis for Catholic engagement with strains of European thought which neo-Thomism viewed as inherently dangerous?

What importance did Chenu attribute to the investigation of patristic and medieval texts? For Chenu "the course of Christian history is the source of theological knowledge, especially in an intelligibility always new for the presentation of the faith in new generations."[25] The key word in this sentence was "intelligibility." The medievalist or the patristic scholar was viewed as seeking further understanding and intelligibility in ancient texts. For Chenu the prime example of such an investigation of the past was the work of St. Thomas.

> All the metaphysics of Aristotle, all the psychology of Augustine, all the mysticism of Denis, all the science of the Arabs, all the asceticism of Gregory and the contemplation of the Victorines did not constitute the soul of brother Thomas, but the soul of brother Thomas had assimilated all that, and that assimilation, that "reduction" of five civilizations in the unity of one spiritual life, ought to be contemplated for itself. That beautiful form which is the intellectualism of St. Thomas is not a pure form; it was born, it lived, it attained its perfection in material, in a time, in a climate, in a context, in a body.[26]

Theologians of the *Saulchoir* were to study history not primarily to discover what various personages said and meant in their own time, but rather to discern, as St. Thomas had done, their meaning for the present. The texts of previous theologians were to be studied like philosophical texts; the questions ought to remain open to the intellects of those who study them. To the neo-Thomists, St. Thomas closed theological options; to Chenu St. Thomas opened theological questions.

### (B) Henri de Lubac

The contemporary reader of the works of Henri de Lubac cannot but be struck by his command of a vast array of patristic and medieval writings. He turned to these sources, Schoof suggests, "for illumination in the relationships between the awareness of God, grace, faith, and human life."[27] De Lubac's ideas concerning our awareness of God and his conception of human nature vis-à-vis grace, topics which were at the center of the controversy surrounding the *nouvelle théologie*, provide ample evidence of his contribution to this movement.

De Lubac's doctrine of God had a strong Augustinian strain which clearly distinguished his position from that of the neo-Thomists. Humanity's initial discovery or awareness of God was not the result of a rational proof drawing on basic characteristics of the world (e.g. movement, degrees of goodness, finitude, efficient causality, governance). Nor should knowledge of God be thought of as an acquisition. Rather, "it is an *image*, an *imprint*, a *seal*. It is the mark of God upon us."[28] The proper sequence is not that the question of God arises and then proofs for his existence are sought, but rather that "it is he who makes himself known to us, It is he who reveals himself to us."[29] The point de Lubac wished to emphasize was that through the working of creation God illumines the mind and that such knowledge "transcends the profane order, wherever we come across it, and leads us into the domain of the sacred."[30] Thus he did not conceive of this knowledge as purely natural as opposed to supernatural. The God encountered was not the God of the philosophers, but rather the personal God of divine revelation.

An unthematic or non-objective knowledge of God, according to de Lubac, was a transcendental precondition for rational activity.

Every human act, whether it is an act of knowledge or an act of the will, rests secretly upon God, by attributing meaning and solidity to the real upon which it is exercised. For God is the Absolute; and nothing can be thought without positing the Absolute and relating it to that Absolute; nothing can be willed without tending towards the Absolute, nor valued unless weighed in terms of the Absolute.[31]

God is the necessary condition for knowledge of truth and willing of the good. In each act of reason and will the reality of God is implicitly and unthematically expressed. For de Lubac God ought not to be conceived of as a principle of being, the first link in the chain, the first in the sequence of causes and effects; He is not a point of origin in the past, but a sufficient reason in the present.[32] Thus as a person turns himself or herself to the good as encountered in the world, God is simultaneously encountered and affirmed in a non-conceptual manner. The person encounters the God of grace.[33]

There was a significant strand of immanence in de Lubac's thought. "Knowledge of God which comes through the external world," he wrote, "is itself, in a sense, a revelation."[34] Through the created order traces of God can be observed which beckon the mind to God. The signs of God permeate his creation. In an important and striking couplet, de Lubac remarked that, "those who uphold immanence deny transcendence, whereas those who believe in transcendence do not deny immanence."[35] The world of the created order had taken on in de Lubac's writings a truly religious significance. Such an interpretation of the human approach to the question of God was a significant deviation from neo-Thomism's emphasis on a sharp separation of the spheres of faith and reason.

De Lubac's theory concerning our knowledge of God occasioned a harsh debate. His *Surnaturel*[36] was probably the most controversial publication of the *nouvelle théologie*. *Surnaturel* traced the development of the concept of the supernatural from Augustine through Aquinas. De Lubac's conclusion was that the authentic thought of Aquinas concerning the distinction between nature and grace had been distorted by sixteenth and seventeenth century commentators. The crux of the problem, as he discerned it, was the emergence of the concept of a pure human nature (*natura pura*) which did not entail a fundamental orientation of human beings to God as their final end. His positive conclusion was that human nature possessed a natural desire for God. To his critics this position appeared at best to de-emphasize, at worst to deny the gratuitous character of grace. What were the issues here?

Kleutgen and the founders of neo-Thomism understood moral theology as an Aristotelian science which directed humanity to the attainment of the supernatural end of its *elevated* nature. Apart from revelation and its theological mediation, the ultimate goal of human life was unknown. Beatitude was the end of elevated nature, not of human nature apart from sanctifying grace. The ultimate end of human nature was understood to fall within the purview of theology, not philosophy. De Lubac contended that it was impossible to conceive of created human nature as having any ultimate finality other than beatitude. Human beings as in fact created by God could never be conceived of as possessing a limited, finite end which could indeed fulfill their deepest longing. His position differed from that of the neo-Thomists not only with regard to a particular doctrine, but also and more basically with regard to their fundamental conception of the relationships between philosophy and theology, nature and grace. From their perspective, de Lubac's conception of human nature limited the freedom of God and thus made grace a demand of human nature, not a gratuitous, free gift.

In 1965, fifteen years after the condemnation of the *nouvelle théologie*, de Lubac returned to these questions in *The Mystery of the Supernatural*.[37] He again depicted human nature as essentially oriented to God as its final end. The call of God was presented as constitutive of human nature.

My finality, which is expressed by this desire, is inscribed upon my very being as it has been put into this universe by God. And by God's will, I now have no other genuine end, no end really assigned to my nature or presented for my free acceptance under any guise, except that of seeing God.[38]

Human nature and its desire for God were depicted as distinct from other created natures and natural drives. Human nature, he suggested, ought more properly to be spoken of as that of a spiritual being, rather than a natural being. Nor is the drive or desire for God like other created appetites which are capable of finite fulfillment; the desire for God is a transcendental drive which stretches beyond the limits of finite, temporal fulfillment. Such is the human paradox: "man cannot live except by the vision of God—and that vision of God depends totally on God's good pleasure."[39] Grace is indeed gratuitous and where grace is not recognized or where grace is rejected human life is necessarily truncated.

### (C) Humani Generis

*Humani Generis* (Aug. 12, 1950) had an impact on the *nouvelle théologie* similar to that which Pius X's *Pascendi Dominum Gregis* had had on modernism. Both encyclicals brought to an end much of the innovative theological speculation within Roman Catholicism which was construed by the papal magisterium as inconsistent with the tradition. Pius XII was quite clear that the tradition to be taught in the schools and seminaries was the teaching of Thomas Aquinas.[40] The crux of this encyclical was not the singling out of particular theological positions as inadequate to the Catholic tradition, but rather once again the dangers which Catholic theologians ought to avoid in contemporary intellectual movements.

The encyclical began by indicating the inadequacies of several important intellectual movements. The theories of evolution, existentialism, communism, historicism, and Protestant neo-orthodoxy were each marked as deficient. The letter then addressed several problems which could be detected in the writings of recent Catholic theologians. There were thought to be some who "challenge the tenets based on law and principles promulgated by Christ and the institutions founded by Him."[41] Those in error whittled down the content of dogma and strove to rearticulate dogma in categories of modern thought; they substituted "new concepts in place of old ones."[42] Later, the encyclical turned to more specific errors to be found in recent writings: denials that the existence of God can be demonstrated from created things, that the world has a beginning, that the supernatural order is gratuitous, that the Mystical Body of Christ is the same as the church. The encyclical also repudiated the contention that the doctrine of transubstantiation rests on an outdated notion of substance.[43]

All of these particular problems were summed up under two related headings which probably indicate the primary thrust of the encyclical: false irenicism[44] and dogmatic relativism.[45] False irenicism presumed that it was possible to express the fundamental convictions of the Catholic tradition in a manner consistent with modern modes of thought. Pius XII's rejection of significant modern intellectual developments was not so much intended to undermine them as secular and Protestant intellectual movements, but rather to deny that they could contribute to a more adequate expression of Catholic religious beliefs. Dogmatic relativism attempted to portray the attempts of some Catholic theologians to alter the manner in which Catholic dogmas were expressed. In the eyes of Pius XII, the *nouvelle théologie* was involved in the same enterprise which Pius X had understood to be the project of the modernists.

A false irenicism and dogmatic relativism were the dangers in modern Catholic thought according to Pius XII, and it was the papal understanding of the tradition that needed to be protected.

> ". . . truth and its philosophical expression cannot change from day to day, least of all where there is a question of the self-evident principles of the human mind or of these assertions which are supported by the wisdom of the ages and agree with divine revelation."[46]

Like his predecessors, Pius XII turned to the Angelic Doctor, Thomas Aquinas, as the paradigmatic expression of Catholic dogma, the definitive expression of the tradition.[47]

*Humani Generis* did not give rise to the same sort of disciplinary decrees that followed upon *Pascendi Dominum Gregis*. However, *Humani Generis* did contain an admonition:

> Let the teachers in ecclesiastical institutions be aware that they cannot with tranquil conscience exercise the office of teachers entrusted to them unless in the instruction of their students they religiously accept and exactly observe the norms which We have ordained. That due reverence and submission which in their unceasing labor they must profess toward the Teaching Authority of the Church, let them instill also in the minds and hearts of their students.[48]

Although Pius did not impose a new oath (the oath against modernism was still required at the beginning of each academic year) he was adamant that papal theology was the theology of the church.

The major theologians associated wih the *nouvelle théologie* were Dominicans and Jesuits. Disciplinary actions were conducted as internal matters of the two orders. Thus, in February, 1951, John Baptist Janssens, the Father General of the Jesuit order, sent a letter to all Jesuits on "The

Encyclical *Humani Generis* of Pius XII."[49] Janssens began his letter by acknowledging that the previous summer he had begun to remove Jesuits from teaching positions. The bulk of the letter was an articulation of theological positions which Jesuits were to maintain. Thus, with regard to the gratuitous character of the supernatural order, he wrote:

> Henceforth then we will not say that the thesis that a spiritual creature could have been not destined to supernatural beatitude is simply an interpretation of dogma by means of defective philosophy, or that this thesis, worked out in order to safeguard the gratuitousness of the supernatural order, is powerless to do so; or that it has no meaning since the mind must go from existing things to possible ones and not vice versa; or again that the supernatural destiny is at the same time essential to man and gratuitous.[49a]

The letter continued in the same vein; it defined the theological positions Jesuits were to teach. The theological positions of Jesuit professors were to be those espoused by Pius XII.

## II. Transcendental Thomism

The origins of transcendental Thomism have been carefully recounted by Otto Muck in *The Transcendental Method*.[50] Karl Rahner's appropriation and development of this mode of thought has been masterfully examined in Peter Eicher's *Die anthropologische Wende*;[51] Bernard Lonergan's contribution has been studied in David Tracy's *The Achievement of Bernard Lonergan*.[52] Certainly our attempt here cannot be to analyze transcendental Thomism as a whole, nor even to provide a comprehensive study of its two most significant theological practitioners, Karl Rahner and Bernard Lonergan. Rather the goal of this brief study will be to set the work of these two major theologians within the context of the developments in Catholic theology discussed in this and the previous two chapters.

Leo XIII's *Aeterni Patris* gave rise to two closely related but distinguishable movements. The first, neo-Thomism, has been referred to repeatedly throughout this study as the dominant and controlling theology within Roman Catholicism from the end of the nineteenth century until Vatican II. As was indicated previously, the theological and philosophical parameters of neo-Thomism were established in Joseph Kleutgen's studies composed in the middle of the nineteenth century. Neo-Thomism consisted in an interpretation of the writings of Thomas Aquinas and required a specific understanding of the relationships and distinctions between nature and grace, faith and reason, philosophy and theology, body and soul. Neo-Thomism throughout this entire period was the dominant position of many Jesuits and Dominicans. It was also the position supported by the papacies of Leo XIII, Pius X, and Pius XII. Because of its strong papal endorsement, neo-Thomism remained the dominant controlling theology within Roman Catholicism for almost one hundred years.

The second movement which stemmed from *Aeterni Patris* was neo-scholasticism. The members of this movement interpreted *Aeterni Patris* as requiring not just a return to the writings of St. Thomas, although he was clearly accorded a privileged position, but also to medieval scholastic philosophy and theology generally. They studied not just Aquinas, but Bonaventure, William of Auxerre, Vincent of Lerins, the Victorines as well as many other scholastics. What in part distinguished the works of Thomas Bouquillon and Dom Odon Lottin from those of the neo-Thomists were the wider medieval sources upon which they drew. The neo-scholastics were also involved in patristic studies because the medieval figures whom they were trying to understand had themselves been attempting to reconcile the inconsistencies in the patristic literature. A further characteristic of neo-scholasticism, which heightens still further its distinction from neo-Thomism, was its willingness to address issues of modernity. Perhaps the paradigmatic neo-scholastic philosopher in this regard was Jacques Maritain.[53] Although this distinction between neo-Thomism and neo-scholasticism is only marginally illuminating with regard to modernism, it clearly depicts the issues surrounding the *nouvelle théologie*. The schools associated with Chenu and de Lubac were clear instances of neo-scholasticism.

The major constructive essays of Rahner (*Spirit in the World*)[54] and of Lonergan (*Insight*)[55] need to be understood as emerging from within the dynamics of neo-scholasticism. This point needs to be carefully understood. Both Rahner and Lonergan possessed a vast knowledge of both the Fathers and scholastic traditions. Rahner's earliest theological publications dealt with patristic issues[56] and many of the essays in the early volumes of his *Theological Investigations* give yet further evidence of his patristic and scholastic learning. Lonergan's *Grace and Freedom*[57] and *Verbum: Word and Idea in Aquinas*,[58] as well as his class notes published as *De Deo Trino*[59] and *De Verbo Incarnato*,[60] clearly demonstrate his knowledge of the Fathers and scholastics. However, when each of these men turned to the task of a constructive theology, of explaining how religious truths could be articulated in the modern world, their point of departure was the writings of Thomas Aquinas. Although St. Thomas was the seminal theological figure for both of them, Rahner and Lonergan were both deeply influenced by the early *nouvelle théologie* theologians, Rousselot and Maréchal. *Spirit in the*

*World* and *Insight* were the result of the *nouvelle théologie*'s emphasis on understanding (*intellectus*) rather than reason (*ratio*).

In the introduction to *Spirit in the World*, Rahner alerted his readers that this work was to be understood as a Thomistic metaphysics of knowledge. He further stipulated that:

> By the Thomistic metaphysics of knowledge we mean the teaching of Thomas Aquinas himself. We presume the right, therefore, to try to understand him from his own writings, without appealing to his commentators and the testimony of his school, and without going into the historical origins of his doctrine.[61]

The task of *Spirit in the World* thus became "an attempt to confront the medieval scholastic philosophy of Thomas Aquinas with the problems of modern philosophy, especially as formulated by Immanuel Kant in his critical and transcendental philosophy."[62]

*Insight* was Lonergan's third major publication. It was preceded by two series of articles: *Grace and Freedom* and *Verbum: Word and Idea In Aquinas*. In the epilogue to *Insight*, Lonergan himself referred to these earlier works as his attempt to reach "up to the mind of Aquinas."[63] His struggle to understand Aquinas had enabled Lonergan to contribute to the task set before theologians by Leo XIII in *Aeterni Patris*, "*vetera novis augere et perficere*" (to enlarge and perfect the old with the new). His early studies enabled Lonergan to grasp what "the *vetera* really were, but also opened challenging vistas on what the *nova* could be."[64] Like Rahner's *Spirit in the World*, so also Lonergan's *Insight* strove to articulate the manner in which Aquinas' theory of knowledge or metaphysics of knowledge could be expressed in a manner philosophically meaningful in the post-Kantian world. *Insight* established a basis for a theory of religious knowledge, that is, for theology.

Because Rahner and Lonergan focused their major constructive works on interpretations of the writings of Aquinas, their studies appear to be of neo-Thomist origin. This, I believe, is an important reason for their rather quick assimilation by theologians and is why neither was ever silenced. One could do what Rahner did, in essence reinterpret every Catholic doctrine, because it was always done within a Thomistic framework. Rahner, in fact, should be understood as offering an alternative to the theology of Kleutgen. From a fundamentally different interpretation of Aquinas, which gave rise to strikingly different understandings of the relationships between nature and grace, philosophy and theology, faith and reason, body and soul, there emerged transcendental Thomism in place of neo-Thomism. The writings of the later Lonergan, unlike those of Rahner, generally did not address specific doctrinal issues, but rather focused on the development of an adequate theological method.

Transcendental Thomism was an effort to establish a response to Kant's philosophy in a manner consistent with the thought of Aquinas. Recall that for Kleutgen and the neo-Thomists after him, Kant's philosophy was the *bête noire* of modern thought. They may also have disagreed with Hegel, Feuerbach, Marx and other molders of modern systems of thought, but the philosophical archvillain, to many the modern Luther, was Kant. Why was Kant viewed as such an implacable foe?

Obviously the answer to that question requires a more complex response than can be given here. In brief, what Kleutgen and the neo-Thomists found in Aquinas was philosophical realism, a system of philosophy which demonstrated how persons could know objects in the world in which they lived. Through sense experience the mind could form an image (phantasm) of the object to be known; the image was then apprehended by the intellect. This theory of knowledge also made it possible to establish a realistic metaphysics; it was possible to determine the common characteristics of everything that exists. The world of sense experience was understood as a world of finite beings composed of potency and act, matter and form, substance and accident, essence and existence. The existence of finite beings in the world and the role of particular beings within this metaphysical worldview were explained in terms of material, efficient, formal, and final causality. In our previous study of the neo-Thomist manuals of moral theology we have seen how these metaphysical categories were used to understand human acts, the relation of the will to the intellect, the specification of sins, and humankind's final end. Finally, the system of metaphysical realism also contended that it was possible to go beyond the world of finite being to affirm the existence of a first mover, a first efficient cause, a necessary being, a cause of every goodness and perfection, and the final cause of all that exists. In the words of Aquinas the mind could move from characteristics of the finite, contingent world to a knowledge of an infinite being which all persons call God.[65]

It was precisely the possibility of such a system of metaphysical realism that Kant denied. Although much of human knowledge depends upon sense experience, the mind does not know the real, the phenomenal, the world of human experience. The categories which constitute the realm of knowledge are properties of the mind, not of the world of objects. Because the mind cannot know the world of finite, contingent being in itself, Kant also considered it impossible to move from characteristics of the world to an affirmation of the existence of God. Human freedom, immortality, and the existence of

God became in Kant's system postulates of practical reason—it was necessary to presume their existence in order to make any sense out of the moral and religious experience of human beings.

For the neo-Thomists there were several dangers in this system. First, they interpreted Kant as embracing a type of subjectivism. Whereas they talked about features of the world, of reality, Kant talked about structures of the mind and postulates of practical reason. Second, because Kant's view could not describe the world in itself, but only the world as known through categories of the mind, it could not demonstrate the existence of God. How could one erect a theological system out of a theory of knowledge which could not demonstrate the existence of God? Third, apart from metaphysical realism, how was the place of human beings in the created order to be determined? The neo-Thomist notion of causality, and especially final causality, provided a very sophisticated manner of explaining the place and purpose of human life within the created order. Finally, if the world in itself cannot be known, how is the natural law to govern human action? For Kant moral activity was to be normed by dictates of practical reason such as, "so act that the maxim of your will could always hold at the same time as a principle establishing universal law."[66] For the neo-Thomists, human beings needed much more specific, concrete moral direction.

What many readers found in Kant was enlightenment, a system of thought which encouraged its practitioners to think and act in accord with reason alone. Traditional manners of construing the world, God's role in the world, and the conditions under which human life was lived were now to be accepted only on the basis of their inherent reasonableness, not solely because they were traditional or the choices of authority. Traditional metaphysics attempted to explain everything about everything, but its findings increasingly came into conflict with the findings of modern science. Realistic metaphysics could address the question of change in terms of potency and act, but could it deal with human historicity? Even if one were to accept a realist theory of knowledge, could one reasonably move from statements about the world to statements about God?

Ultimately Rahner and Lonergan were neither Kantian, nor neo-Thomists, nor neo-scholastics. They were not compelled to refute Kantian thought; rather these transcendental Thomists were able to draw useful elements from Kantian as well as Thomistic theories of knowledge. Rahner began by asking the question "How, according to St. Thomas, can man be spirit in the world?"[67] For Rahner the experience of knowing something was a positive knowledge, a knowledge of something real, even though it was a partial and limited knowledge. But in affirming such limited human knowledge one was also affirming the whole, the unlimited reality of which limited knowledge is but a part. In every act of knowing and loving not only are particular persons or objects known and loved, but also God is known and loved as the condition of the possibility of any human knowledge and love. Rahner takes from Kant the subjective character of human knowing and doing (loving). Human knowing and doing are first of all the result of characteristics of human personhood; they are neither products of the external world nor mirrors of that world. Rahner differs from the neo-Thomists in that for him the affirmation of God arises from fundamental characteristics of human knowing, not from characteristics of the world. His is a metaphysics of knowledge, not of being. He differs from Kant in that he contends that the mind can know the world of objective reality, but the world of objective reality is a fluctuating, historical world about which specific predictions are at best risky. What is important, therefore, is to make as clear as possible the conditions under which human knowing and doing occur; what becomes important is a theological anthropology which can depict the *a priori* and to the extent possible the *a posteriori* conditions under which human life is lived.

Like Rahner, Lonergan is also an epistemological realist. For him, the knowledge affirmed in an act of judgment constitutes the real.[68] Judgments consist of a position (an insight), the conditions (what must be the case for the position to be true) and the fulfillment of the conditions. If the fluid in the glass is water (position), it must be analyzed as $H_2O$ and only water can be analyzed to be $H_2O$ (the conditions); the lab report says this is $H_2O$ (fulfillment of the conditions); therefore this fluid is water. This notion of judgment enables Lonergan to be more confident than Rahner concerning the ability of persons to know the objective world. But it is also important to note that for Lonergan judgments always remain open to revision if the validity of new conditions can be established or if for some reason the conditions are no longer fulfilled. For these two reasons all of human knowledge, and thus the meaning of theological doctrines, is open to the possibility of revision.

In order to comprehend Lonergan's approach to the demonstration of the existence of God it will be necessary to explain his concept of horizon analysis and a moving viewpoint. All human knowing, Lonergan contends, exists within a horizon constituted by the knower and the known, a subjective and objective pole, respectively. The knower is one who poses questions and searches for answers. When the knower thinks a problem has been solved, he or she filters the solution through the process of judgment. The known is made up of that body of learning which is generally considered to be the reliable interpretation of the world in which we live, as well as those areas in which significant investigation is still occurring, (the known unknown) and those areas about which we don't even know at this point in human history (the unknown unknown). Although it is obvious that knowing and understanding occur in us as individuals, nevertheless we as the knowers are most fundamentally parts of a community of knowers seeking further intellectual penetration of the known unknown. The known and the known unknown are not so much that body of learning which I can hold in my head, but rather what the community of human knowers has been able to know. The true does not exist in a world of abstract forms, nor does it consist in things to which the mind conforms; the true is the composite of the knower and known in an act of judgment. So also the real. The real is not defined as a property of things, but rather as what is affirmed in an act of judgment. The true and the real are what can be known within the horizon constituted by the knower and the known.

The "moving viewpoint" suggests a cognate notion. The concept of a moving viewpoint proposes that horizons shift—they move so that the known is focused upon from a different perspective and the knower investigates it with alternative presuppositions or addresses new questions to it. Viewpoints move in order to comprehend a more expansive body of data and in order to meet the challenges that arise from a new approach. A changed viewpoint is the result of changes in both the knower and known. Like the notion of horizon, viewpoints tend to be shared social phenomena; they are the product of the realms of scholarship and learning in which persons are engaged. The significance of the moving viewpoint for the present purpose is that it is what occasions the emergence of the question of God. As persons seek for a higher, more comprehensive viewpoint, one that can comprehend a more vast array of data (known) in a more sophisticated manner (knower), the question of God presses to the fore. For Lonergan, the argument for the existence of God runs as follows: "If the real is completely intelligible, God exists. But the real is completely intelligible. Therefore God exists."[69]

Like Rahner, Lonergan reaches the affirmation of the existence of God through characteristics of knowing, not through a metaphysics of being. Because of his notion of judgment, Lonergan is more confident than Rahner concerning our knowledge of the world; in this regard Lonergan remains closer to Anglo-American philosophy, whereas Rahner is closer to European thought. Rahner develops an elaborate theological system, to a great extent a theological anthropology, by reflecting on the conditions of possibility contained in what we know about human beings and the world, i.e. that it was created and redeemed. Lonergan's system is elaborated by working out the relationships between the knower and known and it attempts to develop a method for theology within which more adequate conceptions of Christian doctrines can be formulated.

The *nouvelle théologie*'s rediscovery of St. Thomas' notion of understanding as a dynamic, open-ended searching after truth which facilitates human comprehension of the physical world and implicitly relates humans to God as the ground of all that is good and true provided the seedbed out of which transcendental Thomism would grow. Although *Human Generis* attempted to terminate the theological activities of many associated with the *nouvelle théologie*, transcendental Thomism emerged from the era largely unscathed. Transcendental Thomism would continue to develop and mature as a system of theology throughout the rest of the 1950s and early 1960s. By the time of the Second Vatican Council, transcendental Thomism had matured to the point of being capable of making a major contribution to contemporary Catholic thought.

In the era from the end of World War I until the eve of Vatican II there also began to appear some developments directly related to moral theology. Although largely unheralded then, it was at this time that the writings of Fritz Tillmann and Dom Odon Lottin offered concrete alternatives to the neo-Thomist manuals. Later in the era the early writings of Bernard Häring and Joseph Fuchs would presage the final stages of moral theology as a theological genre and to shape the possibilities of what its offspring might be. Should the emerging hybrid be grounded in scripture (Tillmann, the early Fuchs, Häring) or systematic theology (Lottin, the later Fuchs)? How was the discipline to be related to nascent transcendental Thomism? It is to questions such as these that we must now direct our attention.

## NOTES

1. Bernard Lonergan, *Insight: A Study of Human Understanding* (New York: Longmans, 1957), 748.
2. "Aeterni Patris" in *One Hundred Years of Thomism*, ed. Victor B. Brezik, C.S.B. (Houston: Center for Thomistic Studies, 1981), 191.
3. Jean Daniélou, "Les Orientations Présentées de la Pensée Religieuse," *Études* 249 (1946):20.
4. Ibid., 17.
5. A. Vermeersch, "Soixante ans dans la théologie morale," *Nouvelle Revue Théologique* 56 (1929):123.
6. Gustav Thils, *Tendances Actuelles en Théologie Morale* (Gemblous: J. Duclot, 1940), x.
7. Ibid., x.
8. Ibid., 31.
9. Jacques Leclerq, *L'Enseignement de la Morale Chrétienne* (Paris: Les Éditions du Vitrail, 1949), 10.
10. Reginald Garrigou-Lagrange, "La nouvelle théologie, ou va-t-elle?" *Angelicum* 23 (1946):125–45.

11. The *nouvelle théologie* is a movement in Catholic theology which needs serious historical investigation. Schoof's *A Survey of Catholic Theology, 1800–1970* (Paramus: Paulist/Newman Press, 1970) contains only a very cursory study of the movement. James M. Donnelley's *Voices of France* (New York: The Macmillan Company, 1961) does not even address Chenu's contribution.
12. Marie-Dominique Chenu, *Une école de théologie: le Saulchoir* (Paris: Les Éditions du Cerf, 1985). This is a republication of the 1937 edition.
13. Ibid., 130.
14. Ibid., 144.
15. Ibid., 134–35.
16. Ibid., 140.
17. Ibid.
18. Ibid., 141.
19. Ibid.
20. Ibid., 148–49.
20a.Ibid., 156.
21. Ibid., 158.
22. Ibid., 162.
23. Ibid.
24. Ibid., 164.
25. Ibid., 169.
26. Ibid., 173.
27. Schoof, *A Survey of Catholic Theology*, 112.
28. Henri de Lubac, *The Discovery of God*, trans. Alexander Dru (New York: P. J. Kennedy and Sons, 1960), 13. This work is a translation of *Sur les chemins de Dieu* (Paris: Aubier, 1956), the third edition of *De la Connaissance de Dieu* (Paris: Editions du Temoignage Chrétien, 1945). References will be to *The Discovery of God* because this work is generally available, but also because its footnotes contain de Lubac's replies to critics of his early versions of what was basically the same text.
29. Ibid., 14.
30. Ibid., 14, footnote 13.
31. Ibid., 40.
32. Ibid., 67.
33. Ibid., 104.
34. Ibid., 94.
35. Ibid., 97.
36. Henri de Lubac, *Surnaturel* (Paris: Aubier, 1946).
37. Henri de Lubac, *The Mystery of the Supernatural*, trans. Rosemary Sheed (New York: Herder and Herder, 1967).
38. Ibid., 70.

39. Ibid., 234.

40. A.C. Cotter, ed. *The Encyclical "Humani Generis"* (Weston: Weston College Press, 1951), #32.

41. Ibid., #31.

42. Ibid., #15.

43. Ibid., #25–29.

44. Ibid., #11.

45. Ibid., #17.

46. Ibid., #31.

47. Ibid., #33, 35.

48. Ibid., #72.

49. John Baptist Janssens, "On The Encyclical Humani Generis of Pius XII" (Woodstock: Woodstock College Press, 1952).

49a.Ibid., 11.

50. Otto Muck, S.J., *The Transcendental Method*, trans. William D. Seidensticker (New York: Herder and Herder, 1968).

51. Peter Eicher, *Die anthropologische Wende*, (Freiburg: Universitätsverlag Freiburg, Schweiz, 1970).

52. David Tracy, *The Achievement of Bernard Lonergan* (New York: Herder and Herder, 1970).

53. See for example Jacques Maritain, *Man and the State* (Chicago: University of Chicago Press, 1951) and *Integral Humanism*, trans. Joseph W. Evans (Nortre Dame: University of Notre Dame Press, 1968).

54. Karl Rahner, *Spirit in the World*, trans. William Dych, S.J. (New York: Herder and Herder, 1968). Original publication date was 1937.

55. Bernard J. F. Lonergan, *Insight: A Study of Human Understanding* (New York: Philosophical Library, 1957).

56. Herbert Vorgrimler, *Understanding Karl Rahner*, trans. John Bowden (London: SCM Press, 1986), 57.

57. Bernard Lonergan, *Grace and Freedom* (New York: Herder and Herder, 1971). These essays were originally published in *Theological Studies* 2 (1941):289–324; and 3 (1941):69–88, 375–402, 533–578.

58. Bernard Lonergan, S.J., *Verbum: Word and Idea in Aquinas* (Notre Dame: University of Notre Dame Press, 1967). These essays were originally published in *Theological Studies* 7 (1946):349–392; 8 (1947):35–79, 404–444; and 10 (1949):3–40, 359–393.

59. Bernard Lonergan, *De Deo Trino, Pars Analytica* (Romae: Apud Aedes Universitatis Gregorianae, 1961).

60. Bernard Lonergan, *De Verbo Incarnato* (Romae: Apud Aedes Universitatis Gregorianae, 1960).

61. Rahner, *Spirit in the World*, xlix.

62. Ibid., xix. The quote is from the Introduction by Francis P. Fiorenza.

63. Lonergan, *Insight*, 748.
64. Ibid., 748.
65. *Summa Theologiae* I, 2.3.
66. Immanuel Kant, *Critique of Practical Reason*, trans. Lewis White Beck (Indianapolis: The Bobbs-Merrill Company, Inc., 1956), 30.
67. Rahner, *Spirit in the World*, 1.
68. Lonergan, *Insight*, Chapter IX, "The Notion of Judgment," (271–278).
69. Ibid., 672.

# 8.

# Four Alternative Manuals
# of Moral Theology

The first five chapters of this study traced the origins and development of the neo-Thomist manuals of moral theology. The theological presuppositions of these manuals as well as the ethical principles and casuistry which shaped their content were investigated. Chapters Six and Seven illustrated the theological developments associated with modernism, the *nouvelle théologie*, and transcendental Thomism—three decisive alternatives to the neo-Thomist tradition. The first two of these movements had no direct influence upon the neo-Thomist manuals of moral theology; the impact of transcendental Thomism would begin to be felt in the 1960s. Throughout this entire period, however, there were theologians committed to premises inconsistent with neo-Thomism, who were also involved in the construction of manuals of moral theology. It is to such efforts that we must now direct our attention.

Fritz Tillmann, Dom Odon Lottin, Bernard Häring, and Joseph Fuchs each authored works which employed theological and philosophical presuppositions different from those of the neo-Thomists. These authors attempted to develop styles of moral theology on the basis of different theological presuppositions as well as distinctive moral theories. The external characteristics of these works gave them a superficial resemblance to the neo-Thomist manuals, but in fact they were significantly different theologies.

## I. Fritz Tillmann

Fritz Tillmann, like Thomas Bouquillon, was primarily a university as opposed to a seminary professor. He continued the strain of Catholic moral theology which had been developed by Hirscher at the University of Tübingen. His work gives striking evidence of the intellectual context out of which it grew. Tillmann was conversant with the writings of Kant and Hegel as

162

well as other important nineteenth and twentieth century scholars. He wrote a number of books dealing with the New Testament and was particularly interested in the Gospel of John. His major contribution to moral theology was his editorship of the four volume work *Handbuch der katholischen Sittenlehre*[1] which included two volumes of his own, *Die Idee der Nachfolge Christi*[2] and *Die Verwirklichung der Nachfolge Christi*.[3] The *Handbuch* was a massive theological undertaking. Its first volume attempted to lay out the philosophical and psychological foundations of Catholic moral theology. Tillmann's two volumes were then devoted exclusively to the theological dimensions of general and special moral theology. In 1937 he published *Der Meister Ruft: eine Laiemoral für glaübige Christen*,[4] a more popular presentation of his theology directed to the needs of educated lay Catholics. Each of these writings mark him as a theologian in a strikingly different mold than the neo-Thomists. In what ways then was he distinctive?

Bernard Häring has remarked that Tillmann's theology was "based entirely on the inspired word."[5] Indeed there were no affirmations in his theology, no theological moves made, which were not based on his interpretations of scripture. This might also be said of at least the intentions, if not the accomplishments, of the neo-Thomists. Tillmann clearly moved beyond them, however, in terms of the manner in which scripture was employed in his writings as well as in his use of contemporary exegetical methods. He did not use the scholastic method; he was not primarily concerned to reconcile the differences in various scriptural passages. Rather Tillmann's method was that of a scriptural theologian; he strove to identify the basic themes of the New Testament which had specific bearing on the conduct of Christians.

Tillmann was also dedicated to the elaboration of these biblical themes into a science of the faith (*Glaubenswissenschaft*). "Catholic moral theology," he wrote, "is the scientific presentation of the following of Christ in the life of the individual and the community."[6] Moral theology entailed a comprehensive study of divine revelation contained in the scriptures, tradition, and the papal teaching office. For Tillmann Catholic moral teaching found its source in "the person of Christ as the original image and the positive form of life set before us."[7] The person of Christ presented in the scriptures was the norm of morality to be imitated by all who would follow him. The kingdom of God was central to Christ's preaching, and its realization was the goal of Christian striving. From the outset, Tillmann's vision of Christian ethics required a social context for personal moral agency. Individuals were thought of as planned and designed for a social, communal existence within the kingdom and were the product of historical and cultural development.[8] Moral theology was a science because it not only identified the source and goal of Christian morality, but also sought to understand the relationship between the distinct elements within the system.

The decisive mark of the follower of Christ was rebirth. Rebirth, as Jesus informed Nicodemus (Jn 3: 1–21), meant the beginning of a new form of existence, the basis of a higher way of being. Rebirth was an ontological re-ordering of creation, which "makes man a new substance," a complete and other way of being, "the bud of divine life."[9] This was not simply a renewal, a healing of wounded human nature, but the creation of a completely other life.[10] The forgiveness of sins was merely the negative side of rebirth, the gift of faith was the positive side. Rebirth was the work of God alone and was received by Christians as a gift.

The preaching of Jesus revealed a God of love and forgiveness; above all a God who was near to his people, wishing them well, and giving them gifts.[11] The divine "Thou" was directly revealed to the human "I" in the person of Christ. In him Christians know the Father. The response of the human "I" was obedience to the will of God. God "demands from each of his children a decision and proof of one's religious-moral power and unfailingly strong will."[12] The basic paradigm at work here was that of the Christian's response to the initiative of God. The response of Christians ought to be one of obedience.

Tillmann repeatedly referred to the "religious-moral" character of the human response. These were two profoundly interrelated aspects of human agency. Tillmann never spoke of a purely moral act; rather, human acts were always characterized as religious-moral.

> In the following of Christ, religion and morality are the two life commandments, which are not independent of one another or strangers to one another; rather they build a living indissoluble unity. The religion of the Gospel cannot be thought of apart from the fulfillment of its moral requirements, because a new morality flows from the new faith and finds in it the power of its development . . . this unity sinks its roots in the ultimate depth of religious faith and moral statements.[13]

The goal of human life was to return to the Creator. Tillmann's discussion of the final end was never elaborated in a metaphysical framework; he did not embrace the neo-Thomist understanding of final causality. Nor did he speculate on what the attainment of this goal might entail; he did not develop a doctrine on beatitude. The goal of the Christian's return to God was important for the present life because it set a context, a perspective from which life in this world needed to be evaluated. The goal of human life also determined Tillmann's position on the relation between nature and grace.

Man stands before the supernatural final end of the unmediated vision of God as it is heard through divine revelation by believing men, and he encounters essential knowledge of God and flowing from that the fullness of divine love.[14]

This was a key element in his doctrine of grace. Revelation obligated believers to God; they knew God and had experienced his love. Thus Tillmann continues:

This is not a miraculous notion of the supernatural, it is not construed as a second framework that can be set outside the natural. [Quoting from Mausbach's *Grundlage und Ausbilds des Charakters*] "The distinction between the natural and the supernatural is based on the subject of morality, on its human and its inner fulfillment; the objective goal of morality, the good, holiness, the lordship of God is enthroned in the inseparable unity of both orders."[15]

Tillmann was clearly rejecting the neo-Thomist distinction between nature and grace. But what was he positively asserting?

Tillmann was asserting, along with the tradition stemming from Aquinas, that there was a common language of morality. The concrete demands of Christian morality were the same as the demands of morality upon the pagans and the Jews. Yet there was truly something distinctive in Christian behavior. First, the norm of Christian morality was the person of Christ whose life was to be imitated—a life lived in accord with the will of God. Although what was concretely demanded of Christians was identical to the demands of morality upon all persons, nevertheless the Christian ought to adhere to these demands because they make possible the imitation of Christ. Second, the Christian through rebirth has become a substantively different person. He or she has now received a new life. Christians were now religious-moral beings who strove to obey the will of God. The Christian was to operate on the basis of this new life and the knowledge given through revelation.

The neo-Thomist manuals of moral theology developed specific moral requirements in relationship to the natural law. In place of the natural law, Tillmann spoke of conversion, faith, and the command to love God and neighbor as the basis of the demands upon the follower of Christ. Conversion was understood as the human counterpart to rebirth whereby "man turns from all his failings and sinfulness so that he can stand before the judge and not be found to be chaff."[16] Faith was construed as the essence of conversion. Faith was "like a grasping of the divine good and life, but also its truthfulness, holiness, and righteousness."[17] In contrast to the neo-Thomists, faith, not charity, was the primordial Christian virtue. For Tillmann faith was not the result of the will, informed by charity, directing human understanding to accept revealed truths; but rather, because faith had been given to Christians, they, as religious-moral persons, were to live in accord with the will of God. Obviously Tillmann did not adhere to the neo-Thomist faculty psychology which sharply distinguished the functions of the intellect and will. His was a more holistic view of human persons.

Rebirth and faith were the first two demands imposed on Christians as a result of their encounter with God. The third demand upon the followers of Christ was the command of love of God and neighbor. This command for Tillmann served both religious and moral purposes.

> The double command of love of God and love of neighbor is not only
> the marriage of the religious and moral, not only the highest union
> of the religious-moral duty and task, it is in its content the highest
> and greatest demand which Jesus imposed on his followers.[18]

The unity of the command stemmed from our love of Christ, God and man, as our brother. It extended to all persons regardless of their nationality or office, even to our enemies.

Fritz Tillmann was neither a Thomist nor a neo-Thomist. He was the expositor of a theological tradition which had its origins among the Catholic theologians of Tübingen in the nineteenth and early twentieth centuries. Like Thomas Bouquillon, he repeatedly referred to the major systematic theologians of his day. He was deeply concerned to develop a theology which would mediate a spirituality that could nourish the lives of Christian men and women. His was not a deductive system, but rather an inductive one which attempted to detail the requirements of the following of Christ on the basis of what Christians know and experience about God through revelation. The most distinctive feature of Tillmann's theology was his attempt to establish all of his theology in direct relation to scriptural themes.

## II. Dom Odon Lottin

The historical investigation of the writings of St. Thomas and medieval theology in general was among the major achievements of Catholic theology between the two World Wars. Dom Odon Lottin made a significant contribution to that task. His *Psychologie et morale aux XIIe et XIIIe siècles*[19] was a masterful study of the moral theology of St. Thomas. Lottin's interests, however, were not just historical. In 1947 he published *Principes de Morale*[20], and then greatly expanded and refined that work into his 1954 *Morale Fondamentale*.[21] He was most certainly a Thomist, one deeply concerned about the manner in which the tradition of St. Thomas might be mediated into the twentieth century. His theology, like that of the Louvain theologians in general, was historical-critical: what can we learn from the past to illumine the present? His *Morale Fondamentale*, which will be examined below, shared several common characteristics with the works of Thomas Bouquillon and Fritz Tillmann. Like them he wrote for graduate students at the university rather than seminarians. He was sharply critical of the neo-Thomist manualists for both theological and philosophical reasons. Indeed, Lottin developed a distinct theological position.

There were numerous grounds on which Lottin criticized the neo-Thomist manuals. Their major fault, he contended, was an excessive orientation toward pastoral ministry.[22] For this reason the manuals attempted to be concise and practical and to eliminate everything that was not interesting to the confessor. Their intellectual integrity was further undermined by the introduction of canon law. Moral theology for Lottin was concerned with the internal forum and private goods, with matters of conscience, whereas canon law addressed the external forum and the public good. The emphasis on pastoral care and canon law tended to remove moral theology from its natural environment: moral philosophy and dogmatic theology.

> Briefly on the one hand, the lack of philosophical speculation in a number of elementary manuals misunderstands the character of the human as well as the nature of reason and Christian morality, and, on the other hand, the lack of theological speculation places its divine and supernatural character in a shadow.[23]

The problem with the neo-Thomist manuals, his critique seemed to suggest, was that they were written from inadequate theological and intellectual premises.

Lottin's critique implied a rejection of the neo-Thomist distinction between philosophy and theology. Philosophy, and moral philosophy in particular, did not just provide the theologian with a metaphysical framework and a set of explanatory categories. For Lottin philosophy was an integral part of the theological project. Adequate conceptions of the human, of reason, and of morality were considered internal to the task of theology; they were not notions conceived philosophically and then augmented by theology's understanding of revelation.

Like Bouquillon and Tillmann, Lottin insisted on the reintegration of moral theology and dogmatic theology. The purpose of moral theology, he wrote, was "to discover an objective norm of supernatural morality . . . a principle which directs our decisions and orients our acts towards a supernatural goal in order to ensure an eternal value."[24] Both dogmatic and moral theology ought to be concerned with the supernatural end which God has proposed and promised to Christians as well as the means given to them to attain that end. Dogma was concerned with the formal exposition of topics such as beatitude, eternal damnation, and the work of sanctification. Moral theology studied the same topics from a practical perspective, as important to human activity, and as the means by which persons ought to be directed to their final end.[25] There can be no doubt that Lottin had Aquinas' *Summa Theologiae* in mind as he pondered the intimate relationship between dogmatic and moral theology.

The methodology employed by Lottin was unique but similar to the transcendental Thomism of Karl Rahner and Bernard Lonergan. His "psychological inductive" approach was an important instance of the turn to the subject in Catholic theology. Whereas the neo-Thomists emphasized an objective moral order grounded in the natural law and the data of revelation, Lottin began with "precise notions taken from experience" and then moved by induction to the primary causes of the moral order.[26] Morality consisted in sentiments and judgments that "sprout spontaneously from the human person."[27] Theologians should strive to discover the cause of these sentiments and judgments using the principle of sufficient reason. What must be the case, if persons experience the reality of such sentiments and judgments? When one answers that question, one will necessarily confront the ground of morality. Lottin proceeded then to examine the psychology of the human act and on the basis of that study arrived at his interpretation of the norms of morality.

The norms of morality which Lottin induced from his analysis of the psychology of moral sentiments and judgments at first appear quite similar to those presented by the neo-Thomists on the basis of their natural law theory. But Lottin's norms must be understood in the light of his own theology. "The good of a being," he wrote, "is that which conforms to its specific nature, a nature given some specific characteristics."[28] The nature of something makes certain activities necessary and naturally appropriate. For human nature this entailed the execution of acts of a reasonable nature; to act in accord with reason was to achieve a true human good (*bonum honestum*). Because the end of human life is a supernatural goal, there must also be a supernatural norm of morality. Through sanctifying grace Christians share in the divine life. "The divine strength which animated the soul of Jesus has become ours [i.e. as Christians]; we live the same life as the Christ . . . we possess an internal principle of divine activity, the same which animated the soul of Christ."[29] The principle of divine life, Lottin maintained, was the supernatural norm of morality. Sanctifying grace in the life of the Christian has the same function as "nature" in purely natural life.[30] Sanctifying grace is the "nature" of the supernatural order.

Sanctifying grace, according to Lottin, was the moral norm of Christian life, but was not immediately a principle of action. The principles of supernatural action for Lottin were the virtues. In a manner similar to that of Tillmann, Lottin attributed to the virtue of faith the knowledge of the supernatural moral norm. Faith, he contended, "transforms our view of the universe."[31] Faith was understood as a source of moral knowledge clearly distinguishable from reason.

> Human reason can establish that God is the author and master of all that is worthy of our religious adoration. But Jesus reveals to us a God who is not only master, but a father who introduces us into a divine family. In one stroke the theory of moral knowledge is transformed.[32]

This knowledge made Christians aware of the dignity of other persons through their participation in the divine nature and united them in Christ. Thus we are all "members of the same family which goes beyond the bonds of language, politics, and race to embrace all humanity, the communion of saints, and the mystical body of Christ."[33]

The understanding of the relationship between nature and grace in Lottin's theology was clearly distinguishable from that of the neo-Thomists. Rational psychology had replaced metaphysics as the fundamental organizing category. Lottin was not primarily interested in two distinct orders of nature and grace, but rather with the characteristics of Christian sentiments and judgments and with the nature of the moral order they indicate. To speak of sanctifying grace as the "nature" of the Christian was to understand the gift of grace in a manner significantly different from the neo-Thomist interpretation of grace as an accidental modification of human nature. The role of human experience in Lottin's theology as well as his emphasis on the proper role of dogma and moral philosophy for moral theology further distinguish his position from that of the neo-Thomists.

## III. Bernard Häring

The publication of *The Law of Christ* was a watershed in the history of moral theology. From the date of its publication (1954) a process was set in motion that would result in the gradual removal of the neo-Thomist manuals of moral theology from the seminaries of Europe and the United States.

There were a number of reasons why this one book was able to have such a decisive impact on the demise of moral theology.

The time was ripe for the publication of such a book. As we already saw in Chapter Seven, World War II had posed questions and issues for Roman Catholicism of an unprecedented nature. The minds and hearts of France were turning from Catholicism to existentialism and communism. In Germany Heidegger's philosophy and situation ethics were capturing the minds of intellectuals. The war had created new problems: To many Europeans reconstruction meant not a return to old patterns of thought, but rather the construction of something new. Neo-Thomism was coming under increasing criticism from Catholic theologians. The *nouvelle théologie* and transcendental Thomism had emerged as critiques of neo-Thomism and, in the case of transcendental Thomism, as an alternative. From 1962 to 1965 the Second Vatican Council turned repeatedly from the preparatory schemas, drafted largely in accord with neo-Thomist presuppositions, to alternative approaches to theological and pastoral questions. *The Law of Christ* was birthed into this theologically changing world. Its use of scripture, its pastoral orientation, its engagement with the intellectual currents of contemporary Europe, its emphasis on the imitation of Christ were likely to be seen as a wise and theologically responsible reading of and response to the "signs of the times."

*The Law of Christ* offered its readers an alternative to the neo-Thomist manuals of moral theology. It differed with regard to both its theology and its moral theory. Its theology was deeply indebted to that of Fritz Tillmann; its moral theory was the particular achievement of Bernard Häring.

Although not the exegete that Tillmann had been, Häring strove in his writing to be responsible primarily to the scriptures. The theological themes he developed were those found in scripture. He did not turn to dogmatic theology for signs of what was theologically relevant; the relationship between nature and grace, body and soul, philosophy and theology were not his organizing categories. Rather the central theological themes of moral theology, he proposed, were the invitation of Christ, the human response, and conversion.

Häring shared with Tillmann a common starting point for Christian ethics. Tillmann spoke of God's initiative and invitation which made possible the response of Christians. This in turn gave rise to his emphasis on the religious-moral character of human agency. Häring's position was essentially the same. "The pure type of religious ethics," Häring wrote, "is of the nature of response, in which moral conduct is understood as response to the summons of a person who is holy, who is absolute."[34] Religion and morality were thus inseparably intertwined. Morality was construed as an essential element in one's responsible response to God's initiative.

Although he did not emphasize the notion of rebirth to the extent Tillmann had, nevertheless Häring stressed that it was the whole person, body and soul, that was "formed in the likeness of the essential image of the Father," the whole person was redeemed "and called to eternal community of love with God."[35] This theological interpretation of what grace accomplishes in human beings was one of the striking features of Häring's theology. The fundamental characteristic of human beings was not seen as human nature, but rather human personhood. Nor did Häring understand personhood in an abstract manner. Rather it was human persons in their concreteness which constituted the subject of theological ethics. Men and women in both their individuality and sociality, their body and soul, their instincts and spirit, their historicity and sense of the present shaped his notion of personhood.

✓ The norm or standard of Christian personhood was the person of Christ.

> Christ stands before us as perfect man, fully spiritual and devoted to the Father, entirely human and open to His brethren, to all the joys and sorrows of the world, absorbed in the majesty of the Father and filled with wonder over the lilies of the field. . . . He appeals to all that is in man: intellect and will, heart and spirit. There is no surer way to the full perfection of the whole man than the perfect following of Christ in the communal life of the Church.[36]

As for Tillmann so also for Häring, Christ was the center of the religious-moral life; he was the norm of Christian morality.

Given the centrality of Christ to this theological ethic, the new law assumed unprecedented importance. Häring provided his readers with a brief history of the natural law as well as its contemporary meaning. The natural law was not, however, a major organizing theme of his general moral theology. Moral norms, he contended, were themselves a "summons and invitation."[37] The new law was "the grace of the Holy Spirit knocking at the door of man's heart. It was the high goal of perfection inviting and summoning."[38] It was in part through the law that persons experience God's invitation, his initiative toward persons. In fact, Häring continued, the law of grace "is gravely endangered by an exclusive orientation according to law, if this is taken in the sense of external prohibitive universal law."[39] In an earlier work, *Das Heilige und das Gute*, Häring argued that:

> Legalism is the greatest moral danger surrounding man; if his morality does not live from the root of religion, from a personal relation to God, then when love becomes difficult the danger of

legalism will surely not be overcome. As soon as Christ appears to the glance of his disciple, abstract duty no longer stands in the moral circle.[40]

Thus the sequence must always be grace and then law; the Christian must first center on the person of Christ and then experience the law as an expression of Christ's summons.

Häring also assimilated Tillmann's concept of conversion as what grace could accomplish in Christians and what Christians could accomplish in their response to the divine initiative. Häring asserted that:

> ... the way to Christ is only through *metanoia*, through conversion that arises from the very depth of the human heart. Christ himself is the messenger of the glad tidings. He himself proclaims that conversion is possible and invites men to turn from sin.[41]

Conversion for Häring entailed the renouncement of sin and the return to God. Corresponding to the social and historical aspects of personhood, conversion implied the restoration of divine sovereignty and the eschatological return of the Lord. Conversion for Häring indicated the *kairos*, the urgency and the timeliness of turning to God. As did Tillmann, Häring associated the paired concepts of conversion and rebirth. For those who have been reborn the law is written on their hearts:

> ... it has become something deep and intimate to the new convert. Now with the eyes of the child, he sees in the law of God the wise dispositions of the heavenly Father. ... The divine life (*Zoe*) itself is now the actual norm of his life.[42]

Conversion was what the divine initiative and the appropriate human response could accomplish within Christians. The primordial sign of conversion was the sacramental life.

Häring's theology was in part the result of his assimilation of Tillmann's earlier work. Häring's unique contribution, however, was the moral theory he related to that theology. Häring's moral theory was not determined philosophically apart from his theology, but was itself the product of his theological position. What distinquished Häring's position from that of Tillmann, on the one hand, and the neo-Thomists on the other, was the role he ascribed to value.

The knowledge of value was the keystone of Häring's moral theory. Its function was similar to the role attributed to faith in *Die Idee der Nachfolge Christi*. Such knowledge was the result of an apprehension of the divine image. As created in the "image and likeness of God," persons possessed a limited but real knowledge of the divine image. Such knowledge was an invitation, "an appeal to us to choose God and His law."[43] The more comprehensive and profound one's understanding was, the greater one's responsibility before God. Knowledge of value was not just intellectual, but rather a dynamic awareness related to the will and emotions as well. It was an appeal to the whole person. Thus it was neither solely theoretical nor legalistic knowledge, but rather "insight into value itself, which is the basis of obligation."[44]

The basis or core of value was construed as an awareness, a cognition of the divinity. Häring was not primarily concerned with basic, abstract, philosophical intuitions of God; such a knowledge was likely to remain vague or to give rise to philosophical and theoretical elaborations. His focus was on what he termed the "practical perception of value" and "the sense of value." In the practical perception, "value is plainly discerned in its clarity and splendor and its concrete worth and claim to our acceptance."[45] The sense of value "attains perfection only in its total response to its word of love."[46] The difference between the practical perception and sense of value was one of degree, the one being less perfect and the other more perfect. In either case, Christians were understood to be aware of the divine image and activity as the center of value which ought to be emulated in their lives. "To a religious morality," he wrote in *Das Heilige und das Gute*, "belongs essentially the personal attraction to the ground of all value and all law, because it is essentially a personal relationship, it is dialogue."[47]

Revelation, the teaching church, and the example of fellow Christians and the saints were presented as the sources of the knowledge of value. The order of creation had been distorted through original sin, but, first in the Old Covenant and then in the New Covenant, God made known the knowledge and foundation of the law. In this manner:

> ... did God exalt this divine instruction and orientation through Christ, who teaches His precepts with words of infinite tenderness, with words filled with impressive and loving earnestness, and not least through acts of His love. Christ gave us a new commandment, the commandment of love. He presented it to us as He Himself lived it, so that we can penetrate into the profound depths of its value and meaning.[48]

A Christian's knowledge of moral good and evil was thus a moral-religious knowledge. Knowledge of God as the basis of value was the source of the Christian knowledge of what was morally right or wrong.

In addition to basic value, Häring also spoke of types of values and particular values. Types of values referred to a set of particular or specific values which shared a more general or generic value. Types of values were associated with Häring's theory of the virtues. Charity, justice or chastity, for instance, were instances of types of values. Particular values referred to the specific values realized in concrete human acts—the avoidance of scandal, feeding the hungry, appropriate sexual behavior.

Types of values were related to the theological and cardinal virtues. They served an intermediary role between basic value and particular value. Their function was to place particular values within a hierarchy of goods (*ordo bonorum*). "The splendor and dignity of particular value can exist only in concert with the whole hierarchy of goods."[49] The life of virtue enables the Christian to prioritize particular values and to do so in relation "to God, the supreme and most loveable good."[50]

Particular values provided the basis of concrete moral norms. "Value dictates norm . . . Mirrored in the objective value itself and its relation to man attracted by value is the rule set up for man as the unalterable standard (norm) of his behavior."[51] Moral norms were not construed as the requirements of pure reason or of an abstract law, but as guides to the realization of particular values. As directive of the objects of human striving, the objective norm could be expressed as:

> . . . the universal moral task of the Christian to cultivate all the natural and supernatural values and use them in rendering homage to God.[52]

From the side of the Christian moral agent, the subjective norm of morality stated that:

> . . . the Christian in spirit and action must develop all his natural and supernatural powers for good and by means of the good overcome all the evil potentialities rooted in him.[53]

Häring's position presented a clear parallel between the objective and subjective aspects of the moral order. There was a hierarchy of objective moral values to be realized through the exercise of natural and supernatural powers. Objective moral values cannot be experienced by the Christian as an arbitrary restraint interfering with freedom, but rather as "the summons and invitation to the exercise of liberty arising from the value in the object, an invitation to preserve and nurture value in freedom."[54] This "summons and invitation" was not just to the inherent good of particular value, but also to the basic value, the divine life, in which all particular values were ultimately grounded.

The natural law and the law of grace reflected the "natural and supernatural powers for good" rooted in the Christian. They were primary sources for knowledge of particular values. For Häring the natural law pertained to the rational capability of persons and was "the norm of free acts discernible through insight into the nature of man and the world by reason itself."[55] The law of grace was "the grace of the Holy Spirit knocking at the door of man's heart. It was the high goal of perfection inviting and summoning, the new law setting the goal to be striven for: *Zielgebot*."[56] Christ as the giver of the Spirit and of the new law was viewed as the center of Christian moral life. Christ was the center of Christian moral life in that he was the norm to be emulated. The law for the Christian was the law of Christ.

Häring's discussion of the natural law and the law of grace sounded similar to that of the neo-Thomists. What distinguished his position from theirs was his rejection of a sharp distinction between nature and grace. His focus remained on persons, not nature. Häring's introduction of the notion of value as the primary concept in his moral theory made it possible for him not just to relate the choice of particular moral values to the order of goods, but also to identify such choices as essential elements within the Christian response to the divine summons and invitation. Thus when he turned his discussion to human acts he could demonstrate the fact that such acts possessed a dual value. The object of the act realized a concrete value in the world, "morally good action enriches the world."[57] But the intention of the act realizes a second value in which the Christian responds to the summons and invitation of God. Drawing upon the German philosopher Max Scheler, Häring referred to this second value as being "astride the action."[58] Thus Häring was articulating further the religious-moral character of his theological ethic. The natural law and law of grace had become for him powerful means of articulating appropriate Christian responses to the divine initiative.

It is somewhat disconcerting to move from *The Law of Christ*'s first volume on general moral theology to the two volumes dealing with specific moral issues. Indeed at many points Häring attempted to discern particular moral values in relation to concrete moral issues. But when he turns to negative prohibitions, the mode of argument and language becomes quite traditional. With regard to sexual morality he referred to "the intrinsic disorder in the sin of impurity,"[59] and to the sin of masturbation as "an unnatural deviation of the sexual craving."[60] The point at issue here is not the moral rightness or wrongness of such actions, but rather that once a theologian has turned to the central role of value for theological ethics and to the centrality of person over nature, it becomes questionable whether such a presentation of specific moral topics remains consistent with or appropriate to the proposed moral theory. Ought not a Christian ethic articulated in the language of Häring's moral theology understand human sexuality as, at least in part, a particular value for persons and not as a particular value exclusively for the good of the species?

*The Law of Christ* was an important work. It was also important for the new ideas and further developments it stimulated in others. Häring's writings were probably the most important single source for the notion of Christian personalism which was to dominate much of Catholic moral theology for the next twenty-five years. As introduced to American readers and then further developed in the writings of Charles Curran, Häring's theology was to have a significant impact upon American Catholicism.

## IV. Josef Fuchs

The extensive writings of Josef Fuchs will be examined in greater detail in Chapters Ten, Eleven, and Twelve. In this context, only his *Theologia Moralis Generalis*[61] will be investigated. This work is important to this study since it maintains many of the external characteristics of the genre of neo-Thomist moral theology. It was written in Latin for Fuchs' seminary students at the Gregorian University in Rome. Unlike Tillmann's and Lottin's books it was written for a clerical audience; it made no overtures to the needs of the laity. But it was also unlike the neo-Thomist manuals in some of its theological affirmations. In fact, what is most interesting about the theology and moral theory of *Theologia Moralis Generalis* is the manner in which it attempted to reconcile the insights of Tillmann and Häring with those of neo-Thomist theology and moral theory. This work may have been one of the last attempts at constructing a manual of moral theology until the recent attempt of Germain Grisez to resurrect the genre in his *The Way of the Lord Jesus*.[62]

Tillmann and Häring had developed their theology directly from the scriptures. Fuchs defined moral theology as "the methodological attempt and scientific understanding of Christian faith in moral matters."[63] Moral theology was presented as theology in the same sense as dogma; they were understood as formally the same. Although dogma gave less consideration to practical affairs than did moral theology, they were essentially the same. The purpose of moral theology "specifically is to elaborate the sense, the character, and the specificity (*proprietatem*) of Christian morality." However, it must also demonstrate "the relation of norms to the truths of dogmatic theology and their foundation in these truths."[64]

Fuchs' moral theology was focused on persons redeemed through Jesus Christ. The first question Fuchs posed was: "who is the man which moral theology considers?" Moral theology, he replied, considered the person "whom God intended and wished through sending his Son into this world."[65] What Christ accomplished was the transformation of persons into sons and daughters of God, which truly enabled them to participate in the divine life through the gift of charity. "To urge and assist Christian moral life pertains to the work of Christ."[66] Christian moral life "is morality lived in the grace and charity of Christ in the Church."[67] Christ urged and assisted Christian life through His example, which was historically concrete.

There was one significant vestige of neo-Thomist theology which Fuchs retained. The notion of a metaphysical finality impelling persons to God as their final end remained a tenet of his theology. "By a metaphysical necessity man desires the final end of beatitude."[68] Neither Tillmann nor Häring doubted that humankind was destined for eternal life with God. But they argued this point on explicitly theological and scriptural grounds. In creation and the Old Covenant, but especially in the New Covenant, a divine initiative towards persons had been undertaken which invited them to fellowship with God as well as a sharing in the divine life. For the neo-Thomists from Kleutgen forward human nature contained as an essential ingredient a metaphysical drive toward union with the divine.

In a manner similar to that of Tillmann and Häring, Fuchs argued for the integral relationship between religion and morality. Morality, he argued, was neither neutral nor impersonal, but rather possessed a religious-personal character. The moral life of Christians was construed as "a personal response to the call of Christ," a response to God.[69] Häring had proposed that Christians experienced the law as God's summons and invitation and that grace needed to precede law. Thus religion and morality were kept together. For Fuchs it was the ordinary situation which "ought to be interpreted as a divine call. . . . Through the very reality of the situation God calls and invites us to something individual and concrete."[70] Universal norms, apart from the situations in which they ought to be applied, were understood as "the voice of God universally speaking through them."[71] Fuchs was proposing that Christian morality was not just concerned with negative moral norms; the concrete situation invites the Christian to a concrete and personal response. However, in situations where the natural or divine law would impose the prohibition of certain acts, there too the voice of God was calling.

Although Fuchs recited the traditional neo-Thomist position on human nature as the basis of the proximate norms of morality, he also contended that recent authors, and not without reason, "think that not human nature, but the human person is the norm of morality."[72] By this they mean not only the nature shared in common by all, but also what is specific and personal in each person. The moral law thus became:

. . . a dictate of practical reason, of reason however enlightened by faith; reason determines the necessity of ends and means from knowledge of man's personal existence (*cognitio Esse hominis personalis*).[73]

In this regard, Fuchs was again quite close to the positions of Tillmann and Häring. He shared their emphasis on faith or knowledge of value as the appropriate type of knowledge of the moral order, as well as their conviction that persons enlivened by grace were the ground of the moral order. But his notion of personal human existence, *Esse hominis personalis*, suggested a lingering bias for a metaphysical grounding of the proximate norms of morality.

Fuchs' basic and most important affirmation about the moral law was that it was the law of Christ. "In justified persons, the law ought to be understood as the imperative of our being in Christ (*Esse in Christo*), as the external explication of the internal movement of the grace of the Holy Spirit."[74] What was central to Fuchs at this point was not the law, but the movement of the Holy Spirit. The law as something external and universal cannot totally determine what a person should do; ultimately that task was assigned to the grace of the Holy Spirit. "Law is not the principal element in the present moral order, the principal element is the movement of the Holy Spirit and grace, which the law, explaining it, serves."[75] Thus the law became a hermeneutical tool for deciphering the requirements of grace; it also served as a hedge against antinomianism.

The significance of Fuchs' phrases *Esse hominis personalis* and *Esse in Christo* came to the fore in his discussion of natural law. "The natural element" in the law of Christ, Fuchs argued, "is very important because it represents the moral order which is known to human reason and thus to all men without supernatural revelation."[76] The basis of the natural law was nature-nature, however, understood not in opposition to spirit, but rather as "the essence of man as both spiritual and corporeal."[77] More specifically nature referred to the essence of human persons, their metaphysical being founded in the creative will of God and the divine intelligence and essence.[78]

The moral law for Fuchs was indeed the law of Christ. But the natural law retained a very specific role. The law of Christ could encourage Christians to creative, positive responses to the concrete situations encountered in their lives. The natural law retained its traditional function of determining moral prohibitions. The natural law was thus an important element within the law of Christ. "The observance of the natural law is a means of expressing the supernatural virtues of faith, hope, and charity, of expressing the following and imitation of Christ, even the vital union with Christ and His mystical body."[79]

The period in which the four manuals of Tillmann, Lottin, Häring, and Fuchs were written continued to be dominated by neo-Thomism. Each of these four authors, however, represented developments beginning to occur among Catholic moralists which would eventually lead to the decline of neo-Thomism. What were the general directions in which these four authors pointed?

First, when these manuals are examined in relationship to one another they point to two major avenues for the development of Catholic theological ethics: a more scriptural approach or one more intimately associated with systematic (dogmatic) theology. Tillmann and Häring opted for the former whereas Lottin and Fuchs chose the latter. Tillmann and Häring were concerned to identify the themes of the New Testament which seemed to clarify the nature of Christian morality. Their use of scripture was markedly different from the neo-Thomists' scholastic approach. Indeed the neo-Thomists had seen a relationship between moral theology and dogmatic theology, but they all relegated major considerations of theological themes such as the final end, the nature of grace, and the meaning of Christ to classes in dogmatic theology. For Lottin and Fuchs theological themes were simply the warp and woof of their theological ethic.

Second, and related to the point made above, these four manuals conceive of the end of humanity, its final end, in a manner strikingly different from that of the neo-Thomist manuals of moral theology. Following Kleutgen, the neo-Thomists considered the ultimate finality of human nature in metaphysical terms and within the *exitus/reditus* schema set forth in Thomas' *Summa Theologiae*. For Tillmann and Häring the final end of persons was construed in the biblical language of the kingdom of God. Indeed the end was the same for both groups of theologians, but their different conceptions of it were profoundly important. The kingdom of God speaks of a God who is near, who is a person, who is actively involved in the lives of persons and to whom persons respond. The God of metaphysical finality is distant, is a principle of being and acts in the world in a very structured manner. For theologians focused more on doctrines than the scripture the task was to comprehend the specific means, the theological and religious resources, which could assist persons in their quest for beatitude.

Clearly with Häring and Fuchs, but also implicitly with Tillmann and Lottin, the notion of person was in the process of replacing human nature as the basis of objective moral norms. The importance of this third development can hardly be overstressed. Human nature is continuous over time and largely impervious to cultural developments. Persons are historical and in many important ways the products of their cultures. Human nature is not conscious; it is an abstract metaphysical generality. Persons are conscious, concrete, and particular. The notion of human nature is apt to distinguish body and soul, to differentiate the faculties of human nature into the rational and volitional, the irascible and concupiscible. The concept of person is more holistic. Although it can distinguish body and soul, intellect and will, it is much less likely to separate them. The common element shared by the notions of human nature and person was the function of reason as a standard of morality. The centrality of personhood among contemporary theologians was not just to have an impact on their moral theory, but would also alter their theology.

Fourth, the theological changes flowing from the turn to person as a central category can be seen in terms of the new understanding of the relationships between nature and grace as well as faith and reason. Grace was no longer viewed as an accidental modification of human nature. There was now a variety of theologies of grace. In one way or another grace was viewed as a gift to persons. Grace did not need to be endlessly parceled out among the different faculties. One example of this, which occurs in the authors examined in this chapter, pertains to reason, charity and faith. As we have seen, the neo-Thomists thought of grace as first turning the will to God as one's final end, and then the will turning the intellect to revelation as what ought to be believed. The priority was on the will and the virtue of charity. Tillman, Lottin, Häring and Fuchs all place a special emphasis on faith enabling persons to discern what is morally good and what is morally evil. They understand faith to work with and through the intellect. None of them speaks of charity turning the will, the will turning the intellect. This is a result of their holistic view of the person and concomitant rejection of faculty psychology. Grace alters persons by inviting from them a response and by facilitating a fitting response.

Collectively and individually Tillmann, Lottin, Häring and Fuchs functioned outside the scope of neo-Thomist moral theology. Although they all retained a manner of describing humanity's yearning for reunion with God, they have largely abandoned metaphysical language as an appropriate means of explaining it. Although they distinguished between nature and grace, body and soul, faith and reason, philosophy and theology, they never allowed one element in these pairs to be separated from its partner. They also understood these distinctions in manners which were fundamentally inconsistent with neo-Thomism.

From this point forward the theology and the moral theory employed by Catholic theological ethicists would become increasingly at variance with the tenets of neo-Thomism. In the years to follow the social and cultural contexts of theological ethics would also begin to change. The university would again become at least as important as the seminary as the social setting in which theological ethics is done. As the understanding of Catholic ministry was broadened beyond the confines of the sacraments and as non-priests became actively engaged in that ministry new demands would be placed on seminary

curricula. In such a world the neo-Thomist manuals would lose their
meaning.

The path from neo-Thomism to contemporary Catholicism spans almost
a hundred years. Indeed it is almost the same hundred years in which
Catholicism took root in the United States. What was the impact of neo-
Thomism on American Catholicism? This is the question to which we must
next turn.

## NOTES

1. Fritz Tillmann, ed. *Handbuch der katholischen Sittenlehre* (Düsseldorf:
   Druck und Verlag L. Schwann, 1934).
2. Fritz Tillmann, *Die Idee der Nachfolge Christi*, vol. 2 of *Handbuch der
   katholischen Sittenlehre* (Düsseldorf: Druck und Verlag L. Schwann,
   1934).
3. Fritz Tillmann, *Die Verwirklichung der Nachfolge Christi*, vol. 3 of
   *Handbuch der katholischen Sittenlehre* (Düsseldorf: Druck und Verlag
   L. Schwann, 1934).
4. Fritz Tillmann, *Der Meister Ruft: eine Laiemoral für glaubige Christen* (Düsseldorf: Mosella, 1937). This has been translated as *The Master
   Calls: A Handbook of Christian Moral Living*, trans. Gregory J.
   Roettger, O.S.B. (Baltimore: Helicon Press, 1960).
5. Bernard Häring, *The Law of Christ*, 3 vol., trans. Edwin G. Kasper,
   C.PP.S. (Westminister: Newman Press, 1966), 1:31.
6. Tillmann, *Die Idee der Nachfolge Christi*, 5.
7. Ibid., 6.
8. Ibid., 61.
9. Ibid., 83.
10. Ibid., 84.
11. Ibid., 114.
12. Ibid., 117.
13. Ibid., 132–133.
14. Ibid., 131.
15. Ibid., 132.
16. Ibid., 162.
17. Ibid., 168.
18. Ibid., 177.
19. Dom Odon Lottin, *Psychologie et morale aux XIIe et XIIIe siècles*, 6 vol.
    (Louvain: Abbaye de Mont César, 1942–60).
20. Dom Odon Lottin, *Principes de Morale*, 2 vol. (Louvain: Éditions De
    L'Abbaye de Mont César, 1947).

21. Dom Odon Lottin, *Morale Fondamentale* (Tournai: Desclée et Cie Éditeurs, 1954). This work is entitled Volume I; however I have not been able to determine whether a second volume was ever published.

22. Ibid., 23.

23. Ibid., 24.

24. Ibid., v.

25. Ibid., 13.

26. Ibid., 35.

27. Ibid., 38.

28. Ibid., 109.

29. Ibid., 152.

30. Ibid., 153.

31. Ibid., 156.

32. Ibid., 155.

33. Ibid.

34. Häring, *Law of Christ*, 1:35.

35. Ibid., 63.

36. Ibid., 72.

37. Ibid., 227.

38. Ibid., 257.

39. Ibid., 260.

40. Bernard Häring, *Das Heilige und das Gute* (Krailling vor München: Eric Wewel Verlag, 1950), 287.

41. Häring, *Law of Christ*, 1:387.

42. Ibid., 403.

43. Ibid., 120.

44. Ibid., 142.

45. Ibid., 125.

46. Ibid.

47. Häring, *Das Heilige und das Gute*, 276.

48. Häring, *Law of Christ*, 1:132.

49. Ibid., 489.

50. Ibid., 487.

51. Ibid., 227.

52. Ibid., 232–233.

53. Ibid.

54. Ibid., 227.

55. Ibid., 237.

56. Ibid., 257.

57. Ibid., 192.

58. Ibid., 191–192.

59. Ibid., 290.

60. Ibid., 301.
61. Josef Fuchs, S.J., *Pars Prima* of *Theologia Moralis Generalis*, editio altera (Roma: Editrice Universita Gregoriana, 1963).
62. Germain Grisez, *The Way of the Lord Jesus* (Chicago: Franciscan Herald Press, 1983). This work is planned as a multiple volume presentation of a contemporary moral theology.
63. Fuchs, *Pars Prima*, 3.
64. Ibid., 13.
65. Ibid., 21.
66. Ibid.
67. Ibid., 35.
68. Ibid., 25.
69. Ibid., 36.
70. Ibid., 40–41.
71. Ibid., 41.
72. Ibid., 37–38.
73. Ibid., 59.
74. Ibid., 62.
75. Ibid., 64.
76. Ibid., 66.
77. Ibid., 68.
78. Ibid.
79. Ibid., 87.

# 9.

# Theology and American Catholicism

Previous chapters have examined the neo-Thomist manuals of moral theology. The existence of competing theological systems such as modernism, the *nouvelle théologie*, and the alternative manuals of moral theology has also been investigated. This entire study has focused on trends and developments in Catholic theology; however, it has done so from an almost exclusively European perspective. The framers of neo-Thomism sought to develop a system capable of competing with Kant's philosophy and contemporary secular European thought in general. Modernism and the *nouvelle théologie* were almost exclusively European movements. It is now time to begin to ask the question: What intellectual and theological challenges faced American Catholicism?

Was there, is there or can there be an American Catholic theology? This is a complex question to answer. We have already seen that Leo XIII in *Testem Benevolentiae* had admonished American Catholics to avoid whatever would give rise to the suspicion that the church in America was in any way different from the church in the rest of the world. The premise of Leo XIII's admonition was that the church was the same in all cultures, that Catholic beliefs and practices were essentially the same in Germany, France, Spain, Italy, and the United States. If Catholic theology was and should continue to be univocal, then there can be no sense in a phrase such as "American Catholic theology." It was precisely such a univocal conception of Catholic theology which neo-Thomism sought to maintain, and which Gabriel Daly has so carefully portrayed as integralism.[1] Integralists, Daly writes, "believed that Catholic orthodoxy is expressed in, and bound up with, a logically organized system of interconnected doctrines each of which goes to make up a divinely guaranteed whole."[2]

To many contemporary theologians, such a conception of Roman Catholic theology is no longer tenable. Theological statements, doctrines and religious practices are viewed as conditioned by the historical circumstances and cultural environments in which they were articulated. Bernard Lonergan, for instance, has contended that "theology is a product not only of the religion it investigates and expounds but also of the cultural ideals and norms that set its problems and direct its solutions."[3] If this is the case, theology will necessarily be viewed as dependent upon and related to the culture from which it arises. More recently, David Tracy defined five basic models of theology which take their distinctiveness from the horizons from which they stem. "Any contemporary Christian theological position," Tracy wrote, "will consider itself obliged to interpret two basic phenomena: the Christian tradition and contemporary understandings of human existence."[4] A theology which takes seriously "contemporary understandings of human existence" must necessarily be tied to cultural and historical conditions.

This chapter will attempt to highlight several ways in which Catholicism in the United States has interacted with Protestantism and American culture. It will be suggested below that there have been at least three manners in which American Catholic thought has addressed its intellectual and cultural milieu. The first will be called the congregational Catholic approach, the second, the cultural Catholic approach. The third approach was a form of neo-Thomism which attempted to present its conception of Catholicism as an alternative to the theological and philosophical strains of American culture.

## I. Congregational American Catholic Theology

The America of 1789, the year John Carroll was named the first American bishop, was strikingly different from Europe. Europe had its great universities, its faculties of theology and its traditions of learning. The intellectual milieu of Europe was rife with Enlightenment philosophy; its social, political and economic world was on the verge of the Age of Revolution; its religiosity was besieged by deism. In America, Harvard, Yale, Columbia were all in existence, but none of them offered graduate courses. They were small fledgling institutions. There were neither Catholic colleges nor seminaries to provide an institutional setting for American Catholic theologians. St. Mary's Seminary (Baltimore) was founded in 1790 and Georgetown Academy in 1791. Although the Enlightenment and deism were to have their influence on American religious life, what was more characteristic of American religiosity was the fact that about fifty years earlier America had gone through the First Great Awakening and was on the eve of the Second. America had already had its revolution and, although there were still monarchists and Tories, there were not yet the long traditions and factions steeped in the history of the country that could make the post-revolutionary era as divisive and strife-torn as would be the case in Europe. The American revolution did not cause the domestic political, social, or economic turmoil which the Age of Revolution would unleash in Europe. The constitution was written and ratified; America was in the process of creating the social, political, economic, and religious institutions which would forge its way of life.

As it is used here, the notion of congregational Catholic thought was suggested by Jay Dolan's *The American Catholic Experience*.[5] Dolan uses the term to portray Archbishop John Carroll's conception of a sort of congregational church order which he envisaged for American Catholicism.[6] Carroll sought to establish "an independent national church with separation of church and state."[7] He attempted to ensure that episcopal appointments would be determined by the local clergy and ratified by Rome. James Hennesey comments on this matter that "his vision was of a local church in communion with the bishop and see of Rome (a communion which he always emphasized as essential), but internally autonomous, self-perpetuating, and free of the least taint of foreign jurisdiction."[8] This church order also involved a great deal of lay involvement in the administration of the churches. Congregational Catholicism also attempted a Catholic Enlightenment, an effort "to reconcile Catholicism with the new questions raised by the Age of Reason."[9] This entailed developing theological positions which were responsive to the American political, social, and religious environment.

There were perhaps two reasons why Carroll elected Congregational Catholicism, and both had to do with his Maryland upbringing and experience. First, he may have seen a positive value in the Protestant church orders which existed in Maryland. More likely, however, his proposed model of church government reflected the manner in which Catholicism in Maryland already existed. Carroll had served as the elected leader of the remnants of the Jesuits in the United States after the suppression of the order. Whatever his theoretical position might have been, in point of fact Carroll sought to develop a church in America which would be both Catholic and American. As a well-educated and thoughtful cleric who served an almost equally well-educated congregation, many of whom were intellectually tied to the ideologies which justified the Declaration of Independence and the Constitution, it is not surprising that Carroll would be open to the intellectual currents of his environment.

But Congregational Catholicism was not the achievement of Bishop Carroll alone. The origins of Congregational Catholicism lie among Catholics who were in the United States at the time of the revolution and their descendants, or American converts to Catholicism. Congregational Catholic thought emerged in the early period of American history, from the 1790s to the 1830s, when throughout the nation "Catholics and Protestants were learning how to live together; mutual respect had improved. . . . Such amicable relations were ... signs of a fundamental shift in the mentality of the people."[10] Congregational Catholic theology was made possible because religious toleration had been embodied in the nation's new Constitution. Catholics at this time, perhaps only because they were such a small proportion of the population, did not experience the bigotry that would mar the second half of the nineteenth century.

Congregational Catholicism was not a theology. Rather it was an approach adopted by individual figures in the Republican era to organize and identify Catholicism in America. It was an approach of Catholics who had been raised in America and deeply identified themselves as both Americans and Catholics. It was an approach made possible in part because Catholics and Protestants in America were relatively at ease with one another. Catholics and Protestants saw each other as equally American. Congregational Catholicism was a phenomenon of several individuals; it was not a movement within American Catholicism nor was it a policy of the bishops in general. It was a model which would soon be abandoned as the church of the immigrants replaced the church of the English Catholics centered in Maryland and as the relations between Catholics and Protestants deteriorated.

## II. Cultural Catholicism

Beginning in the 1840s and then again after the Civil War large numbers of Catholics immigrated to the United States. The massive growth of American Catholicism was the consequence of the large number of immigrants. Catholics were no longer stereotypically viewed as simply another Christian group in America, but rather as a foreign church controlled by a foreign ruler. Americans were white, Anglo-Saxon, Protestants. Immigrant Catholics were German and Irish, Polish and Italian. They spoke strange languages, or English with a brogue or heavy accent. They were clearly different from Americans. The American Catholicism of the Republican era was overwhelmed by and then assimilated by the church of the immigrants. Relations between Catholics and Protestants deteriorated with remarkable speed.

Cultural Catholicism had two specific sociological contexts. The first was among a segment of the Catholic hierarchy who believed that the interests of American Catholics would best be served through their assimilation into American culture. The second context was primarily associated with the Catholic University of America, but also with other institutions of higher education as well as scholarly journals. The university context was an attempt to engage American scholarship and cultural developments from the perspective of Catholic theology.

## (A)  The Episcopal Context

As the number of immigrant Catholics rose the Catholic episcopacy took upon itself the welfare of these new Americans. The primary figure in this movement was John Ireland, but Dennis O'Connell, Cardinal Gibbons, and those usually associated with Americanism were also among its proponents. The church leaders who sided with Ireland were convinced that immigrant Catholics needed to be acculturated into American society. One context of cultural Catholicism was the episcopacy itself, its internal discussions, its relations with Rome, and the public statements and actions of the leading bishops. Unlike Carroll, the bishops who were dedicated to the policy of acculturation had themselves immigrated to the United States and had developed a deep admiration for the institutions and culture of their adopted land. They strove to demonstrate their affection for the American way of life.

There were three major issues which the American Catholic hierarchy had to face in the closing years of the nineteenth century, each of which was in some way a consequence of immigration: the establishment of the parochial school system, whether or not the American Catholic church was to be organized along nationality lines, and the question of secret masonic organizations. The details of these questions have been adequately discussed elsewhere.[11] What will be important for our purposes will be to determine how they gave rise to a distinctive form of American Catholic thought.

The parochial schools were organized in order to protect the Catholicism of the children of the immigrants. The problem with the public school systems from the Catholic perspective was that they were not religiously neutral; rather, they were at least implicitly Protestant. From 1884 onward, the American Catholic hierarchy was committed to the establishment of independent Catholic schools. In order to lessen the financial burden these schools imposed upon the church, John Ireland, the Archbishop of St. Paul, worked out an exploratory plan by which the local public school board would rent two Catholic school buildings and pay the salaries of the Catholic teachers in these schools. Explicit religious education would take place after the official school day. Opposition to this plan arose among Ireland's colleagues within the hierarchy. What caused the opposition was the concern that such a plan seemed to recognize the state, rather than parents or the church, as the party primarily responsible for the education of children. This dispute produced a "pamphlet war" between Thomas Bouquillon, then a faculty member of the Catholic University of America, and Peter Holaind, S.J., of Woodstock College, the recently founded Jesuit seminary outside of Baltimore. The basic question became whether the primary right and authority in education lay with parents and the church, or whether the state had the primary right and authority in this regard. If indeed the state possessed such a right, might it not coerce Catholic children into the public system? Ireland and his supporters were willing to work closely with the state to provide for the education of children. They did not view the state as essentially antithetical to the interests of Catholicism. This was difficult for Roman authorities of the 1880s to understand because the situations regarding both education and church/state relations in Italy, France, and Germany were so different. The papacy's response was that Ireland's plan could be "tolerated." The ideal solution would leave education solely in the hands of parents and the church. Given the social and political realities of America, however, Ireland's plan was accepted as a tolerable compromise.

At approximately the same time, there was also a growing concern among some bishops in America, as well as persons in Germany and Austria, that the Catholic identity of the immigrants could only be maintained if they also maintained their ethnic identities. The Catholic schools were to nurture both the Catholic and ethnic identities of their students. German Catholics were to be cared for by German-speaking priests who would maintain the traditional religiosity. They should also be provided with German bishops. Either "nationality bishops" would serve as auxiliaries in the larger sees, or the bishoprics in America could be divided along ethnic rather than geographical lines. Ireland and his supporters rejected all such proposals and contended that the immigrants needed to be assimilated into American society. They indeed needed assistance in maintaining their faith, but they also needed to speak, think, and act in a manner consistent with American customs. American Catholics ought to be like their Protestant compatriots in all things save one: they were to be Catholics. This was difficult for European Catholics, with their history of Catholics and Protestants divided into separate enclaves, to accept. Many in Europe as well as some members of the American hierarchy feared that such a deep immersion of Catholic immigrants into American culture would lead not just to the loss of their ethnic identity, but also to a loss of their Catholic identity.

European Catholicism had condemned many secret or masonic organizations as part of its response to the Enlightenment and the revolutionary movements of the eighteenth and nineteenth centuries. Such movements were almost by definition atheistic and anti-Catholic. As the labor movement in the United States began to take shape, some bishops were concerned that groups such as the Knights of Labor were secret societies and that Catholics ought to be forbidden to be members. Cultural Catholicism tended to view the Knights of Labor, and the labor movement in general, as potential instruments which might alleviate the poverty experienced by so many of the immigrants. The preference of Rome was that Catholics form their own distinct organizations for the amelioration of social conditions. The fear was that the involvement of Catholics in organizations which were predominantly Protestant, or not totally governed by Catholic principles, would involve material if not formal cooperation in the evil of others. Could Catholics and Protestants really cooperate on social questions which involved moral issues without compromising their respective religious identities? Ireland and other members of the hierarchy believed such cooperation was both possible and desirable.

The cultural Catholicism which was present among some members of the hierarchy proposed that Catholicism in the United States could exist in harmony with American Protestantism and the social and cultural institutions of America. However, other members of the American hierarchy, as well as many members of Roman congregations, had severe reservations about such a possibility. They feared that to become American would mean becoming Protestant. It was such fear, coupled with Ireland's and O'Connell's growing assertions that the American Catholic experience might well provide the model for church/state relations in Europe, that eventually led to *Testem Benevolentiae*.

### (B)  The University Context

The scholarly context of cultural Catholic theology is a phenomenon about which we perhaps have a great deal to learn. Recent studies of American Catholicism such as Dolan's and Hennesey's barely allude to the role of theologians. Fogarty suggests that *Testem Benevolentiae* and the condemnation of modernism destroyed the possibility of innovative theological scholarship in the United States until the 1940s. In a generally insightful essay on American Catholic thought, John Coleman has proposed that "there are only three deceased American Catholic theologians still worth reading today for more than historic interest."[12] He then lists Orestes Brownson, John A. Ryan, and John Courtney Murray. This is perhaps a too pessimistic reading of the history. Such a list must be amended to include at least John Zahm, Augustine Hewit, and Gustave Weigel.

Congregational Catholicism did not possess a fixed institutional context. It found expression in the writings of Orestes Brownson and Isaac Hecker. Brownson and Hecker were adult converts to Catholicism and thus some aspects of their thought were fixed prior to their conversion to Catholicism. Both went through phases of transcendentalism which continued to influence their work. What one finds in the writings of Brownson and Hecker are bridges between Catholicism and American Protestantism and American philosophy.

The opening of the Catholic University of America made possible a significant Catholic intellectual presence in the United States. Of the eleven original faculty members of the University only John Keane, the rector, Augustine F. Hewit, and Charles Warren Stoddard were born in the United

States. George M. Searle was English-born, but educated at Harvard. Hewit, a graduate of Amherst and Hartford Theological Seminary, and Searle were both converts to Catholicism. The remainder of the faculty were drawn from Germany, France, Ireland, and Belgium.[13]

Bouquillon and Edward Pace, who joined the faculty shortly after the university opened, have left us memorials of what they hoped the Catholic University would accomplish. Bouquillon envisioned an increase in the number of American priests who would be educated at home.

> The great majority of our priests must be educated at home, in the midst of the people to whom their lives are devoted. Their minds, even while they are being imbued with theological learning, must be kept in touch with the actual environment. Their studies must be made, not merely in an abstract manner, but with a view to practical application in this age and in this country. . . . By thus adapting their mode of thought and action to the conditions of priestly life in America, they will, from the very outset, be able to understand their people and make themselves understood by the people.[14]

The graduates of the university would also become the faculty members of the American seminaries as well as the progenitors of a truly intellectual apostolate.[15]

In "Our Theological Seminaries" Edward Pace outlined the theological approach which he envisioned at the university. Having acknowledged the significance of *Aeterni Patris* and of the Thomistic revival, he went on to emphasize the need of theology to be responsive to the developments of modern science. The language of scholasticism, he suggested, "is not the language of the present day, nor are its axioms, sound as they may be, the norm of modern thought."[16] The facts of science are undeniable, the principles of Thomism self-evident, thus "how to focus the principles upon the facts in an orderly unit of knowledge is the question."[17] The study of scripture and history "demand erudition rather than speculation, a painstaking search for documentary evidence rather than severe deduction from well-known principles, the application of critical methods where *a priori* reasoning is of little avail."[18] Such research, Pace wrote, requires specialists trained in the methods appropriate to discrete disciplines.

Through its journal, *Catholic University Bulletin*, the Catholic University provided a platform for Catholic reflection on contemporary American issues. In 1898, Bouquillon published "Catholicity and Civilization."[19] On the surface, the essay was a response to an article by a French economist, Emile de Laveleye, *Le protestantisme et le catholicisme dans leurs rapports avec la liberté et la prosperité des peuples"* (Protestantism and Catholicism in relation to the liberty and prosperity of people). De Laveleye had argued that the political, social, and economic principles of Catholicism were inherently opposed to cultural development and incapable of providing for the needs of persons living in the Catholic countries. Bouquillon responded that geographical and environmental features of a country as well as its ideology influence cultural development. The church, both historically and in the present, encourages progress. Although the dogmas of Catholicism remain the same over time, their progressive application facilitates cultural change.[20] "By the Catholic Church and in it are developed the first elements of all progress, labor, instruction, charity; in it are safeguarded the three great factors of civilization—unity, authority, liberty."[21] This essay, however, was not merely a response to a European discussion. Rather it attempted to portray the manner in which the Catholic tradition could contribute to American culture. It was an early attempt to articulate the value and significance of the Catholic tradition for American society and culture.

In 1896 the same journal carried an essay by John Zahm entitled "Leo XIII and Science."[22] Zahm's basic claim was that in Leo XIII modern science had a true friend and supporter. Leo XIII had championed the cause of science not only in theology, but also in the physical sciences. He quotes Leo XIII as writing:

How grand and majestic is man when he commands the thunderbolt and causes it to fall harmless at his feet; when he summons the electric flash and sends it as the messenger of his will through the depths of the ocean, over precipitous mountains and across boundless deserts.[23]

The essay recounts the many occasions before and after his ascent to the throne of St. Peter that Leo XIII strongly endorsed modern science, and makes the point that Leo's endorsement of science was increasingly being recognized by European intellectuals.

One of the more insightful, but also paradoxical, pieces to appear in the *Catholic University Bulletin* was written by W.R.A. Marron, a faculty member of the St. Paul Seminary in St. Paul, Minnesota: "Pragmatism In American Philosophy."[24] "In its upbuilding, its defenders and above all, in its spirit," Marron wrote, pragmatism "smacks decidedly of the American."[25] The essay is a cursory review of the writings of Royce, Pierce, James, Caldwell, and Dewey. Marron faults pragmatism for its rejection of theory and its acceptance of value, affective meaning, and activity-experience as the norm of truth.[26] But the author goes on to stress the positive contributions of pragmatism. This new American philosophy:

. . . has brought philosophy in touch with real life and has thereby purified religion of numberless conceits and much hollowness and superficiality. It has elevated the moral beliefs of those who, though professing Christianity, subscribe to no particular religion. . . . [27]

In the work of the pragmatists, the philosophy of religion could be seen retreating from mechanism; the days of Darwin, Huxley and Spencer were past. Pragmatic philosophy required God, freedom, and immortality. America stood on the edge of a new day, a new generation of scholars, "whose hearts and minds are with us [Catholics] regarding the cardinal truths of Christian philosophy, though their method of arriving at them and defending them is manifestly unsound."[28]

Cultural Catholic theologians attempted to relate Catholic religious life and its doctrines to aspects of American society and culture. Two of its most articulate spokespersons were John Zahm and Augustine Hewit. John Zahm, the son of an Alsatian immigrant, was a member of the Congregation of the Holy Cross and received his education at the University of Notre Dame. Zahm's two major books, *Bible, Science, and Faith*[29] and *Evolution and Dogma*[30], attempted to indicate the manner in which contemporary science, and particularly the theory of evolution, could be understood as consistent with the principles of Catholic theology. Zahm understood St. Augustine as being the first theologian to arrive at the conception of the fact that:

. . . the world is under the reign of Law, and that God in the government of the physical universe acts not directly or immediately, but indirectly and through the agency of secondary causes, or what we are pleased to denominate "the laws and forces of nature."[31]

Zahm contended that a theistic notion of evolution, i.e. a theory which "admits the existence of a God, and the development, under the action of his providence, of the universe and all that it contains,"[32] was accepted by both Greek and Latin Fathers of the Church. In addressing the question of the relationship between Catholic doctrine and the theory of evolution Zahm was involved in one of the most significant intellectual and theological disputes of his day.

Augustine Hewit was one of the founders, along with Isaac Hecker, of the Paulist Fathers. He was a regular contributor to the Paulist journal, *The Catholic World*. In *Problems of the Age*,[33] Hewit attempted to present the doctrines of Catholicism to Protestant America. His concern was to demonstrate that the Catholic faith is in accordance with reason and to show "the

internal coherence and symmetry of the Catholic doctrines, and their corre-
spondence or analogy with rational truths."[34] There was at least one important similarity between the theologies of Zahm and Hewit: both were Augustinian theologians rather than Thomists.

Cultural Catholicism was an effort on the part of some members of the
episcopacy and some theologians to present Catholic theology as a resource
for a burgeoning American society. The Catholic tradition could contribute to
the still developing American culture. Cultural Catholicism also considered
the established social, political, and economic institutions of America as not
necessarily inimicable to the Catholic way of life. The episcopal branch of
cultural Catholicism attempted to create American Catholic institutions and
to develop relations with Protestantism and American society which would
foster a sense of harmony and mutual respect. The theologians attempted to
present the Catholic faith as consistent with reason and thus capable of
entering into the major intellectual discussions of the day.

## III. The Reign of Neo-Thomism

First *Testem Benevolentiae* and then the condemnation of modernism
marked the death knell for this fledgling cultural Catholicism. "With the
condemnation of modernism following so closely on the condemnation of
Americanism," Fogarty writes, "the American Catholic church lapsed into
an intellectual slumber from which it did not awaken until the 1940s."[35]
Dolan recounts that:

> . . . seminary libraries closed their doors except for a few hours a
> week, suspicious books were removed from library shelves, secular
> newspapers and periodicals became forbidden reading for seminar-
> ians, intellectual curiosity was discouraged. Brain rot set in, a
> climate of fear gripped the academy. . . . The fear of heresy settled
> over episcopal residences, chanceries, seminaries and Catholic in-
> stitutions of higher learning. Free intellectual inquiry in ecclesias-
> tical circles came to a virtual standstill. . . . Contact with Protes-
> tant and secular thinkers was broken off. It was as though
> someone had pulled a switch and the lights failed all across the
> American Catholic landscape.[36]

The Catholic University of America became a conservative institution which
would no longer tolerate the positions of cultural Catholicism.

The seminaries had been largely American translations of European
institutions. The faculties tended to be European, the textbooks the same as

those used in Ireland, France, or Germany. The dominant influence in the early years was the spirituality of St. Vincent de Paul and Jean Jacques Olier, both of whom placed a much higher value on the spiritual formation of seminarians than on their intellectual formation.[37] The intellectual component of seminary education was generally very weak. As Stafford Poole has written:

> The theological curriculum itself was almost entirely of post-Reformation, polemical vintage. Its teaching was static and unimaginative, and many texts in the theological sciences remained standard for an incredible number of years, usually untouched by any but the most superficial revisions. In many crucial areas, such as the theology of non-Catholics, the application of the virtue of justice to modern business life, apologetics, new movements in theology and exegesis, the American seminary remained staunchly backward.[38]

The textbooks, John Tracy Ellis has reported, were European manuals, especially Perrone's *Compendium Dogmaticae Theologiae* and Jean-Pierre Gury's *Compendium Theologiae Moralis.* Bishop Francis Patrick Kenrick had composed a manual of moral theology which the American bishops endorsed in 1843, but the Sulpician Archbishop of Baltimore had never promulgated the order. Preference for European texts predominated.[39]

In 1884, thus after the publication of *Aeterni Patris*, the bishops directed the American seminaries to comply with the wishes of Leo XIII by faithfully following the teaching of St. Thomas. Poole has noted that in the years following the condemnation of modernism, the seminary instructors turned again to the European manuals. "The theological manuals," he writes:

> are often less concerned with teaching principles or outlook than with grinding out ready made answers and apologetic refutations of long dead errors, shooting, as the saying goes, where the enemy was last seen. Biblical texts and quotations from the Fathers are generally used only as polemical weapons, and this frequently out of their original context. Historical development is usually overlooked in favor of the scholastic approach.[40]

Neo-Thomism became the dominant approach in American Catholic theology throughout this period.

By 1964 the number of Catholic colleges and universities had mushroomed to 278.[41] The theology of the colleges was also that of neo-Thomism. What is important to realize with regard to the presence of neo-Thomism in both the seminaries and colleges was that it purported to offer a cultural and intellectual alternative to the American system. "Thomism provided a sense of security in a world of change and furnished the intellectual cement that could bind religion and culture together."[42] There are several points that must be noted in this regard.

From its inception in the writings of Joseph Kleutgen, neo-Thomism was self-consciously an alternative to the larger culture in which it existed. For Kleutgen this larger culture was the intellectual world of Kant and his followers. Unlike Congregational or Cultural Catholicism, neo-Thomism tended to be a separatist theology. The manuals used in American Catholic seminaries prior to *Aeterni Patris* were eclectic; they did not offer a tightly defined theological system as neo-Thomism proposed. Neo-scholastic manuals, which were in part concerned to address the culture in which they existed, were rarely adopted in American seminaries, although Bouquillon's work was to have some influence at the Catholic University. Neo-Thomism was the theology which permeated American Catholic colleges and seminaries until the eve of Vatican II.

John Tracy Ellis[43], Robert Cross,[44] Gustave Weigel[45] and others have offered a number of reasons why American Catholicism has failed to produce intellectuals proportionate to its numbers in the population. The immigrant status of the church throughout much of this period and the hostility which many Catholics experienced from the nativists have contributed to this phenomenon. It was also certainly a factor that Catholic colleges and universities in the United States were, for the most part, small and insignificant institutions until the years following World War II. Their departments of theology were given more to catechesis and apologetics than to theological inquiry. Most of these institutions were administered by members of religious orders who "were more apt to be missionaries of European ultramontanism than heralds of harmony between Catholicism and America."[46] Whatever the reasons might have been, it remains something of a tragedy, as Hennesey remarks, that after three hundred years of Catholics living in the United States there still exists "no significant body of writing which could be said to represent American Catholic thought."[47] American Catholicism has not produced a Jonathan Edwards, nor a Reinhold or H. Richard Niebuhr. Catholic thought in America did not need to draw upon American culture, especially its intellectual strains, because it possessed a closed system of thought sufficient to its needs, neo-Thomism.

Clearly the major exception to this general depiction of Catholic intellectual life was the writing of John A. Ryan. A student of Thomas Bouquillon at the Catholic University of America, Ryan took Bouquillon's natural law theory and conception of the relationship of theology to the social sciences and built upon it a creative Roman Catholic analysis of the economic and social issues of the period. Ryan inherited from Bouquillon a neo-scholastic approach to theological and ethical issues which left him free to discover authentic values in American society.

The revival of Catholic theology in the United States began in the 1940s. Hennesey indicates the role played by Americans in the early stages of the liturgical renewal movement and their concern for the social implications of the liturgy; he refers to Virgil Michael, O.S.B., Martin Hellriegel, William Leonard, S.J., and Gerald Ellard.[48] It was also in the 1940s that John Courtney Murray and Gustave Weigel were added to the faculty of Woodstock College. The renewal of theological inquiry among American Catholics began in the seminaries. It would not be until after Vatican II, with the exception of the Catholic University of America, that theology would find an academic home in the Catholic universities.

It is both interesting and provocative to review some of the American theological journal articles stimulated by the *nouvelle théologie* and *Humani Generis*. *Theological Studies* published essays by Philip Donnelley,[49] Walter Burghardt,[50] Cyril Vollert,[51] and Gustave Weigel.[52] *The American Ecclesiastical Review* carried articles by John Clifford Fenton[53] and J. Clayton Murray.[54] Not once in any of these writings is there even an allusion to Americans being part of the *nouvelle théologie* or even to persons having strong sympathies with it. In 1947 Philip Donnelley proposed that American theologians should become more interested in the movement.

> Because of the lofty and apostolic motives of these writers and their recognized theological stature, and because the problems they are confronting are similar to ours, it is almost essential that American Catholic leaders, and especially theologians, follow closely the major trends and controversies of European theological thought.[55]

The trend of American Catholic theology of the period was accurately portrayed in Donnelley's proposal. European theologians may have developed an answer to the spreading of atheism and agnosticism. Although American theologians could assimilate European thought, there was little expectation for the development of an indigenous American Catholic theology. Fenton's essay concluded that *Humani Generis* was applicable and binding on American theologians, but he did not suggest that there were American members of the movement. With the exceptions of John Courtney Murray and Gustave

Weigel, American Catholic theology continued to be dominated largely by European concerns and European authors. American Catholic theologians were commentators on and assimilators of European developments. It is little wonder that in the 1960s, as the American Catholic colleges and universities were attempting to vitalize their theology departments for a more significant role in the academic life of these institutions, they would discover that they lacked the theologians and exegetes necessary to implement their goals.[56]

## IV. The Post-Vatican II Era

Among the many beneficial outcomes of the Second Vatican Council (1962–1965) has been a revitalization of Roman Catholic theology. The Council turned away from neo-Thomism and developed its own biblically-oriented theology. One of its most significant documents, "The Church in the Modern World," reflected a much more open and responsive attitude to societies and cultures than that of which neo-Thomism had been capable. What had been the dominating theology among Catholics for almost a century now became the theology of only a staunchly conservative element within the church.

In the United States, Vatican II was to have a significant impact on both the seminaries and colleges. Seminary curricula were almost completely redone. The manuals of moral theology, as well as their dogmatic counterparts, were replaced. Many seminaries were moved from their rural environments into cities, in many instances forming some sort of relationship with either a large academic institution or a number of Protestant seminaries. A declining proportion of faculty members received their terminal degrees either at Rome or the Catholic University of America, a growing proportion obtained their degrees at Yale, the University of Chicago, and Harvard.

Vatican II gave renewed stimulus to the growth of American Catholic higher education. The first real change had occurred after World War II. Suddenly a large number of Catholic young men could afford college because of the G.I. Bill of Rights. These young men came to college in such large numbers that quonset huts needed to be erected in order to house them. In the 1950s American Catholic colleges were adding new dorms and libraries, science centers and administrative offices. A process was in motion which would lead some of these colleges and universities to become major institutions of American higher education. Vatican II encouraged these colleges and universities to reconsider their religious identity.

What Vatican II seemed to require in many of these institutions was a significant redefinition and development of their theology departments.

Alongside major medical centers and law schools, schools of business and engineering, ought not Catholic schools to have prestigious departments of theology? Vatican II had awakened new religious interests in many young people who wished to major or minor in theology, an impossibility at the vast majority of American Catholic colleges until after Vatican II. For the first time in their history the Catholic colleges and universities were prepared to provide an appropriate academic setting for their theology faculties.

As a consequence of these developments American Catholic theology has taken an unprecedented turn. The majority of persons teaching theology in Catholic colleges and universities are lay women and men. The number of priests and religious men and women has dropped dramatically. At no previous time in its history, and nowhere else in the world, has the church possessed such a large number of lay theologians. Although a significant number of these theologians were educated in Europe, the majority received their Ph.Ds. from American universities, both Catholic and Protestant.

For the first time in its history American Catholicism possesses two strong institutional settings for its theologians: the university and the seminary. The university has become the context from which Catholicism addresses and interacts with American culture and scholarship. The seminary is the context in which the pastoral theology of the American church is developed.

Was there an American Catholic theology? No, there were only innovative approaches to the relationship between American culture and scholarship and Catholic theology. Had cultural Catholicism been given the time to mature into a definite theological school it might have given rise to an American Catholic theology. But that was not to be. Is there at present an American Catholic theology? Probably not. But for the first time in the history of American Catholicism the resources for such a development are in place.

## NOTES

1. Gabriel Daly, *Transcendence and Immanence: A Study in Catholic Modernism and Integralism* (Oxford: Clarendon Press, 1980) and "Catholicism and Modernity," *Journal of the American Academy of Religion* 53 (1985):773–796.
2. Daly, "Catholicism and Modernity," 776.
3. Bernard Lonergan, "Theology in its New Context," in *A Second Collection*, William F. Ryan and Bernard Tyrrell, eds. (Philadelphia: The Westminister Press, 1974), 58.

200 Time Past, Time Future

200 *Time Past, Time Future*

4. David Tracy, *Blessed Rage for Order: The New Pluralism in Theology* (New York: Seabury Press, 1975), 23.
5. Jay Dolan, *The American Catholic Experience* (Garden City: Double-day and Company, 1985), 112 and 118.
6. Ibid. 172.
7. Ibid., 108.
8. James Hennesey, *American Catholics: A History of the Roman Catholic Community in the United States* (New York: Oxford University Press, 1981), 85.
9. Ibid., 108.
10. Ibid., 102–103.
11. Thomas T. McAvoy, C.S.C., *The Great Crisis in American Catholic History, 1895–1900* (Chicago: Henry Regnery Company, 1957); Gerald P. Fogarty, *The Vatican and the American Catholic Hierarchy*, Band 21 of *Papste und Papstum*, ed. Georg Denzler, (Stuttgart: Anton Hiersemann, 1982), 1–194.
12. John Coleman, "Vision and Praxis in American Theology: Orestes Brownson, John A. Ryan, and John Courtney Murray," *Theological Studies* 37 (1976):3.
13. John Tracy Ellis, *The Formative Years of the Catholic University of America* (Washington: American Catholic Historical Association, 1946), 371–373.
14. Thomas Bouquillon, "Theology In Universities," *Catholic University Bulletin* 1 (1895):27.
15. Ibid., 28.
16. Edward A. Pace, "Our Theological Seminaries," *Catholic University Bulletin* 1 (1895):392.
17. Ibid.
18. Ibid., 394.
19. Thomas Bouquillon, "Catholicity and Civilization," *Catholic University Bulletin* 4 (1898):467–480.
20. Ibid., 478–479.
21. Ibid., 479–480.
22. John Zahm, "Leo XIII and Science," *Catholic University Bulletin* 2 (1896):21–38.
23. Ibid., 27. Zahm does not give a reference to the writings of Leo XIII.
24. W.R.A. Marron, "Pragmatism In American Philosophy," *Catholic University Bulletin* 10 (1904):211–224.
25. Ibid., 211.
26. Ibid., 222.
27. Ibid., 223.
28. Ibid., 224.

29. John Zahm, C.S.C., *Bible, Science, and Faith* (Baltimore: John Murphy and Co., 1894).

30. John Zahm, C.S.C., *Evolution and Dogma*, reprint edition (New York: Arno Press, 1978). Originally published in 1896.

31. Zahm, *Bible, Science, and Faith*, 79–80.

32. Zahm, *Evolution and Dogma*, 279.

33. Augustine F. Hewit, *Problems of the Age* (New York: The Catholic Publication House, 1868).

34. Ibid., 12.

35. Fogarty, *The Vatican and the American Hierarchy*, 193.

36. Dolan, *The American Catholic Experience*, 319.

37. Stafford Poole, C.M., *Seminary In Crisis* (New York: Herder and Herder, 1965), 38–39; see also John Tracy Ellis, *Essays in Seminary Education* (Notre Dame: Fides Press, Inc. 1967), 138.

38. Ibid., 53.

39. Ellis, *Essays*, 144.

40. Poole, *Seminary In Crisis*, 110–111.

41. Daniel Callahan, "The Catholic University: the American Experience," in *Theology and the University*, ed. John Coulson, (Baltimore: Helicon Press, 1964), 67, footnote 1.

42. Dolan, *The American Catholic Experience*, 352.

43. John Tracy Ellis, *American Catholics and the Intellectual Life* (Chicago: The Heritage Foundation, 1956).

44. Robert D. Cross, *The Emergence of Liberal Catholicism in America* (Cambridge: Harvard University Press, 1958).

45. Gustave Weigel, "American Catholic Intellectualism—A Theologian's Reflections," *Review of Politics* 19 (1957):275–307.

46. Cross, *The Emergence of Liberal Catholicism*, 36.

47. Hennesey, *American Catholics*, 258.

48. Ibid., 257.

49. Philip Donnelley, "Current Theology: On the Development of Dogma and the Supernatural," *Theological Studies* 8 (1947):471–491; "Discussions of the Supernatural Order, *Theological Studies* 9 (1948):213–249; "The Gratuity of the Beatific Vision," *Theological Studies* 11 (1950):374–404.

50. Walter Burghardt, "On Early Christian Exegesis," *Theological Studies* 11 (1950):78–116.

51. Cyril Vollert, Book Review of *Surnaturel* in *Theological Studies* 8 (1947):288–293 and "Humani Generis and the Limits of Theology," *Theological Studies* 12 (1951):3–23.

52. Gustave Weigel, "The Historical Background of the Encyclical Humani Generis," *Theological Studies* 12 (1951):208–230.

53. John Clifford Fenton, "The Lesson of the Humani Generis," *American Ecclesiastical Review* 123 (1950):359–378 and "The Humani Generis and Its Predecessors," *American Ecclesiastical Review* 123 (1950): 452–458.

54. J. Clayton Murray, "Dogma and Intellectual Freedom," *American Ecclesiastical Review* 123 (1950):443–451.

55. Donnelley, "Current Theology," 471.

56. Hennesey, *American Catholics*, 323.

*10.*

# The Impact on Moral Theology of Post Vatican II Theological Developments

It is impossible in the limited space of a single chapter to survey the many and divergent ways in which theologians have attempted to displace neo-Thomist moral theology during the past quarter century. However, it is readily apparent to anyone who has followed their writings that contemporary Catholic moralists have been producing a theological literature which is inconsistent with the theological premises of neo-Thomist moral theology. The purpose of highlighting these inconsistencies is to propose that such theological developments are really no longer instances of moral theology as the discipline has been defined in previous chapters, but rather such developments are evidence of the emergence of new theological genres. It is also important to note that the inconsistencies to be examined below do not pertain to specific moral teachings concerning birth control, sterilization, topics of death and dying, or social justice; nor do they deal with moral theories such as proportionalism. Rather the issues to be discussed pertain to specifically theological topics.

This chapter will explore the writings of Bernard Häring, Karl Rahner, Bruno Schüller, Josef Fuchs, Richard McCormick, and Charles Curran. These authors have been selected because their works have had a lasting and significant impact on American Catholic moralists. Although there are affinities in Curran's writings to positions taken by Häring, and in Fuchs and McCormick to the theology of Rahner, these authors do not in any way constitute a new school of Catholic theology. On the contrary, they exemplify the plurality of theologies which form the contemporary Catholic environment.

The theologians whose writings will be examined in this as well as the next two chapters are increasingly referred to as revisionist theologians.

Each of these theologians has attempted in one manner or another to revise, to bring up to date the moral theology which dominated the discipline in the years of their seminary and graduate education. Revisionist moral theology has not led all of its proponents along the same path. For Louis Janssens and others it has meant a more adequate understanding of the writings of Thomas Aquinas. For Häring and indirectly Curran, revisionist theology has meant not only the further development of insights originally developed by the Tübingen theologians, but also the employment of the philosophy of Max Scheler and H. Richard Niebuhr. Schüller and McCormick have clearly attempted to distinguish their positions from that of neo-Thomism. An important claim of this study is that the word "revisionist" is too weak. As revisionist theologians move further and further away from the neo-Thomism which predominated in the early years of their careers the links between the past and the future have become more tenuous. Through a process of organic development new theological genres, indeed rooted in the past, have emerged as distinct genres. The *Summae Confessorum* were distinct from the monastic penitentials. The university theology of Aquinas was distinct from that of the *Summae Confessorum*. The manualist theology of the counter-Reformation was distinct from the university theology of Aquinas. So in turn the writings of the revisionist theologians are becoming increasingly distinct from those of their neo-Thomist predecessors.

## I. Bernard Häring

The publication of Bernard Häring's *The Law of Christ*[1] presaged many developments which were to become more explicit in later years. *The Law of Christ* deviated from the structure of the manuals, from their intellectual isolation, and in some important regards from their theological presuppositions as well. Häring's work retained the structural elements of general and special moral theology and discussed all the usual topics within each part; however, the work did not contain a section dealing with the canon law of the sacraments. The exclusion of this one element had two related consequences. First, it minimized the legalism of his moral theory. The manuals of moral theology, like their predecessors the *Summae Confessorum*, were steeped in the close association of legal and moral theory which resulted from Gratian's *Concordance of Discordant Canons*. The discussions of justice in the manuals, for instance, were deeply indebted to the tradition of Roman law on such topics as ownership and restitution. Häring's work attempted to develop positions on specific topics in relation to a theory of morality, not to law. Second, *The Law of Christ* does not suggest a juridical model for pastoral ministry, but rather proposes a *medicus*, a "healing" model. Häring's introduction of concepts such as invitation and response, conversion, and the following of Christ provides a significantly different orientation in terms of the cure of souls.

Häring's doctoral thesis, *Das Heilige und das Gute*,[2] was a study of the works of Max Scheler and Rudolf Otto. In that work Häring examined the relationship between freedom and grace from the point of view of the holy and the good. The footnotes and bibliography of *The Law of Christ* gave ample evidence of his indebtedness to a wide spectrum of European philosophy and theology. Unlike that of his neo-Thomist colleagues, Häring's theology is not a closed system, but rather remains open to scholarship from any source that would permit him to decipher more accurately the fundamental characteristics of Christian morality.

There are many ways in which the theology of *The Law of Christ* can be distinguished from that of neo-Thomism. Although Häring retains the significance of the final end or beatitude and the supernatural characteristics of meritorious acts, these doctrines take on a distinct meaning in his theology. First, the concept of personhood replaces "nature" as the primary category by which moral agents are depicted. The return of Christians to God is not analyzed in relation to the needs and requirements of a metaphysical essence, but rather in relation to the imitation of Christ. Exemplary causality tends to replace final causality. The theocentric ethic of neo-Thomism is replaced by a Christocentric ethic. Neo-Thomism's rational psychology of will and intellect, its understanding of grace turning the will and intellect to humankind's final end, are replaced by the notion of conversion: "the most utterly personal movement, the restoration of the bonds of personal intimacy with God, a recovery and reacceptance of the most personal and holy rights, the rights of the child which had been lost until now . . . "[3] Not only was Häring developing a series of theological propositions significantly different from those of the prevalent neo-Thomism, he was also rejecting its distinctions between philosophy and theology and body and soul. The metaphysics and rational psychology of neo-Thomism were challenged by a position which intermingled philosophy and theology and embraced a holistic notion of persons.

In 1978 Häring produced a second systematic Christian ethic, *Free and Faithful in Christ*.[4] This work maintains a substantial continuity with *The Law of Christ*, but it also demonstrates the maturity of the author's position. The latter is the case particularly with regard to three topics: the nature of moral theology, refinements in the notion of responsibility, and the concept of the natural law.

Perhaps the most significant advance in Häring's thought has been his approach to what moral theology is. In *Free and Faithful* he explicitly moves away from an emphasis on normative ethics and instead defines the task of moral theology as gaining the right vision or perspective.[5] Later in the work, in the context of a discussion of natural law, he again stresses the need for a vision prior to the development of a normative position.[6] His discussion of the nature of moral theology is immediately followed by an examination of the Old and New Testaments. His use of scripture to define a Christian vision for an ethical theory is one of the most innovative uses of scripture by a contemporary moral theologian.

The notion of responsibility plays as central a role in the theology of *Free and Faithful* as it had in *The Law of Christ*. If anything, there is now even more emphasis on the historical, social, and interpersonal nature of responsibility. What is new is the manner in which Häring qualifies responsibility as "creative and faithful." These two terms define for Häring the distinctively Christian aspect of his ethical theory.[7] The notion of faithfulness indicates the kind of responsibility Christians have both to God and to one another. His use of fidelity has connotations similar to Josiah Royce's and H. Richard Niebuhr's notion of loyalty. The creative aspect of responsibility is the consequence of Häring's conviction that moral theology is primarily a matter of vision, rather than rules and duties. Thus in loyalty and fidelity the Christian community must search out those ways of living that are responsive to the invitation of Christ. Since Häring understands freedom (creativity) and fidelity as fundamentally biblical themes he has forged his moral theology within a biblical perspective.

The natural law has lost all of its traditional metaphysical foundations in *Free and Faithful*, and it does not any longer provide access to an objective moral order which the Christian need only look at in order to see. Rather the natural law suggests that "man has to discover what is good and evil, he cannot determine it arbitrarily."[8] Given the historical, social, and cultural contexts in which persons seek the good, the only caveat that remains of the traditional natural law is that it not be sought arbitrarily. "There are," he contends "abiding truths. And we can even hope that, throughout history, humankind will come to acknowledge ever more clearly those abiding human rights and moral values."[9] This is not, however, a call to return to a static moral system. Rather Häring's purpose is to set a curb to moral relativism and to stress that meaningful and binding moral responsibilities can be articulated. As he states somewhat later in his text, the natural law pertains to people's "capacity to listen and learn and to know in dialogue with others, with a vivid sense of the continuity of life."[10] Further, the natural law ought not to be understood as some sort of autonomous ethic. Christ did not come to restore an autonomous system of natural law, but rather "to restore, confirm, and bring to fullness the original design of

God."[11] Thus the natural law is not merely a philosophical doctrine upon which theology can build, but rather it is itself a theological doctrine stemming from creation. The natural law and the new law are both in fact given in revelation. The significant differences between the Häring of *Free and Faithful* and the theology of the neo-Thomists should be readily apparent to any reader of this study.

## II. Karl Rahner

Karl Rahner's theology constitutes a major alternative to neo-Thomist moral theology. Rahner's central achievement was to relocate the topics associated with moral theology into a systematic theology and, within that context, to elaborate a theological anthropology. In an early essay he commented that:

> ... it is the business of dogmatic theology itself comprehensively and with uniform thoroughness to establish the authentic foundation of the Christian can, ought, and may; to answer the question "what must I do to enter eternal life?" All that dogmatic theology can say is that moral theology should concern itself with what, once this question is proposed, remains to be done.[12]

This statement must be read, I believe, as a specific rejection of the fundamental premises of neo-Thomist moral theology.

Rahner's articulation of "the authentic foundation of the Christian can, ought, and may" entails the development of a revised natural law theory (an essential ethic) as well as a formal existential ethic. These two distinct but complementary moral theories depict the common morality we share as human persons as well as the moral demands which confront persons as individuals. They are both grounded in Rahner's theological anthropology.

Rahner's critical natural law theory rests upon the *a priori* conditions of human personhood which establish specific guides to human action. James Bresnahan has written:

> The category "person," therefore, appears as the constant correlative of "nature" wherever the latter has normative import. This is so much the case that human nature for Rahner consists of nothing more nor less than the conditions of possibility of conscious freedom by which the "spirit/person" shapes himself in time and history.[13]

Besides freedom, Rahner also indicates at least two other *a priori* conditions of human personhood. Power, he argues, is:

> ... a certain self-assertion and resistance proper to a given being and hence is its innate possibility of acting spontaneously, without the previous consent of another. ... All beings, simply because they exist—in themselves and in contrast to others—inevitably have power in a certain sense and to a certain degree.[14]

God's offer of grace constitutes the third "existential." Gerald McCool has described this as a "permanent modification of the human spirit which transforms its natural dynamism into an ontological drive to the God of grace and glory."[15] Freedom, grace and power, as the *a priori* conditions of human personhood, constitute the normative sources of human action. To violate these fundamental structures in another or in one's self is to risk violations of the moral order. To exercise one's power in relation to the freedom of another is to take the moral risk that the other will forever be different than he or she chooses to be. May one do such a thing?[16]

The answer to such a question, Rahner maintains, cannot be determined by simple reflection on or deductions from the *a priori* conditions of human personhood. Rather in addition to attending to the *a priori* conditions, the moral agent must also attend to the concrete possibilities, the *a posteriori* conditions latent in human experience. Specific moral norms are the product of an apprehension of the conditions of personhood and an empirical appraisal of concrete human experience. "The normative content that results from this dialectical process," Bresnahan argues:

> ... must be explicitly recognized to be time conditioned and culture related, potentially incomplete and partially inadequate—and, therefore, for another time and culture than that in which it was elaborated, possibly misleading.[17]

In *Foundations of Christian Faith*, Rahner writes that:

> ... very many individual moral norms which are binding on Christians reflect structures which belong to concrete reality which is different from God. Social justice and certain norms of sexual morality are in the first instance descriptions of the structures of created reality, of finite, conditioned and contingent realities, and they are descriptions which have been transposed into normative language.[18]

Rahner's critical natural law theory establishes primarily proscriptive moral norms; it excludes whatever endangers the existentials of and thus the integrity of personhood.

Rahner complements his critical natural law theory or essential ethic with what he terms "a formal existential ethic." If critical natural law theory can proscribe certain forms of actions as immoral, the question remains, what ought one to do? This question, Rahner argues, cannot be answered in terms of the realization of a universal ideal, i.e. the *a priori* conditions of personhood, actualizing themselves here and now.[19] A human act has meaning and significance. Through one's choices and actions, one affirms the reality of one's personhood, thus one creates self-identity and uniqueness. One's choices constitute the "coming to light of his ineffable moral individuality and are not just a merely arbitrary selection from among certain possibilities."[20] The uniqueness and individuality of such actions have eternal significance as embodying the concrete, material will of God addressed to the individual. The material will of God to which the individual must respond is not a deduction from a universal norm, but rather an individual or existential norm unique to the person to whom it is addressed. Rahner's formal existential ethic focuses on the coming-to-be of the unique, individual person.

Rahner's ethic is clearly distinct from that of the neo-Thomist manuals, and intentionally so. His emphasis on the conditions of possibility for individuals to develop a rich, mature relationship with God in their struggle to be what they ought to be, and his emphasis on an empirical approach to concrete moral norms as well as their cultural relativity sharply distinguishes his position from the manualists' stress on a universal human nature and absolute moral norms. His understanding of the relationships between nature and grace, faith and reason, philosophy and theology clearly move his theology into a distinct theological genre. His acceptance of the Kantian tradition and modern philosophy's turn to the subject enabled him to embrace positions which the neo-Thomists explicitly repudiated. Even more importantly, Rahner's ethic, theology of grace, and theory of the person were developed in explicit opposition to neo-Thomist theology.

## III. Bruno Schüller

The German Jesuit theologian Bruno Schüller has been a third major critic of the neo-Thomist manuals of moral theology. The opening chapter of his *Gesetz und Freiheit*[21] is an examination of the manualists' presentation of divine law. Schüller argues that the traditional manuals contain nothing which could not be found in philosophical ethics and church law. Further, their presentations were both theologically and philosophically unsatisfying. Finally, the law was conceived in these treatises as static, as unchanged in whatever ethical or salvation-historical context humankind might find itself.[22]

In his copious writings Schüller has attempted to develop an autonomous theistic ethic. His theory of morality is typified by two characteristics:

> (1) It thinks of a moral demand as that which is morally right by nature, thereby distancing itself from every species of moral positivism; (2) It ascribes the logically original insight into moral demands to reason (*ratio*), insofar as reason is gnoseologically distinguished, in the Augustinian sense, from faith (*fides*).[23]

His ethic is autonomous in that the requirements of the moral order can be known independently of faith and revelation. It is theistic in that the moral order itself is understood as "the command of the creator,"[24] or as he asserts elsewhere:

> This state of goodness is independent of and prior to any freely chosen position that man may take towards himself, his fellow human beings, and the world around him. It is *not* the result of any decision but can, it seems, only be the object of rational perception.[25]

The fundamental position which underlies the extensive writings of Schüller is his notion of ethical reflection. The task of ethical reflection is to elevate into critical consciousness the possible conditions for morality in general.[26] Ethics requires that one search for the intrinsic reasons for moral precepts,[27] namely the question "under what conditions can a moral rule be justified?"[28] It is this conviction concerning the fundamental nature of ethical reflection which constitutes the unifying thread in his work.

But what is morality for Schüller? Morality is the result of two fundamental aspects of human existence: creatureliness and freedom. Creatureliness indicates the dependence which characterizes human existence; freedom and personhood reflect the independence of human existence. The presence of both of these defining characteristics in every human being creates the experience of moral obligation (*das unbedingte Sollen, die Notwendigkeit des Sollens*). Moral obligation:

> ... is the form which total dependence assumes insofar as it is dependence coupled to independence. If we establish creatureliness for total dependence—creatureliness is the unique form of total

dependence—freedom and person for independence, then one could say: unconditional obligation is the form in which one's creatureliness translates itself toward personhood.[29]

Creatureliness and independence (freedom) are the necessary conditions for morality and moral obligation.

But if these are the conditions of morality, it is the movement from undecidedness to decidedness which constitutes moral experience. This movement is initiated as one becomes aware of one's self as a personal creature who encounters the divine law (creatureliness) and in deciding (freedom, person) realizes one's freedom. The relationship between the creator and the personal creature is not only the existential basis, but also the cognitive basis of unconditional obligation.[30] The divine law is critical to the nature of morality. The law is the address of God to humankind to decide for or against God.[31]

The theistic character of Schüller's position must again be noted. His definitions of morality and moral obligation are intrinsically bound up with a creationist doctrine and humankind's absolute dependence on God. According to these definitions there can be no purely human or natural morality, if by those terms one intends to suggest a morality which does not base itself in humankind's relationship to God.

Schüller consistently uses three terms to refer to the law which is at the center of morality: the unconditional obligation of the law (*das unbedingte Sollen des Gesetzes*), the divine law (*Gesetz Gottes*), or simply the law (*das Gesetz*). He is hesitant to employ the traditional divisions of the divine law and natural law. The reason for this is his understanding of creaturehood: one's self is a gift from God. A person stands indebted to God for everything and is called to live his or her life in accord with God's grace.[32] The word "nature" in this usage intends to indicate creaturely existence as such insofar as this anticipates the free and unqualified love of God.[33] What lies behind this usage is Rahner's distinction between person and nature.[34] Nature indicates the unfulfilled, undeveloped, unassimilated aspects of one's reality; personhood is what one has fulfilled, developed, and assimilated. The unconditional obligation of the law is the demand to actualize decisively one's nature toward personhood. "The law is a form that grace adopts insofar as it is intended for a person."[35] Thus one becomes through a free decision what was made possible by nature and grace.

God is first and foremost the free giver of gifts and then the maker of demands, but He is never the one without the other. Therefore the content of divine grace and divine commands are the same. It is God himself given to man in the medium of his human existence and then imposed on him for his free acceptance.[36]

A number of points need to be clarified with regard to this position. First, creaturely existence pertains to the realm of grace; it ought not to be construed as natural (as distinct from supernatural) existence. Nature is one's givenness antecedent to one's free self-determination.[37] Secondly, there is a correlation between God's gifts and his demands. As the gifts are assimilated into one's personhood, they impose demands. Being grounds obligation. The indicatives of God's dealing with humankind contain the imperatives of divine commands.[38]

Schüller's theology was developed in counter-distinction to the neo-Thomist manuals of moral theology. His starting point has been culled more from neo-scholastic moral philosophy than from moral theology.[39] The manner in which Schüller blends philosophy and theology, his Rahnerian notion of nature and grace, and his considerable dependence upon contemporary philosophy clearly distinguish his position from that of the neo-Thomist manualists.

## IV. Josef Fuchs

The significance of Josef Fuchs' career as a theologian is difficult to assess. In many ways the modifications which have occurred in his conception of moral theology have been the result of his contact with other theologians, especially Rahner, but this fact cannot be allowed to diminish his own significance. As the author of several editions of a manual as well as numerous articles and books he and his writings serve as something of a weathervane of the manner in which moral theologians since the late 1940s have been appropriating developments within their own discipline as well as within systematic theology.

In 1955 Fuchs published *Natural Law*.[40] In that study he clearly demonstrated his affinities for some aspects of neo-Thomism and introduced some positions which he himself had developed. Like the neo-Thomists, Fuchs maintained an ontological or metaphysical foundation for the natural law and its role in founding the objective moral order. "There is an objective order defined by natural law and this in the final issue is based on being."[41] Human nature remained a vehicle for the mediation of God's moral order. "God speaks through it and reveals himself in it. It bears his features and it is his image."[42] What distinguished his position from that of the neo-Thomists with regard to the natural law was that he considered it a theological rather than a philosophical doctrine. He viewed the natural law as a theological doctrine because it was among the Christian truths revealed in the scriptures and because it was a frequent topic of papal discourses and writings.

In his 1970 *Human Values and Christian Morality*[43] Fuchs continued to maintain the theological character of the natural law. "The elements of the natural law," he wrote:

> are, in fact, elements of a supernatural moral order, although they are not supernatural in the same way as those elements that are inherently supernatural and do not, therefore, belong to the natural order.[44]

The development of Fuchs' thought which occurred between *Natural Law* and *Human Values and Christian Morality* becomes evident in relation to two specific topics: the metaphysical basis of the natural law and the role of Christ in the moral life.

With regard to the former, Fuchs has moved to ground his natural law theory in transcendental Thomism. He no longer speaks of an objective moral order, but rather proposes that it is up to human persons to determine what the specific requirements of the natural law are—what it means to be a person in the world.[45] When persons discover those modes of human behavior which protect and enhance human dignity, then they have arrived at "a knowledge of the natural law."[46] There are few purely *a priori* or metaphysical assertions concerning a person's moral conduct. Rather he contends:

> *A priori* moral norms relate primarily to man's personal, responsible, social and historical nature which, as in all human behavior, demands consideration in the realization of his mandate and desire for progress. These general moral principles are of considerable importance and have their consequences in all human conduct, but alone they scarcely produce concrete guide-lines for human behavior and human progress. More concrete guide-lines presuppose experience and knowledge of concrete reality and its possible method of realization—together with the consequences.[47]

At this point in his career Fuchs had clearly distanced his theology from that of the neo-Thomists. Not only had he rejected an objective metaphysical order as the basis of Christian moral obligation, but he had also moved to a more empirical grounding of concrete moral norms. Person and experience have replaced human nature as the sources of concrete moral norms.

The second important development was his more detailed portrayal of the fundamentally christological character of his ethic. Natural law reasoning, Fuchs argued, consists in "explaining more realistically, more profoundly, and more completely, our life in Christ."[48] Drawing upon Häring he stated that the "foundation of Christian morality is the sublime call which has become our portion in the person of Christ."[49] It is at this point that

Fuchs' theological understanding of the natural law again becomes significant. "Natural law morality," Fuchs contended:

> ... is ordered to the redeeming Christ and his grace. ... Only insofar as such deeds and virtues (i.e. those required by the natural law) are born and filled with the love of Christ blooming in us, are they in a full sense, Christian deeds.[50]

The law of Christ is not considered materially, i.e. it does not impose moral requirements distinct from those of the natural law. What makes those requirements truly christological is that the Spirit of Christ living in Christians permeates their lives and activities and becomes expressed "in prescriptions and commandments" which constitute the law of Christ.[51] The distinctive element in Christian ethics is "a specific Christian intentionality which transcends and fulfills all human moral values."[52] What Fuchs has thus accomplished is a Christocentric moral theology. Christ is not viewed as a new lawgiver, but rather as the animating principle in the moral conduct of Christians. Again this is clearly different from the perspective of the neo-Thomists. The animating function of Christ is attributed by Fuchs to grace and its workings in the human person; it is not construed in relation to traditional faculty psychology. Fuchs' appeal is to the person of Christ working in a spirit of love and redemption in the lives of persons. It has been to these basic themes that Fuchs has returned in his more recent studies *Personal Responsibility and Christian Morality*[53] and *Christian Ethics in a Secular Arena.*[54]

## V. Richard McCormick

No individual has contributed as much to contemporary American discussions of the development of moral theology as has Richard McCormick. His many essays dealing with topics of general moral theology and especially medical ethics reflect the concerns of a scholar steeped in the tradition and sensitive to current developments within it. His "Notes on Moral Theology" appeared regularly in *Theological Studies* between 1965 and 1984 and provided a sort of clearinghouse for issues pertinent to moral theology. These "Notes" bear a strong resemblance to what Bernard Lonergan termed "dialectics."[55]

In an article published relatively early in his career, "Human Significance and Christian Significance," McCormick formulated five premises assumed by the majority of Catholic moral theologians: the primacy of charity, the essential interiority of law in the New Covenant, the existence of the natural law, the relationship of the natural law to gospel morality, and the rejection of moralism.[56] By the "primacy of charity" McCormick intended to suggest that the call of Christ is an invitation to a way of life, a way of being.[57] "Ethical reflection, if it is to be Christian, must begin from the fact that the human personality has, so to speak, been seized by the divine grasp, quickened with a new life so that every virtue and virtuous act is an expression, a mediation of this new life tendency."[58] The life and being of the Christian have been transformed and now constitute the ground of Christian action. (The indicative, what we are in both the order of creation and the order of redemption, is the ground of the imperative, what we ought to do.) The interiority of the new law suggests its capacity "to move men to action *ad extra*."[59] This understanding of the new law of grace strives to remove any legalistic, externally coercive characteristics from Christian morality. The new law, as an essential element in the life of the Christian, is the movement of the Holy Spirit. The natural law is analogous to the new law. It too reflects the imperative of our being. "The natural law is fundamentally man's being as implying his becoming, it is above all an inner reality or imperative, and therefore, as *law*, is analogous as is the *Law of the Spirit*."[60] The relationship between the natural law and the new law is such that they cannot ground two separate moralities. "There is only Christian morality, not a natural and a Christian morality."[61] The good acts of the non-Christian, even of the atheist or agnostic, are materially the same, and "are often or at least potentially performed out of a believing, a Christian love."[62] Finally the rejection of moralism entails the rejection of a preoccupation with individual, external acts, a rejection of legalism in favor of the discernment of a Christian way of life.[63]

McCormick warned the readers of "Human Significance and Christian Significance" that he did not wish "to be understood as sharing these assumptions in every respect."[64] In several more recent essays, McCormick has formulated more clearly the theological and ethical perspectives which permeate his own position. Although a detailed discussion of his moral theory, especially his understanding of proportionalism, will be delayed until Chapter Twelve, a brief presentation of it will be necessary here in order to highlight his theology.

According to McCormick, moral norms are statements about value and disvalue. They are "statements of the value or disvalue of concrete acts, the significance of the acts."[65] Values define opportunities for human flourishing.[66] The values which ground material moral norms are "utterly original, we can only point to and assert their significance, we cannot prove it."[67] The values which are directive toward authentic human goods can only be discerned in their relation to the basic human inclinations: to preserve life, to mate and raise children, to explore and question, to enter into friendships and relations with unknown higher persons, to use intelligence in guiding action, and to develop skills for play and the fine arts.[68] "In these inclinations our intelligence grasps the possibilities to which they point and prescribes them."[69] The normativity of essential human ethics is thus grounded in these spontaneous inclinations. Specific moral judgments are "incarnations of these more basic normative positions."[70] Values are the objects of moral intending; moral intending ought to be correlated to the basic human inclinations. Concrete moral acts intend specific values and attempt to realize those values in the concrete and culturally affected world of reality.

McCormick has adopted and revised an interpretation of St. Thomas' natural law theory initially proposed by Germain Grisez[71] and John Finnis.[72] This position is a refinement of Thomas Aquinas' elliptical discussion of the three precepts of the natural law (*Summa Theologiae*, I–II, 94.2). The list of basic inclinations which can be found in the writings of each of these contemporary authors attempts to define the drives and orientations of human nature towards basic human values. Values such as friendship, play, and the preservation of life are never simply accomplished and possessed. Rather, persons intend these values, but what they realize concretely are the human goods of this specific friendship, the enjoyment of this specific game, and the protection of this individual life (*bona honesta*).

Drawing upon an essay by James Gustafson, McCormick has proposed that theology is a decisive way of viewing and intending the world.[73] Christians are formed by the religious stories and symbols which constitute their body of beliefs. Such a theology steadies "our gaze on the basic human values that are the parents of more concrete norms and rules."[74] A theological ethic strives to keep attention focused on the values which are the objects of the basic human inclinations. Christian stories and symbols assist the Christian in identifying the basic values in oneself so that they can be known apart from the manner in which they are concretely realized in a given society. Such a theological perspective intends to enable Christians to see the pure value of the protection of life, to see beyond the limited ways in which life is protected in this society. Theological ethics seeks to ensure that basic values are being realized as completely as possible.

Theological ethics is also "a decisive way of viewing and intending the world"; it provides "stories and symbols that affect our perspectives."[75] McCormick lists thirteen key elements in the Christian story, such as "God is the author and preserver of life," and "in Jesus' life, death and resurrection we have been totally transformed into new creatures, into a community of the transformed."[76] As a way of viewing and intending the world, the Christian story provides a sensitivity to the values and meanings expressed in the natural inclinations. Theological ethics seeks to correlate cultural expressions of basic human values with the vision grounded in the Christian story.

McCormick's theology has journeyed far from that of the neo-Thomist manuals. The manualists' distinctions between theology and philosophy, faith and reason, nature and grace have not been maintained in his theology. There are, however, even more significant comments that need to be made in relation to McCormick's accomplishments. It has been through his "Notes on Moral Theology" as well as his numerous journal articles that the theologies of Häring, Schüller, Fuchs, and numerous other European theologians have been introduced to American readers. In this regard his work has been consistent with post-Americanism Catholic thought; it has been deeply reliant upon European figures. Such a comment, however, needs to be moderated by a yet more important factor in McCormick's career. No other American Catholic theologian has more frankly and openly striven to engage issues of contemporary American life, especially developments in medical technology, from the perspective of the tradition of moral theology. The institutional setting for the bulk of his writings has been the university, not the seminary. In the judgment of this author McCormick could never have engaged American culture as profoundly as he has in fact done if he had remained in a seminary setting. Part of what made his accomplishments possible was that he took it upon himself to learn the theologies of his Protestant colleagues, especially those of James M. Gustafson and Paul Ramsey. This broader perspective made him sensitive to the Protestant dimensions of American culture, a culture indeed not fundamentally inimical to a Catholic way of life.

## VI. Charles E. Curran

The impact of Charles Curran on the post-Vatican II American Catholic church has been considerable. As a faculty member at the Catholic University of America he has educated numerous theologians, many of whom have become seminary professors, thus channeling Curran's theology to the next generation of priests. The many books he has published over the past twenty-some years have been carefully read not only by his professional peers, but also by a large following of Catholic priests seeking to keep their pastoral skills up-to-date. His explicitly theological contributions to contemporary moral theology involve his use of the responsibility/relationality ethical model and the theological methodology which he employs.

The ethical model which Curran has adopted is one which he describes as the model of relationality and responsibility.[77] The manner in which Curran develops his understanding of this model represents an innovative blending of European Catholic theology and American Protestantism. When Curran speaks of responsibility and relationality he clearly has in mind the creative work of his mentor, Bernard Häring. But in those passages in which he was first developing this model he also made repeated references to

H. Richard Niebuhr's *The Responsible Self.*[78] Like Niebuhr, Curran understands the model of relationality and responsibility as providing a third alternative to the moral theories of teleology and deontology.

It is especially important to notice that it was in part theological reasons, and not just concern for an adequate ethical theory, which induced Curran to embrace the model of relationality and responsibility. In *Themes in Fundamental Moral Theology* he wrote:

> Such a model seems to be more in keeping with both theological and ethical data. Theology views the life of grace and the reality of sin primarily in terms of relationships as is evident in the concepts of covenant and love. In the perspective of Christian eschatology the individual does not have that much power and control over one's end and destiny. The cross and the paschal mystery reminds us that our end or goal is not completely in our hands. We as Christians live in the hope that the evils and problems of the present can be transformed somewhat now by the power of God and ultimately transformed into the fullness of life.[79]

Thus he understands the model of responsibility/relationality as an especially provocative category in which he can account for both the moral and the theological experience of Christians.

Like Fuchs and McCormick, Curran does not think that there is a specifically Christian ethic, if one means by that material moral norms which impose moral obligations on Christians which do not exist for non-Christians as well.[80] Curran goes on to suggest, however, that the attitudes, the dispositions or virtues, the goals and ideals, the moral judgments of Christians give rise to an authentic Christian way of life.[81] These definitive characteristics of Christian life are the product of one's stance and thus constitute the manner in which the concrete historical order of morality is interpreted.

By "stance" Curran means a perspective or angle of vision which directs one's view of the world. He describes his own stance as one constituted by the fivefold Christian mysteries of creation, sin, incarnation, redemption and resurrection destiny.[82] This stance sheds light on the Christian meaning of death, on life as the living of the paschal mystery, and thus gives rise to attitudes, dispositions, and goals specific to such a Christian perspective. These central Christian mysteries shape the manner in which the Christian views the world.

The world in which life is lived is a concrete, historical order shaped by the creation, fall and redemption of humankind. These are the most significant characteristics of the world; they define fundamental traits of the human habitat.[83] The actual world order constitutes the objective counterpart to Curran's notion of stance. Christian doctrines are not mental constructs that enable the Christian to view the world and to react to it in a distinctive manner; they are not a set of Christian "rose-colored glasses." Rather the doctrines of creation, sin, incarnation, redemption, and resurrection destiny enable the Christian to see the world as it really is, i.e. as created, sinful, and redeemed. Thus the Christian attempts to construe the historical human moral order in "the light of the Christian story, symbols, and self-understanding."[84]

In the work of Charles Curran theology and ethical theory have become as intricately related as in any contemporary theology, with the possible exception of Karl Rahner's. That Curran's work needs to be clearly distinguished from that of the neo-Thomist manualists is immediately obvious. His emphasis on responsibility/relationality is different from the teleological emphasis of the manualists. His conceptions of nature/grace, philosophy/theology, faith/reason are clearly at variance with these hallmarks of the neo-Thomist tradition as the manualists understood them. Curran's belief that theological convictions shape both the objective and subjective dimensions of the Christian world yet further distinguishes his theology.

As we have seen, there were a number of theological reasons which led contemporary theologians to distinguish their positions from that of neo-Thomism. Changing perspectives concerning the nature and adequacy of neo-Thomist moral theory would lead to yet further grounds for abandoning that position. It is to those discussions that we must now direct our attention.

## NOTES

1. Bernard Häring, C.SS.R., *The Law of Christ*, 3 vol., trans. Edwin G. Kaiser, C.PP.S. (Westminster: The Newman Press, 1961).
2. Bernard Häring, C.SS.R., *Das Heilige und das Gute* (Krailling: Erich Wewel Verlag, 1950).
3. Häring, *The Law of Christ* 1:392.
4. Bernard Häring, *Free and Faithful in Christ*, 3 vol. (New York: The Seabury Press, 1978, 1979, 1981).
5. Ibid., 1:6.
6. Ibid., 317.
7. Ibid., 59.
8. Ibid., 323.
9. Ibid.
10. Ibid., 325.
11. Ibid., 327.
12. Karl Rahner, S.J., *God, Christ, Mary and Grace*, vol. 1 of *Theological*

Investigations, trans. Cornelius Ernst, O.P. (Baltimore: Helicon Press, 1961), 16–17.

13. James Bresnahan, "Rahner's Ethics: Critical Natural Law Theory in Relation to Contemporary Ethical Methodology," Journal of Religion 56 (1976):41.

14. Karl Rahner, More Recent Writings, vol. 4 of Theological Investigations, trans. Kevin Smyth (New York: The Seabury Press, 1974), 391–392.

15. Gerald McCool, A Rahner Reader (New York: Seabury Press, 1975), 185.

16. Rahner, More Recent Writings, 405.

17. Bresnahan, "Rahner's Ethics," 42. See also Ronald Madras, "Implications of Rahner's Theology for Fundamental Moral Theology," Horizons 12 (1985):74–76.

18. Karl Rahner, Foundations of Christian Faith: An Introduction to the Idea of Christianity, trans. William V. Dych (New York: Crossroad, 1985), 408–409. See also, Madras, "Implications," 82–83.

19. Karl Rahner, Man in the Church, vol. 2 of Theological Investigations, trans. Karl-H. Kruger (Baltimore: Helicon Press,1963), 224; see also Rahner, The Dynamic Element in the Church, trans. W. J. O'Hara (Montreal: Palm Publishers, 1964), 18.

20. Rahner, Man in the Church, 227.

21. Bruno Schüller, S.J., Gesetz und Freiheit (Düsseldorf: Patmos Verlag: 1966).

22. Ibid., 2–8.

23. Bruno Schüller, S.J., Wholly Human: Essays on the Theory and Language of Morality, trans. Peter Heineg (Washington: Georgetown University Press, 1986), 2.

24. Ibid., 44.

25. Ibid., 92.

26. Schüller, Gesetz und Freiheit, 16.

27. Bruno Schüller, S.J., "Zur theologischen Diskussion über die lex naturalis," Theologie und Philosophie 42 (1966):496.

28. Bruno Schüller, S.J., "Die Personwurde als Beweisgrund in der normativen Ethik," Theologie und Philosophie 53 (1978):552.

29. Bruno Schüller, Gesetz und Freiheit, 18.

30. Ibid., 19.

31. Ibid. 23–25; see also Bruno Schüller, S.J., Die Herrschaft Christi und das weltliche Recht (Roma: Verlagsbuchhandlung der Päpstlichen Gregorianischen Universität, 1963), 331.

32. Schüller, Gesetz und Freiheit, 42.

33. Ibid. See Schüller's footnote on page 42.

34. Karl Rahner, *God, Christ, Mary and Grace*, 346–382.
35. Schüller, *Gesetz und Freiheit*, 43.
36. Ibid., 43–44.
37. Schüller, "Zur theologischen Diskussion," 40.
38. Schüller, *Gesetz und Freiheit*, 44.
39. Schüller, *Wholly Human*, 44.
40. Josef Fuchs, *Natural Law*, trans. Helmut Reckter, S.J., and John A. Dowling (Dublin: Gill and Son, 1965).
41. Ibid., 6–7.
42. Ibid., 60.
43. Josef Fuchs, *Human Values and Christian Morality* (Dublin: Gill and Macmillan Ltd., 1970).
44. Ibid., 2.
45. Ibid., 181.
46. Ibid., 183.
47. Ibid., 189.
48. Ibid., 31–32.
49. Ibid., 58.
50. Ibid., 65.
51. Ibid., 76.
52. Ibid., 123.
53. Josef Fuchs, *Personal Responsibility and Christian Morality* (Washington: Georgetown University Press, 1983).
54. Josef Fuchs, *Christian Ethics in a Secular Arena* (Washington: Georgetown University Press, 1984).
55. Bernard Lonergan, *Method In Theology* (New York: Herder and Herder, 1972), 235–266.
56. Richard A. McCormick, S.J., "Human Significance and Christian Significance," in *Norm and Context In Christian Ethics*, eds. Gene Outka and Paul Ramsey (New York: Charles Scribner's Sons, 1968), 234–243.
57. Ibid., 235.
58. Ibid.
59. Ibid., 240.
60. Ibid., 241; see also Richard A. McCormick, S.J., "Notes on Moral Theology," *Theological Studies* 26 (1965): 615.
61. McCormick, "Human Significance," 242–243.
62. Ibid.
63. Ibid., 245.
64. Ibid., 233.
65. Richard A. McCormick, "Does Religious Faith Add to Ethical Perception?" in *Readings in Moral Theology #2*, eds. Charles E. Curran and Richard A. McCormick (New York: Paulist Press, 1980), 164.

66. McCormick, "Human Significance," 246.
67. McCormick, "Does Religious Faith," 165.
68. Richard A. McCormick, S.J., "Theological Dimensions of Bio-Ethics," *Logos* 3 (1982):27; see also McCormick, S.J., *How Brave A New World?* (Garden City: Doubleday and Co., Inc. 1981), 5.
69. McCormick, "Theological Dimensions," 27.
70. Ibid., 28.
71. Germain Grisez, *Beyond the New Morality* (Notre Dame: University of Notre Dame Press, 1974).
72. John Finnis, *Natural Law and Natural Rights* (Oxford: Clarendon Press, 1980).
73. McCormick, "Theological Dimensions," 30.
74. McCormick, *How Brave A New World?*" 10; see also his "Theological Dimensions," 29.
75. McCormick, "Theology and Biomedical Ethics," 30.
76. Ibid.
77. Charles Curran, *Themes In Fundamental Moral Theology* (Notre Dame: University of Notre Dame Press, 1977), 136–139; *Catholic Moral Theology in Dialogue* (Notre Dame: Fides Publishers Inc., 1972), 32; *Contemporary Problems in Moral Theology* (Notre Dame: Fides Publishers Inc., 1970), 235–238.
78. Curran, *Contemporary Problems*, 140, 234–238; *Catholic Moral Theology*, 104–110, 154.
79. Curran, *Themes In Fundamental Moral Theology*, 137–138.
80. Charles Curran, "Is There a Catholic and/or Christian Ethic?" in *Readings in Moral Theology #2*, eds. Charles E. Curran and Richard A. McCormick, S.J. (New York: Paulist Press, 1980), 75.
81. Ibid., 67; see also Charles Curran, *Toward an American Catholic Moral Theology* (Notre Dame: University of Notre Dame Press, 1987), 58.
82. Charles Curran, *Moral Theology: A Continuing Journey* (University of Notre Dame Press, 1982), 38.
83. Curran "Is There a Catholic and/or Christian Ethic?" 77.
84. Curran, *Toward an American Catholic Moral Theology*, 58.

# 11.

# Moral Theology and the Situation Ethics Debate

The nature and role of the moral theory employed by contemporary Catholic theological ethicists are, in many instances, significantly different from those of their neo-Thomist predecessors. The general parameters of neo-Thomist moral theory have already been discussed in Chapter Four. The task of this chapter and the next will be to give an account of the manner in which the Catholic discussion of situation ethics and "proportionalism" has led to the abandonment of neo-Thomist moral theory.

The decisive moment in the transition from neo-Thomist to revisionist moral theology has usually been associated with the publication of Paul VI's encyclical *Humanae Vitae* and the theological debate which it engendered. In *The Making of Moral Theology*, John Mahoney has aptly commented that:

> . . . the entire methodology of moral theology was in question, and the relationship between the theologians and the Magisterium became the subject of innumerable conferences and statements . . . The Church, and with it moral theology, have been changed immeasurably by Pope Paul's letter.[1]

What is important to understand, however, is why a document such as *Humanae Vitae* could have had such a profound impact on the church and, particularly in relation to the interests of this study, on moral theology. Indeed what was different was neither the style nor the content of the papal encyclical, for it certainly could have been published under the signature of Pius XII, Pius XI, Pius X, or Leo XIII. Why in 1968 were Catholic theologians prepared to voice public dissent to a papal directive? Mahoney has suggested one important reason: the manner in which the encyclical seemed to differ from the spirit of the Second Vatican Council.[2] However, as important as the role of the Council was for the manner in which theologians would react to the encyclical, the foundations of their response can only be adequately assessed in relation to the discussion of situation ethics in the 1940s, 1950s and 1960s. The question of moral absolutes, the nature of the natural law and the binding force of the ordinary, i.e. non-infallible, papal magisterium had been heatedly discussed among theologians and commented on by the papal magisterium prior to the publication of *Humanae Vitae*.

From the perspective of American Catholicism there are three distinct phases to the discussion of situation ethics. The first pertains to the manner in which Pius XII articulated his opposition to the introduction of situation ethics to European Catholicism. The second encompasses the discussion of German theologians, especially the writings of Josef Fuchs and Karl Rahner, which attempted to identify the dangers associated with situation ethics as well as what Catholicism might glean from this movement. The third phase occurred in the United States in the mid-1960s as at least two Catholic ethicists attempted to demonstrate what they considered to be the positive elements in the situation ethics of Joseph Fletcher. This chapter will examine each of these three phases of the situation ethics debate.

There is one further comment which is crucial to the manner in which one attempts to construe this history. Our focus here is on moral theory. Contemporary revisionist theologians understand the term "moral theory" differently than their neo-Thomist predecessors. For the neo-Thomists, philosophy provided a metaphysical framework within which revelation could be more adequately comprehended. Neo-Thomism's philosophical presuppositions determined the manner in which the nature of moral obligation, law, conscience, and the human act could be construed. The moral theory of revisionist theologians is much more likely to be determined by their theological convictions. Bruno Schüller and Bernard Häring could both speak of moral obligation stemming from a person's encounter with an unconditional demand, but for them the unconditional demand flows from a God with a face, not from a metaphysical being; in the language of Bernard Lonergan, it flows from the God of Abraham, Isaac, and Jacob, not the God of the philosophers. Rahner could focus his incredible philosophical acumen on how one is to determine what ought to be done in light of concrete, *a posteriori* data, but he could do so only because he had previously elaborated his conception of the supernatural existential. Charles Curran and Richard McCormick turn to a proportionalist methodology to resolve complex moral dilemmas, but only after the former has elaborated the manner in which a specifically Christian stance can influence one's worldview, and the latter the manner in which the Christian story can steady one's gaze on the moral values at stake. The moral theory of these authors is directly the product of their theology.

# I. Pius XII and Situation Ethics

Pius XII's first clear indication of his significant concern about situation ethics occurred in *Humani Generis*. The ways in which this encyclical attempted to address issues posed by the *nouvelle théologie* and to defend the theological and philosophical premises of neo-Thomism have already been examined in Chapter Eight. The encyclical was also concerned to curb the potential impact of these new ways of thought on ethical considerations. The philosophical positions which opposed Catholicism's *philosophia perennis* were viewed as a conglomerate of "immanentism, or idealism, or materialism, whether historic or dialectical, or even existentialism . . ."[3] Whatever name was most appropriate for this new foe of Catholic teaching, its core danger consisted in a denial of immutable essences.[4] The aspects of Catholic teaching most immediately threatened by this new philosophy were theodicy and ethics.

In *Humani Generis* the specific enemy of Catholic thought remained amorphous. The encyclical took somewhat of a "shotgun" approach: rather than drawing a sharp bead on a specific target, it was content to scatter its objections over a broad area in the hope of mortally wounding all potential foes. What needed to be protected by such a broadside were the central philosophical positions of neo-Thomism which provided the framework for the tenets of systematic theology. If philosophy was not capable of knowing immutable essences, how could theologians determine which moral acts were objectively sinful? If so much of Catholic thought was threatened by these new philosophies, then was not the papacy's role as a teacher of moral norms itself being challenged?

In 1952 Pius XII delivered two addresses which focused much more directly on situation ethics. In the first, a radio message, he alluded to the presence in the church of "some who would like to make a radical revision of Catholic moral law in order to arrive at a new appraisal of its value."[5] These persons seemed to make the conscience of the individual absolute and thus to free Catholics from what they perceived to be "the narrow and oppressive overseeing by the authority of the Church."[6] In his allocution to The World Federation of Catholic Young Women, Pius XII referred to a new conception of moral life which does not premise the principles of the moral life on the truths of faith.[7] This new morality, he contended, was not based on universal moral laws, but on the real and concrete circumstances in which Christians must act. Although this new conception of morality did not completely deny general moral principles, it did move them from the center of ethical reflection to the periphery. The pope countered that the "fundamental obligations of the moral law are based on the essence and nature of man, and on his essential relationships, and thus they have force wherever we find man."[8] The final Roman reaction to situation ethics occurred in 1956 when the Holy Office forbade and prohibited the doctrine of situation ethics "to be taught or approved in Universities, Academies, Seminaries and Houses of formation of Religious or to be propagated and defended in books, dissertations, assemblies. . . ."[9]

In this series of addresses the papal concerns had become much more focused than they had been in *Humani Generis*. The target had been narrowed to situation ethics, not existentialism in general. The foes Pius XII wished to target did not simply dismiss moral principles or norms; rather they allowed other elements such as the object or circumstances of an act to be at least as decisive in assessing its morality. It was moral absolutes, intrinsically evil acts, which had been attacked by these enemies of the faith. The reason that these theologians and philosophers had been deceived concerning moral absolutes was because they had failed to adequately understand the essence or nature of human beings. These innovators had denied the role of the magisterium as a moral teacher, as an authentic source of moral norms and especially those moral absolutes which ought to guide the conduct of individual Catholics. Theologians and philosophers were beginning to discuss the binding force and importance of the ordinary papal magisterium.

## II. Situation Ethics in Germany

Much remains to be learned concerning the emergence of situation ethics among Catholic intellectuals in post-World War II Germany. Men and women were questioning the morality which had permitted or at least tolerated the atrocities and evils of the war. How could so many Germans have complied with the demands of such an unjust regime? With the social and political framework of their lives destroyed, how were persons to deal with the many concrete moral issues which confronted them? As young Germans surveyed their world from the ruins of Berlin or Dresden, would they, like their parents, simply marry and raise a family? Or did the absence of a legitimizing social order suggest that sexuality might be understood independently of marriage and the rearing of children? To what extent ought the bizarre and difficult concrete situations of the post-war era determine younger people's moral practices? Precisely what the issues were for Germans of the late 1940s and early 1950s, and the manner in which a growing number of philosophers and theologians were being swayed in the direction of situation ethics, remain a largely untold story.

The aims of this section must remain limited. It must suffice to provide a brief account, drawn from a number of significant theological essays written during this period, of the development of a Catholic situation ethics. Note that a number of key topics were repeatedly addressed in this literature: 1) the authority of the church over the moral lives of its members; 2) the binding force of universal moral laws, i.e. are there intrinsically evil acts? 3) human nature as the basis of Christian morality as opposed to the concepts of "person" or "individual"; 4) a new understanding of the natural law; and 5) the relationship between theological motifs and moral theory.

In 1946, the influential journal *Stimmen der Zeit* carried an essay by Karl Rahner entitled *"Der Einzelne in der Kirche."*[10] Rahner began his essay by proposing that the individual and the community must be understood as analogical and correlative concepts.[11] The danger, he continued, was to absolutize one term, especially the individual, so that the other becomes meaningless. Rahner's line of thought focused on the individual, rather than nature, as the key characteristic of human beings. As material-biological, human beings are individuals; each is one of many similar individuals. But human beings are not just material-biological, they are also spiritual. As spiritual the human is more than an individual person, more than an instance of a law, more than the individualization of a universal model. As spiritual the human is "a son of God, created by God as an individual who lives from grace and is addressed by God as a beloved You (*Du*) and by the Son and Spirit as well."[12] As spiritual, the individual is a transcendental concept, analogous to the concept of "being." The individuality of the human, Rahner concluded, ought to be understood in relation to the individuality of the persons of the Trinity.

There were two key aspects of the human according to Rahner. First, the human exists in a tension between the individual and the community; to deny or even inappropriately de-emphasize one side of the polarity is to deny an essential aspect of the human. Second, the individual is both material-biological and spiritual. The individual is a material-biological being and, as such, similar to many individuals; but at the same time the individual is also a spiritual, transcendent being, addressed by God as a particular, unique individual. This understanding of the individual had several implications for moral theology.

First, with regard to concrete moral decision-making, a distinction needs to be made. Inasmuch as an individual is material-biological, universal moral norms ought to define his or her moral obligations. Rahner was quite clear in maintaining the significance of universal moral norms. Second, Rahner also proposed that the spiritual dimension of the individual heard "the particular call of God intended only for him and not mediated through universal moral norms."[13] The material-biological and spiritual dimensions of the individual have become complementary elements in the moral decision. Where a universal moral norm applies, it ought to bind the conscience of the

Christian; but there remain critically important spheres of moral decision-making which ought to be determined, not by reference to a universal moral law, but rather in response to the address of God. Rahner would need to clarify this latter point in a subsequent essay. It seems that some of his readers accepted his position on the spiritual dimension of the individual and ignored his comments on the material-biological dimension. From such a false reading, Rahner would appear to have been advocating a form of situation ethics.

The second implication of Rahner's interpretation of the individual influenced his understanding of the teaching church. Since the individual has been graced, the church has become the correlative to community. As the graced individual is material-biological, he or she is "one of many similar beings whose ontological and moral subjectivity can and must be influenced by law and external authority."[14] Rahner was perfectly clear about the abiding significance of the magisterium. But he also contended that:

> ... there is a zone which is personal and graced which belongs to
> the individuality of each person and this is a sphere of the private
> which ought not be dependent upon the Church.[15]

Thus he was also clear that there is an important dimension in the religious life of the individual that ought to be free of ecclesiastical guidance. With regard to universal moral norms as opposed to a free response to the call of God, as well as with regard to the role of the magisterium vis-à-vis individual freedom (recall that freedom for Rahner is always most basically the freedom to respond to God), Rahner required that the material-biological and spiritual dimensions be maintained in a dialectical, complementary, and analogous relationship. To deny or minimize either side could only lead to a diminishment of the individual.

In 1949 Hans Wulf called attention to two distinct movements within the church. The first sought to make the church more secure by stressing organization and the official ministry of the church, by emphasizing law and authority. The second sought to nurture the church by calling for the freedom of the individual, encouraging verbal expression on important issues, and fostering independent decision-making.[16] In the writings of the German intellectual Ernst Michel, Wulf saw an important attempt to foster the second of these movements. As Wulf understood Michel, the kernel of Christianity is the good news which makes possible the purer and deeper living of Christianity.[17] Revelation is the call of God to be a partner; the person is to answer out of the depths of one's freedom. The problem of contemporary Catholicism was that the kernel had become obscured by the concrete church as well as by the practice of believers. The essence of

Christianity had become falsified and transformed into legal categories. Thus the Christian was placed in a tragic situation in which it was impossible to fulfill the law; the Christian had fallen into sin, lived in error and was under judgment.[18] The Christian should be able to respond to God as a person and out of faith, hope and love. Michel viewed love as the creative principle of morality—love and do what you will. He was careful to stipulate that he did not wish to disavow totally the role of law, but only the "unchristian interpretation of the law presented by the teaching Church."[19] Michel's position, at least as summarized by Wulf, might well have been the sort of theology Pius XII had in mind in his addresses on situation ethics. Michel at best minimalized the role of moral rules and viewed the teaching church as more of a danger than an asset to Christian living. As was the case with Rahner's *"Der Einzelne in der Kirche,"* Michel was concerned to articulate clearly a religious basis, not simply philosophical criteria, for moral decision-making. The response of the individual to the call of God was becoming a central element in moral theory.

One attempt to make situation ethics more palatable to Catholic theologians proposed that it was merely a new form of casuistry. In response to an essay of Richard Egenter, Hans Hirschmann, S.J., argued that this analogy was simply false. Whereas casuistry was concerned with the application of universal laws to specific cases, situation ethics stressed that moral awareness arises from the fullness of concrete reality, especially as historical. Situation ethics focused on the person as dialogical and stressed the social nature of human existence—my being with others, existence with others, my meeting with others.[20] Only in faith, Hirschmann continued, can one adequately comprehend the components of our situation. Every situation involves our relationship with the living God. The indwelling of the personal, indeed tri-personal God, is central to moral decisions. The ultimate question is, "Lord, what do you wish that I should do?"[21] Again, the religious context as well as the significance of the individual or person were the central issues. The concrete, historical situation had become the context from which the individual must respond.

In light of the sort of theological developments reported by Wulf and Hirschmann, Rahner was quick to provide a further clarification of his position. He began his essay, *"Situationsethik und Sündenmystik,"*[22] by attempting to delineate two significant tendencies within German Catholicism. The first was a growing trend toward an extreme situation ethics. This position made much of the moral complexity of the contemporary world. The social and cultural structures which had guided the moral decisions of previous generations were no longer functioning. Many, especially the younger generation, found it increasingly difficult to decipher their moral obligations. This trend toward an extreme situation ethic also drew upon Protestant theology and its opposition to material moral norms. What was emerging was:

> An extreme existential philosophy which holds that where spirit, person, and freedom are present, no universal essence of man and his affairs ought to determine the moral decision; there are no universally binding moral norms, there are only non-deducible individual decisions which are in no way instances of a universal norm.[23]

What resulted was a greater emphasis on intention than on the moral action itself. It was not what one did that was important, but only the intention with which one acted. Only the intention was considered good; it was the only thing of value before conscience and before God. Universal moral laws, the natural law, revelation were all to be set aside and in their place the central question was: Is the person loving? Then everything is in order.[24]

The second major tendency Rahner alluded to was called the "mystique of sin." This mystique resulted from an undue emphasis on sin, both individual and social. There was a growing conviction that Christians could not fulfill their moral obligations and thus stood ever convicted of their sin. All that was left was reliance on the mercy and forgiveness of God, faith that God calls sinners to redemption.[25] The position of Ernst Michel, as reported by Wulf, would be one instance of the mystique of sin. This mystique also found expression in Pius XII's rejection of positions which suggested that young persons ought not be expected to live a life of chastity.[26]

In response to the dangers posed by an excessive situation ethic, Rahner returned to the position developed in *"Der Einzelne in der Kirche"* and emphasized the material-biological dimension of the individual. "Man has the duty," Rahner wrote, "to form his conscience according to an objective measure of moral worth, to be educated and instructed. This is the role of the magisterium."[27] Although there is an individual ethic, he continued, this does not eliminate the universal in the individual or its role in decisions of conscience. There is an individual ethic only in dialectical relationship with the ethic of universal moral norms.[28] The majority of Christian consciences do not shake off the gospel and the church teaching concerning universal moral norms. For the Christian the fulfilling of a command is not a mere matter of ethics, but an essential element of Christianity.[29] Although Rahner continued to maintain the existence of the spiritual dimension of the individual and thus an area of free response to God, his emphasis in this essay was clearly and emphatically upon the significance of moral norms and the role of the teaching church.

The following year Walter Dirks, the editor of the widely-read journal of lay Catholics, *Frankfurter Hefte*, published a carefully drafted response to Rahner's recent essay.[30] Dirks' essay made four major points; the first two pertained to the origin of situation ethics, the latter two to specific claims concerning the nature of situation ethics. The first two of these points can be summed up in the phrase "historical consciousness." Situation ethics arose, Dirks argued, when persons became aware that historical change was occurring now in the spatial and temporal world in which they lived.[31] Thus his first point was that situation ethics developed within the context of historical change. The historical developments which bedeviled the men and women of the 1950s, according to Dirks, were the product of a destroyed social order. In a changed world it had become more difficult to determine what one should do; the son of a peasant could no longer simply follow in the footsteps of his father. The collapse of an objective social framework *de facto* left persons more free, more conscious, and more fully responsible for their decisions.[32] The loss of an objective social framework was the decisive historical change. But not only was there historical change, for of course historical change had been occurring for millennia, but now persons were *aware* of historical change. What distinguished the situation of post-war Germans from that of earlier generations was that they were aware, conscious of the historical change occurring around them.

Dirks' third point attempted to clarify the relationship of moral rules to concrete situations. Situation ethics, Dirks contended, did not intend to be a criticism of the commandments, but rather of the casuistic manner in which they were interpreted in concrete situations. The law ought not to be construed as an end unto itself; the law could never be itself an absolute. Rather the law must be seen as an instrument which enables the Christian to say, "Yes, Lord."[33] Situation ethics also demanded that the application of the law take seriously the corporeal, psychological, and intellectual needs of persons. The methodology of situation ethics "often placed material needs in bold relief, and this situational imagination sometimes discovered needs which are quite different from those generally conceded and presented as the standard."[34] What situation ethics asked of a moral rule was: what sense does its application make in this situation? Does it serve the needs of persons in such a manner that in acting in accord with a moral rule one serves the material needs of one's neighbor and in doing so says "Yes, Lord"? Moral norms, Dirks seems to have meant, find their meaning and thus their moral significance not in relation to some abstract theory of human nature, but rather in relation to the concrete needs of historical and social persons.

Dirks' final point with regard to situation ethics was the most important. The moral decisions of persons "move to place order in a small section of this world and to advance a few steps towards its own salvation."[35] Germans in the 1950s, he argued, found themselves caught in a world which appeared chaotic and as moral agents they were invited to give that world meaning. "To act within this situation means . . . to confer meaning on that which was without meaning."[36] At this point Dirks challenged the deepest presupposition of neo-Thomism. He rejected the notion of a pre-existent moral order which only needed to be adequately discovered and which could then serve as the ultimate basis of human meaning. According to the neo-Thomists, if one conforms to the objective moral order, one will live a life of love of God and service to one's fellows. For Dirks this order needed to be created.

Dirks' position challenged that of Rahner in two important ways. First, Dirks questioned whether Rahner's individual could be adequately divided into the material-biological and the spiritual, the one normed by universal moral principles, the other governed by the free response of the individual. Moral rules remained important for Dirks, but they were not absolute. One needed to ask what a rule means, what it could contribute to human flourishing in a particular situation. Second, the area of human freedom which Rahner had excluded from the realm of universal moral rules and binding church teaching tended to focus on the individual's relation to God, in effect to be more religious in nature than moral. Dirks insisted that all moral decisions must include a social dimension, must include their impact on the lives of other persons. Human freedom must always act in a manner which is responsible to the legitimate needs of the other.

In later years Rahner would refine yet further his understanding of ethics within systematic theology.[37] And indeed the social nature of Christian moral decision-making would become more explicit in his thought. Rahner would also become increasingly aware of the manner in which human decisions altered the structures of the world in which Christians live. He seems in fact, however unconsciously, to have assimilated the basic challenges Dirks had directed against him. However, the complementarity and analogical relationship between the individual as material-biological and spiritual would remain at the center of his ethical position. Since our goal here is not an exhaustive examination of Rahner's ethic, but rather of his contributions in the area of moral theory which would ultimately lead to the rejection of the moral theory of neo-Thomism, it will be necessary to refer to only one further essay.

For the neo-Thomists, as we saw in Chapter Four, the object, end, and circumstances were the determinants of morality. The object—the act itself apart from the reasons why it was done and the circumstances under which it occurred—was judged morally in relation to divine law, natural law, or canon law. Because of their objects some acts were deemed intrinsically evil. Regardless of why they were done, such acts always were considered to entail serious sin. It was the objective nature of neo-Thomist moral theory that was challenged by situation ethics. In one manner or another, the new morality, as situation ethics came to be called, questioned the existence of universally binding moral norms. Situation ethics contended that either the particularities of the concrete situation or the direct address of God dictated what was to be done. Object, end, and circumstances were co-equally the determinants of morality.

In his essay *"Situationsethik und Sündenmystik"* Rahner had alluded to a growing tendency to claim that the basic determinant of morality was good intention. He saw within situation ethics not only a tendency to give priority to circumstances over objective morality, but a correlative move to view the intention of the act as more important than the act in its objectivity. In an essay written in the 1960s, Rahner seems to have moved somewhat closer to the position he criticized in *"Situationsethik und Sundenmystik."* In "Some Thoughts On A Good Intention," he proposed that nothing definite about the value of a person and his actions can be decided solely by the correctness of his external actions. Morally good acts must be assessed in relation to the intention of the agent. Only with human freedom and the heart can a person make a decision which has its source in God and which leads to God.[38] Thus from the perspective which seeks to determine the eternal significance of an act, its intention becomes crucial. "True Christian morality," he continued,

> . . . is a balance between the internal intention of the heart and the external act, a balance which always goes from one to the other without resting or taking root in either one of them.[39]

Rahner does not say, nor does he suggest, that a good intention can make an objectively evil act good. But what happens when one begins to question, as proponents of situation ethics had already done, whether there were in fact no intrinsically evil acts? In such a case the object, end, and circumstances might be viewed as co-equal determinants of the morality of a specific act. And, if indeed one can accept that position, then one has embraced one of the key tenets of proportionalism.

Between 1952 and 1954 Josef Fuchs published a book-length manuscript[40] and two influential journal articles[41] dealing with situation ethics. In each of these writings Fuchs strove to clarify the meaning of situation ethics, to defend something of a traditional natural law position and to ferret out the positive element latent within the new morality.

Situation ethics, Fuchs wrote in *Situation und Entscheidung*, developed as Christians became more conscious of their individual and personal relationship to God, more aware that they were individually addressed by God.[42] More specifically, situation ethics posed several concrete questions.

First, and on strictly theological grounds, it queried whether universal moral norms were appropriate for every individual case and whether they in fact mediate into the present the actual will of God. Second, if universal moral norms were not mediations of the divine will, how did God inspire the individual with regard to specific moral questions?[43] At issue were the significance of universal moral laws and their claim to allow no exceptions. The situation ethicists whom Fuchs was reviewing did not deny the existence of moral rules, but they questioned their applicability in concrete cases pertaining to marriage, military service and murder.[44]

The natural moral law, Fuchs argued, is nothing other than the being of a creature created in the divine image; thus ultimately the ethical demand is grounded in the essence of God.[45] "The natural law means nothing other than the inner ordering, the being of creation created in God's image, and thus ultimately grounded in the being of God."[46] Situation ethics, according to Fuchs, made two fundamental errors. The first was theological. The new morality based created goodness and obligation in the free will of God, not in the divine essence.[47] Situation ethics sought to safeguard the immanent sovereignty of God; it wished to stress the personal relationship which unites God and the Christian. From this theological point of view, heavily influenced by Protestantism, the natural law appears as an alien factor which belies the fundamentally human relationship between God and the Christian.[48] Second, situation ethics tended to view the person as free-floating; it did not allude to human nature and therefore provided no continuity between the past and present situations.[49] For Fuchs such a position was excessively influenced by the actualism of Emil Brunner,[50] Rudolf Bultmann,[51] Dietrich Bonhoeffer,[52] and Karl Barth.[53]

Fuchs went on to suggest that the totality of the moral universe consisted of two planes. First, on the plane of universal essences, universal moral norms remained binding within every situation and ought to be the object of every moral choice. But, he continued, there was also a plane of absolute originality on which the individual responded in a personal manner to the call of God. This was a supernatural plane in which persons were in communion with the Trinity, experienced objective redemption, celebrated the sacraments, and expressed their personal love of God.[54] Within this supernatural plane the Christian responded to the divine gift and call in a manner which fundamentally determined his or her existence.[55] But this response remained a heightening, an intensification of the demands of natural morality.

> By means of inspiration God so leads man, not so that He imposes duties where the moral order leaves man free, or that He establishes freedom where the moral order places commands, but rather

that through an inner effect one might have a more adequate insight and place a more adequate act of the will.[56]

Thus Fuchs ended up in a position quite similar to that of Rahner. Both continued to maintain the moral significance of universal norms grounded in a metaphysical notion of essences. Both, however, found it necessary to carve out an area which would acknowledge the ability of Christians to determine their own unique response to the personal call of God. For Fuchs, the supernatural sphere, in a manner reminiscent of the neo-Thomist manuals, made it possible for the Christian to know more completely what ought to be done and to set one's will more completely on the moral good. There was, however, a poignant tension in each of these essays. The language of a human and divine essence remained central to Fuchs' position, but at the same time "person" was consistently introduced to depict the supernatural component of the human.

## III. Situation Ethics in the United States

Throughout the 1950s the various authors of *Theological Studies'* "Notes on Moral Theology" chronicled events in Europe pertaining to situation ethics. In 1953 Gerald Kelly, S.J., reported on the various papal addresses dealing with the new morality.[57] Two years later, J. J. Farraher, S.J., recounted yet another address of Pius XII dealing with situation ethics and provided his readers with a brief synopsis of Fuchs' "Morale théologique et morale de situation."[58] John J. Lynch, S.J. contributed in 1958 still another review of European theological developments pertinent to situation ethics. He too stated that the entire discussion would seem to have no specific relevance to American Catholicism: ". . . none of our Catholic theologians in this country has attempted—or even been tempted I would presume to say—to defend any theory of situational morality. . . ."[59] Some, and especially priests in the hearing of confessions, Lynch explained, perhaps began to approach the position of situation ethics when they permitted the circumstances of a particular situation to soften the requirements of objective morality. They permitted the circumstances of an act to become excuses for disregarding a natural law prohibition whose absoluteness was not denied, but was not sufficiently appreciated. Thus the principal error of situation ethics was seen as the failure:

. . . to grasp the ultimate practical implication of intrinsic evil as predicated of certain human acts—failure, in other words, really to appreciate the full significance of an absolute natural law prohibition.[60]

In a few paragraphs, Lynch encapsulated the manner in which much of the situation ethics debate would be carried on by American Catholics. The principal issue was the binding force of natural law moral norms, especially the role of intrinsically evil acts. In the same year, John Connery agreed that although "the circumstances should not be neglected in the consideration of the moral act," such attention to the circumstances does not call for a shift of emphasis away from the object. The assessment of the moral significance of such acts as homicide, fornication, stealing, masturbation, calumny, etc., unquestionably dealt with categories of sin (i.e. acts which are wrong *ex objecto*) which no circumstance could alter.[61] For neither Lynch nor Connery were the specifically theological issues of the Christian's relationship to God and the ability of the Christian to respond to God important or even peripheral issues.

Situation ethics did not become a topic of intense controversy among American Catholics until the mid-1960s. The initial catalysts were the publication of John A. T. Robinson's *Honest to God*[62] and Joseph Fletcher's *Situation Ethics*.[63] Robinson sought to legitimate the role of those in the church who were only able to question the prevailing dogmatic and ethical orthodoxy.[64] Fletcher attempted to present a method of moral decision-making which discerned moral obligations in the light of concrete situations. Fletcher's goal was not to provide an ethical system, a set of material moral norms; specific moral duties could only be determined in the light of a given situation.[65] Fletcher's book gave ample evidence of his having been influenced by Barth, Bonhoeffer, Bultmann, and especially Brunner.

Fletcher's and Robinson's books would cause a considerable stir among both Protestant and Catholic ethicists in the United States. John Giles Milhaven, S.J., and David J. Casey, S.J., have provided an excellent historical account of both the European and American background of the new morality.[66] They are particularly helpful in the manner in which they present the contributions of H. Richard Niebuhr and Joseph Sittler to the development of situation ethics in America. The present study must limit its investigation of these matters to a brief presentation of Fletcher's position (Robinson fundamentally endorsed Fletcher on ethical issues) and then to the manner in which two American Jesuits attempted to relate Fletcher's work to the Catholic tradition.

It is important to keep in mind that Fletcher was not opposed to moral principles. In contrast to French existentialism, which he considered antinomian,[67] Fletcher conceived of the situation ethicist as one who "enters every decision-making situation fully armed with the ethical maxims of his community and his heritage, and he treats them with respect as illuminators of his problems."[68] Where he differed from Catholicism and much of American Protestantism was in his assertions that the only universal law was love, and that an absolute moral obligation was the product of a specific situation, not an abstract moral rule;[69] moral obligations could be absolute only in relation to a specific situation. Thus in every situation one ought to strive to maximize love, and the specifics of one's actions ought to be determined by the situation. A moral maxim might well be an instructive guide for what ought to be done, but the ultimate criterion of moral action for Fletcher remained the norm of love.

Fletcher's "principled relativism" proposed that Christians ought to follow moral norms if they serve love, but he also maintained that in specific circumstances the Christian might need to reject the applicability of any of the ten commandments.[70] Fletcher's method, therefore, possessed three basic characteristics. First, love was its only rule. Second, it respected the *sophia*, the wisdom of the church and the culture which had each formulated significant moral maxims. Third, the *kairos* was the concrete situation in which the moral agent determined whether the moral wisdom of the church and culture could serve love in this situation. Fletcher considered both his concept of love as the moral absolute as well as the significance attributed to the *kairos* to be based on theological convictions. With regard to these two points he was deeply influenced by dialectical theology, especially that of Brunner.

The knotty question for Fletcher's situation ethics was how to determine the manner in which love was to be served. In matters of social policy, he turned to utilitarianism. Its strategic principle was the greatest good for the greatest number.[71] Love was also to be discerning and critical. His ethic would not prefer one person to another, but rather would prefer the neighbor whose need was greater.[72] Certainly his proposed ethic was empirical and consequentialist. But ultimately for Fletcher the when, where, which and how were *kairos* factors which could be determined only by looking carefully at the full play of ends, means, motives, and result. "The rightness is in the gestalt or shape of the action as a whole, and not in any single factor or ingredient."[73]

The Jesuit philosopher Thomas Wassmer was one American Catholic who was significantly influenced by the writings of Joseph Fletcher. Although his writings reflect the considerable influence of situation ethics upon him, it is important to realize that Wassmer maintained a position distinct from that of Fletcher, a position affected by his concern to influence his own Catholic tradition.

First, Wassmer consistently maintained that an "authentic morality is one resulting from the dialectical tension of two ethics, the ethic of responsibility and the ethic of conviction."[74] By an ethic of responsibility he meant something closely akin to Fletcher's situation ethics. It was situational and relied upon empirical evidence in making moral decisions. An ethic of conviction, on the other hand, was a position ultimately concerned for principles and norms of moral conduct, and thus akin to traditional Catholic morality. Wassmer's position could be clearly distinguished from that of Fletcher by his insistence that the two ethics needed to be kept in a dialectical tension. "These two ethics serve the function of thesis and antithesis, and the synthesis is the personal, incommunicable, moral struggle toward a decision that respects both."[75] An ethic of conviction was just as essential to Wassmer's position as was an ethic of responsibility.

"In the ethic of responsibility, empirically verifiable evidence is of great importance, and is sought to demonstrate the value in the existential moral act here and now."[76] Wassmer's point was not just the obvious one, that empirical evidence is critical to a situational approach to morality; he also made the more nuanced point that empirical observations ought to illumine the central values which an ethic of conviction sought to protect. The ethic of responsibility must acknowledge that the ethic of conviction seeks to protect basic human values; the ethic of conviction must recognize that the values its precepts seek to protect might not be jeopardized or even involved in the light of concrete empirical investigation. Thus Wassmer maintained that:

> Any value (life, promise keeping, fidelity, whatever) should never be seen in isolation, but in a constellation of other values and disvalues; none should be so polarized or absolutized that it is viewed essentially and not existentially in concrete phenomenological experience.[77]

Moral values must be discerned in a manner which acknowledges the complex realities in which they exist; where they "are surrounded by a multiplicity of other values and disvalues which have to be harmonized and synthesized into a reasonable ethical whole."[78] The danger inherent in an ethic of conviction was to absolutize a value, to form an exceptionless moral norm, which separated that value from the wide range of values which might be present in a concrete situation.

This last element was indicative of the most consistent theme in Wassmer's writings: a rejection of moral absolutes. In this matter he was closest to Fletcher and was engaged in an attempt to alter the Catholic tradition. His fundamental objection to the notion of moral absolutes was that they represented an abstract, theoretical view of morality, whereas moral decisions always need to address the concrete, thus they need to be informed by the circumstances or situation.[79] The circumstances of an act are always essential elements in the determination of its morality.[80]

The position of John Giles Milhaven was perhaps even closer to a pure form of situation ethics than was Wassmer's. His numerous essays in the late 1960s and early 1970s attempted to portray a view of the new morality from a Catholic perspective and to depict how specific moral norms consonant with such a view might be developed.

Milhaven shared with Fletcher the conviction that "the only absolute the new morality recognizes in practice, the only thing a man has to do always and in all situations, is to love."[81] The dictates of this morality could be discerned through good, experiential consequences. There is also a specific image of God which provided theological grounding for the position being developed. God ought not to be viewed as a lawgiver who seeks from human beings simply the response of obedience; the Christian understanding of the relationship between God and humanity is not that of a father to his children. Rather the Christian stands before God as an adult man or woman. God watches over with pride and love, but leaves the Christian free to make his or her own responsible decisions.

> Man is responsible for the experienced consequences. God does not save him from them. This is the only way we and God judge the man: through the experienced consequences he has chosen to bring about. God's saving love in Christ bears him up and gives his life its ultimate meaning, yet in his particular moral judgments and decisions he stands alone, free, responsible.[82]

The theological warrant for this view of Christian morality lies in the fact that God has given humankind dominion and sole responsibility for what goes on in this world.[83]

Like Wassmer, Milhaven was concerned to dislodge the notion of moral absolutes from their dominant place in Catholic thought. Neither the theology of the new morality nor its method of determining moral obligation could provide a basis for moral absolutes. Moral absolutes, Milhaven pointed out, pertain to only a small portion of the moral decisions a person is called upon to make.[84] The natural law tradition which contended that the essential purpose of a particular act suffices to determine its moral and immoral use attempted to understand moral duties in terms of God's general purpose in creation. Milhaven's notion of morality sought to determine the particular purpose in God's creation, which can then serve as the norm of morality.[85] This position, although clearly rejecting moral absolutes, maintained an important place for moral norms. Milhaven proposed that the new morality would in fact generate far more general principles and far more concrete obligations than had the traditional morality.[86] How then ought such moral norms and obligations to be determined?

The basis for every moral determination is the divine command to love.[87] What distinguishes the new morality from the old is its greater emphasis on love and lesser emphasis on law.[88] More concretely, then, how ought moral rules and obligations to be determined?

> To understand what is good for a person, he, a man of the twentieth century, relies exclusively on experience. For him, love knows no *a priori* laws, sees only the ones loved and what experience shows is happening or likely to happen to them. Love is, therefore, pragmatic, hard-headed, often unromantic.[89]

And more concretely yet:

> . . . it is empirical evidence, not direct insight into what something is, but the observation, correlation, and weighing out of numerous facts, which reveal the value of most human acts; for they show what effect these acts will have in the concrete, existing world on those absolute values a man discerns by immediate insight.[90]

Thus, in a manner similar to the methodology proposed by Wassmer, so also Milhaven's approach relied upon empirical evidence to decipher the meaning and impact of specific values in concrete situations.

Values and principles remained important to the new morality, but their applicability and significance could only be determined in concrete circumstances. The notion of a hierarchy of values could serve as a general rule of thumb for determining the selection of conflicting values, but it might also be misleading because "the priority or proportion between given values is not a fixed one when applied to concrete situations."[91] The ultimate criteria by which the moral significance of empirical data could be determined were the insights generated within the moral agent by affective and appetitive orientations.[92] Ultimately, Milhaven seems to embrace knowledge by connaturality. As one is disposed by one's virtues, loves and drives, those personal characteristics of the moral agent, so one is enabled to discern true instances of good through an empirical investigation of a particular situation.

Both the European and American discussions of situation ethics challenged three related tenets of neo-Thomist moral theory. Key to the entire situation ethics debate was the question of moral absolutes. The existence of intrinsic, i.e. *ex objecto*, moral evil was rejected by all the situation ethicists. The neo-Thomist tradition had contended that such absolute moral norms could be known in either of two manners: through an apprehension of the natural law or through the magisterium of the church. The sort of considerations which led a growing number of theologians to deny the existence of concrete moral absolutes also impelled them to rethink their basic conceptions of the natural law and the binding force of the ordinary papal magisterium. What was beginning to emerge was a sense of the moral whole, of the scope and depth of the values and data which needed to be assessed in order to make a valid moral judgment. In the situation ethics discussion the circumstances and intention of the moral act were to take on an importance which the neo-Thomists would never have attributed to them. At the heart of these reconsiderations of traditional Catholic moral theory was the conviction that the relationship between God and the moral agent was the predominant criterion by which the adequacy of any such theory was to be judged.

## NOTES

1. John Mahoney, *The Making of Moral Theology* (Oxford: Clarendon Press, 1987), 301.
2. Ibid., 259–301.
3. Pius XII, "Humani Generis," *Acta Apostolicae Sedis* 42 (1950): 573.
4. Ibid.
5. Pius XII, "De Conscientia Christiana in Iuventibus Recte Efformanda," *Acta Apostolicae Sedis* 44 (1952):273.
6. Ibid.
7. Pius XII, "Ad Delegatas Conventui Internationali Sodalitatis Vulgo Noneupatae," *Acta Apostolicae Sedis* 44 (1952):414.
8. Ibid., 417.
9. Cardinal Pizzardo, "Acta SS. Congregationum, Summa Sacra Congregatio S. Officii," *Acta Apostolicae Sedis* 48 (1956):145.
10. Karl Rahner, S.J., "Der Einzelne in der Kirche," *Stimmen der Zeit* 39 (1946–1947):260–276.
11. Ibid., 261.
12. Ibid., 263.
13. Ibid., 266.
14. Ibid., 267.
15. Ibid., 268.
16. Hans Wulf, S.J., "Gesetz und Liebe in der Ordnung des Heils," *Geist und Leben* 22 (1949):356.
17. Ibid., 357.
18. Ibid., 358.
19. Ibid., 364.
20. Hans Hirschmann, S.J., "Im Spiegel der Zeit," *Geist und Leben* 25 (1951):301–302.
21. Ibid., 303.
22. Karl Rahner, "Situationsethik und Sündenmystik," *Stimmen der Zeit* 145 (1949–50):320–342.

23. Ibid., 331.
24. Ibid., 332.
25. Ibid., 334.
26. Pius XII, "De Conscientia Christiana," 274–275.
27. Ibid., 336.
28. Ibid.
29. Ibid., 337.
30. Walter Dirks, "How Can I Know What God Wants of Me?" *Cross Currents* 5 (1955):76–92. This is a translation by Sally S. Cunneen of Dirks' essay in *Frankfurter Hefte*, April 1951.
31. Ibid., 79.
32. Ibid., 81.
33. Ibid., 84.
34. Ibid., 85.
35. Ibid.
36. Ibid., 86–87.
37. Karl Rahner, *On Heresy*, vol. 11 of *Quaestiones Disputatae*, trans. W.J. O'Hara (Montreal: Palm Publishers, 1964); *The Dynamic Element in the Church*, vol. 12 of *Quaestiones Disputatae*, trans. W.J. O'Hara (Montreal: Palm Publishers, 1964); *The Christian of the Future*, vol. 18 of *Quaestiones Disputatae*, trans. W.J. O'Hara (Montreal: Palm Publishers, 1967); "On The Question of a Formal Existential Ethics," in *Man in the Church*, vol. 2 of *Theological Investigations*, trans. Karl Kruger (Baltimore: Helicon Press, 1963), 217–234; "Some Thoughts On A Good Intention," in *Theology of the Spiritual Life*, vol. 3 of *Theological Investigations*, trans. Karl-H. and Boniface Kruger (New York: The Seabury Press, 1967), 105–128; "The Theology of Power," in *More Recent Writings*, vol. 4 of *Theological Investigations*, trans. Kevin Smyth (New York: Seabury Press, 1966), 391–410; "The Theology of Freedom" and "Reflections on the Unity of Love of Neighbor and Love of God," in *Concerning Vatican II*, vol. 6 of *Theological Investigations*, trans., Karl-H. and Boniface Kruger (New York: Seabury Press, 1969), 178–196 and 231–249; "The Experiment with Man" and "The Problem of Genetic Manipulation," *Writings of 1965–67*, vol. 9 of *Theological Investigations*, trans. Graham Harrison (New York: Seabury Press, 1972), 205–224 and 225–252.
38. Rahner, "Some Thoughts on A Good Intention," 107.
39. Ibid., 109.
40. Josef Fuchs, S.J., *Situation und Entscheidung* (Frankfurt am Main: Verlag Josef Knect Carolusdurckerei, 1952).
41. Josef Fuchs, S.J., "Situationsethik in theologischer Sicht," *Scholastik*

27 (1952):161–182; "Morale théologique et morale de situation," *Nouvelle Révue de Théologie*, 76 (1954):1073–1085.

42. Fuchs, *Situation und Entscheidung*, 29.
43. Fuchs, "Situationsethik in theologischer Sicht," 161.
44. Fuchs, "Morale théologique et morale de situation," 1073.
45. Fuchs, *Situation und Entscheidung*, 34.
46. Fuchs, "Situationsethik in theologischer Sicht," 163.
47. Fuchs, *Situation und Entscheidung*, 35.
48. Fuchs, "Morale théologique et morale de situation," 1074.
49. Fuchs, *Situation und Entscheidung*, 42.
50. Emil Brunner, *The Divine Imperative*, trans. Olive Wyon (Philadelphia: The Westminster Press, 1947).
51. Rudolf Bultmann, *Jesus and the Word*, trans. Louise Pettibone Smith and Erminie Huntress Lantero (New York: Charles Scribner's Sons, 1934).
52. Dietrich Bonhoeffer, *Ethics*, trans. Neville Horton Smith (London: Collins, 1964); *Letters and Papers From Prison*, trans. Reginald Fuller (New York: The Macmillan Company, 1953).
53. Karl Barth, *Ethics*, trans. Geoffrey W. Bromiley (New York: Seabury Press, 1981); *The Doctrine of Creation*, Part 2 and Part 3, vol. 3 of *Church Dogmatics*, eds. G. W. Bromiley and T. F. Torrance (Edinburgh: T and T Clark, 1960).
54. Fuchs, "Morale théologique and morale de situation," 1078–1079.
55. Fuchs, "Situationsethik in theologischer Sicht, " 177.
56. Ibid., 175.
57. Gerald Kelly, S.J., "Notes on Moral Theology, 1952," *Theological Studies* 14 (1953):273–274.
58. J.J. Farraher, S.J., "Notes on Moral Theology," *Theological Studies* 15 (1955):233–235.
59. John J. Lynch, S.J., " Notes on Moral Theology," *Theological Studies* 19 (1958):168.
60. Ibid., 169.
61. John Connery, S.J., "Notes on Moral Theology," *Theological Studies* 19 (1958): 592.
62. John A. T. Robinson, *Honest to God* (London: SCM Press Ltd., 1963); see also his *Christian Morals Today* (Philadelphia: Westminster Press, 1964).
63. Joseph Fletcher, *Situation Ethics: The New Morality* (Philadelphia: Westminster Press, 1966).
64. Robinson, *Honest to God*, 8–9.
65. Fletcher, *Situation Ethics*, 11.

66. John G. Milhaven, S.J. and David J. Casey, S.J., "Introduction to the Theological Background of the New Morality," *Theological Studies* 28 (1967):213–244.

67. Fletcher, *Situation Ethics*, 24–25.

68. Ibid., 26.

69. Ibid., 27.

70. Ibid., 71–74.

71. Ibid., 95.

72. Ibid., 104.

73. Ibid., 142.

74. Thomas Wassmer, S.J., "Contemporary Situational Morality and the Catholic Christian," in *To Be A Man*, ed. George Devine, (Englewood Cliffs: Prentice-Hall, 1969), 94.

75. Joseph Fletcher and Thomas Wassmer, *Hello Lovers*, ed. William E. May (Washington: Corpus Books, 1970), 96.

76. Wassmer, "Contemporary Situational Morality," 97–98.

77. Thomas Wassmer, S.J., *Christian Ethics for Today* (Milwaukee: Bruce Publishing Company, 1969), 9.

78. Ibid.

79. Thomas Wassmer, "A Re-examination of Situation Ethics," *Catholic Educational Review* 57 (1959):33.

80. Thomas Wassmer, "Is Intrinsic Evil a Viable Term?," *Chicago Studies* 5 (1966):310–314; see also his "A Re-examination," 337.

81. John Giles Milhaven, S.J., *Toward A New Catholic Morality* (Garden City: Doubleday and Company, 1970), 14.

82. Ibid., 18–19.

83. Ibid., 32.

84. Ibid, 13–26.

85. John Giles Milhaven, S.J., "Towards An Epistemology of Ethics," *Theological Studies* 27 (1966):228–229.

86. Milhaven, *Toward A New Catholic Morality*, 24.

87. Ibid., 58.

88. John Giles Milhaven, S.J., "Objective Moral Evaluation of Circumstances," *Theological Studies* 32 (1971):408.

89. Milhaven, *Toward a New Catholic Morality*, 59.

90. Milhaven, "Towards An Epistemology of Ethics," 235.

91. Milhaven, "Objective Moral Evaluation," 415.

92. Ibid., 423.

# 12.

# Proportionalism and Contemporary Moral Theory

The debate concerning situation ethics was an important moment in the history of Catholic theological ethics which undoubtedly contributed to the decline of neo-Thomist moral theology as a theological genre. However, one would be hard pressed to find a contemporary Catholic theologian who would espouse today the principles advocated under the aegis of situation ethics. Proportionalism, on the other hand, appears to have taken a solid hold in the thinking of a growing number of European and American theologians. These theologians have articulated a position which is a logical development from the principles of the tradition of moral theology, but which is also clearly an alternative which can no longer be assumed under the mantle of the traditional genre. It is new wine which cannot be contained in the old wineskin.

In the past twenty years the discussion over what proportionalism is and its relevance to Catholic theology has spawned an enormous amount of literature in both Europe and the United States. Each successive volume of *Theological Studies'* "Notes on Moral Theology" from 1971 to the present, with the exception of 1974, has continued to discuss aspects of this developing theory. Furthermore, there is no reason to believe that the discussion of proportionalism will soon become a moot point.

It is simply impossible to attempt to present all the interpretations of proportionalism which have emerged to date or to present the specific position of each of the major authors. Rather, what will be attempted is a summary of what seem to be the main tenets of proportionalism based on the writings of Peter Knauer, Louis Janssens, Bruno Schüller, Josef Fuchs, Charles Curran and Richard McCormick. The danger in such a presentation, besides the obvious problem of sketchiness, is that proportionalism may as a result appear to be a univocal concept. Although there is clearly a "family resemblance" which makes it possible to group a large number of diverse writings together, nevertheless it must also be mentioned at the outset that there remain significant differences between ethicists who would consider themselves to be proportionalists. Many of these differences have been noted in Richard McCormick's seminal contribution to this discussion, "Ambiguity In Moral Choice,"[1] and in his "Notes on Moral Theology."

This chapter will first examine proportionalism as an alternative moral theory to that of neo-Thomism. Second, it will explain what proportionalists mean by ontic or premoral evil. Third, the nature of proportionate or commensurate reason will be investigated. A final section will indicate the manner in which both situation ethics and proportionalism have altered the ways in which the natural law and the ordinary magisterium are understood by revisionist theologians.

## I. Proportionalism as an Alternative Moral Theory

What makes proportionalism such an important factor in contemporary Catholic ethics is that it presents itself not just as an element within a moral theory or as a tool of casuistry such as the principles of double effect and totality had been (see Chapter Five), but rather proportionalism is presented as in itself a consistent moral theory. Proportionalism does not understand itself as one means of determining moral goodness in contrast to other acceptable means, nor does it understand itself as limited to certain types of moral decisions such as was the case with the traditional understanding of the principles of double effect and totality. To anyone operating within the ethical premises of neo-Thomist moral theory proportionalism must appear as a clear alternative.

Proportionalism developed, in part, out of several reconsiderations of the principle of double effect. In the essay which first introduced the concept "proportionalism," Peter Knauer's "The Hermeneutic Function of the Principle of Double Effect,"[2] the author argued that the principle of double effect "provides the criterion for every moral judgement."[3] His contention was that the principle of double effect's standard of commensurate reason is decisive for the determination of both the object and end of the moral act, and therefore that commensurate reason is the decisive criteria for the determination of the appropriateness of a means to an end. Commensurate reason became the ultimate criterion of the morally good. McCormick[4] and Schüller[5] maintain that the presence of commensurate or proportionate reason can justify either the direct or indirect willing of a nonmoral, premoral, or ontic evil.

The principle of double effect was developed to deal with conflict situations, situations in which one act had both a desirable and an undesirable effect. The neo-Thomist manualists, it will be recalled, employed it in relation to such topics as indirect abortion, self-defense, and material cooperation in the evil of another. The principle was limited to a specific range of moral issues, although as was discussed in Chapter Five that range was expanding. Proportionalists, on the other hand, understand proportionate reason to be relevant to every moral decision, even those in which a conflict of values may not be immediately apparent. This is the key reason why their moral theory is a comprehensive theory; it is understood as relevant to every moral decision. Why is this the case?

The major reason for this is that proportionalists view every human act as imperfect in some way. If an act does not involve conflict between ontic good and evil, or between greater or lesser evil, it is nevertheless limited by the spatio-temporal characteristics of human existence. Charles Curran has alluded to four sources of the conflictual character of human acts: 1) the difference between the subjective and objective aspect of human acts; 2) creaturely finitude and limitation; 3) eschatological tension; and 4) the presence of sin in the world.[6] Josef Fuchs has described the same factors as inhibiting the ideal realization of ontic values; he related them to a theory of compromise. Although both Curran and Fuchs have articulated positions with some similarity to the "mystique of sin" mentality associated with situation ethics, their positions are clearly distinct from those challenged by Rahner. "The compromise solution," Fuchs has written, "does not allow the simultaneous realization of the morally right and the morally wrong, but only of the morally right, which, however, contains both nonmoral right (good/value) and nonmoral wrong (evil/disvalue)."[7]

The first step in correctly understanding proportionalism is to grasp both the fact of and the reasons for its rejection of absolutely binding concrete moral norms. The neo-Thomists, as was explored in Chapters Four and Five, considered the object, end, and circumstances of an act to be the determinants of morality. There were also some acts which were considered immoral *ex objecto*, i.e. by their very nature. Among such intrinsically evil and thus sinful acts were included the direct killing of the innocent, formal cooperation in the evil of another, contraception, the sexual sins against nature (*contra naturam*), as well as rape, incest, adultery, and fornication. The inherent malice of these acts was known through the natural law and/or the teaching of the magisterium. It was precisely the notion of intrinsic evil in moral theology which was the object of criticism by the situation ethicists. Proportionalists readily concede that in such actions there may well be ontic or premoral evils, terms which will be explained anon, but they also maintain that there may well not be moral evil in these acts. For proportionalists no act, apart from acts immediately directed against God or direct involvement in the sin of another, is immoral and sinful by its very nature. The morality of the act must be assessed in relation to its circumstances and end as well. Such an assessment is what is meant by proportional reason.

Proportionalists have rejected the notion of intrinsically evil acts because of the manner in which concrete moral norms had been traditionally justified. In 1965 Bruno Schüller wrote that:

> The most pressing task of moral theology today is the rethinking of the particular character of moral knowledge and ethical proof. This can be accomplished only by intensive philosophical work.[8]

It has been exactly to such a task that proportionalists have dedicated themselves. According to Schüller, there are two types of moral norms. To the first type belong norms having to do with a person's relation to God as well as analytic norms such as "you shall always act justly," or "you shall never kill a person without just cause." Such norms are absolute. The second type of norms are synthetic; their binding force is dependent upon the fulfillment of contingent conditions: "You must keep a secret entrusted to you, unless through revealing it you would avert a greater evil than would be done to the entruster of the secret through this revelation." The obligation imposed by this rule is contingent upon the fact that greater evil will not befall the granter of the secret or someone else by maintaining its confidentiality. If this turns out not to be the case, if events become such that there is a conflict between the value of maintaining the secret and significant disvalues which will result from complying with the rule, then the rule of promise-keeping might not apply. The validity of these synthetic norms, Schüller has argued, is determined in relation to a basic preference principle:

> Of two evils, the worse is to be avoided; of two values, the more important is to be realized; but causing an evil is only justified by its being the only means to realizing a good of proportionate importance.[9]

Thus Schüller formulates his basic hypothesis with regard to moral norms:

> All ethical norms which have to do with our actions and undertakings in relation to our fellow man and the world can only be particular formulations of this more general preference rule.[10]

Concrete synthetic moral norms ought to be understood as contingent, not absolute. In a given set of circumstances a synthetic norm might not be applicable. The goals and realities of our actions in relation to our neighbors and the world are never absolute goods or absolute evils; therefore the meaning of such goals and realities must be judged in relation to the preference principle. Even the moral prohibition against the direct killing of an innocent must be assessed in concrete cases in relation to the preference principle. Such a teleological approach, i.e. an ethical approach focused on the ends or consequences of a moral act, requires that the morality of an act can only be determined in the concrete. And if indeed one can legitimately determine that the direct killing of another can be morally permissible, then the distinction between direct and indirect killing is no longer morally relevant.[11]

Louis Janssens rejected the neo-Thomist notion of moral absolutes as inconsistent with both the teaching of St. Thomas and the requirements of a contemporary theology. According to St. Thomas, Janssens argued, the understanding of the structure and morality of human action is tied to the subject. The *finis operantis* (the end of the agent), not the *finis operis* (the end of the act itself) determines the moral nature of an act. "An exterior action considered as nothing but the material event is an abstraction to which moral evaluation cannot be applied."[12] The moral object ought to be seen as the material of the moral act which receives its specifically moral characterization, its form, from the end or intention of the act.

Fuchs examined scripture, the magisterium and the natural law, the purported traditional sources of moral absolutes, and concluded that they could not produce such norms. Scripture provides a series of transcendental norms, similar to Schüller's analytic norms, and indeed a set of objective values, but not concrete moral absolutes. The magisterium and the natural law indeed generate moral norms, but they are bound to specific cultures and historical epochs. If scripture, the magisterium and the natural law do not contain the sort of moral absolutes the neo-Thomists described, then such absolutes must not exist.[13]

## II. The Meaning of Ontic, Premoral, or Nonmoral Good/Evil (Value or Disvalue)

The terms ontic evil, premoral evil, and nonmoral good/evil have been employed several times in this discussion; it is now time to clarify their precise meaning. In his very important essay "Ontic Evil and Moral Evil," Louis Janssens defined ontic evil as:

... any lack of perfection at which we aim, any lack of fulfillment which frustrates our natural urges and makes us suffer. It is essentially the natural consequence of our limitation.[14]

The specifically evil character of these obstacles to human flourishing which result from our finite and sinful natures can be seen in the manner in which persons experience "a lack and want, and to the extent that [they are] detrimental and harmful to the development of individuals and communities."[15]

In a similar manner, Fuchs speaks of premoral values and disvalues. If, for example, someone were to regard contraception as an evil, but were also to acknowledge some justifiable circumstances in which contraception might be used, then such a person must also understand that the evil of contraceptive use so affirmed lies in the premoral sphere.[16] If the applicability, in Schüller's sense, of a moral norm is contingent upon the fulfillment of certain conditions, the evil involved cannot be an absolute or intrinsic moral evil. If it were, one who followed a legitimate exception would be acting against a moral good, which no ethicist would allow. Thus the evil to which concrete moral norms point are first of all premoral evils.

McCormick, as we have seen, describes basic tendencies which orient persons towards specific goods or values which create opportunities for human flourishing. These fundamental goods lie deeply embedded in the human reality; they were present before cultures and societies began to specify the manners in which they might concretely be realized. The inclinations point to such basic goods as: the tendency to mate and raise children; the tendency to explore and question; the tendency to seek out others and obtain their approval-friendship; the tendency to use intelligence in guiding action; the tendency to develop skills and exercise them in play and in fine arts. It is the relationship between these basic tendencies and the goods or values which satisfy them that constitutes the realm of morality. To mate and raise children is a basic human good, but how is this good to be concretely realized? In a tribe or clan structure? In the inclusive family structures of China or India? In the nuclear family structure of late twentieth century America? To mate and raise children is first of all a premoral good towards which human persons are oriented. These basic goods are simply premoral goods prior to any moral specification.[17] Schüller perhaps has something similar in mind when he defines a physical good as "what does not have its origin in the free self-determination of man."[18] But how do ontic or premoral good/evil become moral good/evil?

Knauer's answer is perhaps the briefest and thus most elliptical. Moral evil "consists in the last analysis in the permission or causing of physical evil which is not justified by commensurate reason."[19] Moral evil is the result of the will causing or permitting a physical evil without commensurate reason. The act and the intention form a single unit which yields to moral assessment. Independently of one another neither the act nor its end can be morally assessed.[20]

Janssens depicts the object of morality as the promotion of the truly human growth of individuals and social communities.[21] We have the duty to remove as much as possible the ontic evil which comes about when we act. The norm by which specific ontic evils might be caused or permitted is proportionate reason. Moral evil is again determined in relation to that which the will commands, which is always both an act situated within specific circumstances and the reason for the act. Janssens writes:

> In the actualization of a good end and the deliberations about the means to this end, the genuinely important question is what place this end has in the totality of human existence.[22]

Like Janssens, Fuchs understands morality as set within a fundamentally social, or perhaps more accurately, interpersonal context. Morality seeks to determine:

> ... the significance of the action as value or non-value for the individual, for interpersonal relations and for human society, in connection of course, with the total reality of man and his society and in view of his whole culture.[23]

Human action ought to be deemed morally good when one intends and effects an ontic good, for example life, health, joy, culture; human action ought to be deemed morally evil when one has in view and effects an ontic evil such as death, wounding, deprivation of property without a proportionate reason. In a conflict situation proportionate reason could justify the selection of a nonmoral evil as the necessary means for the achievement of an essential nonmoral good or value. Nonmoral evil can be effected for a proportionate reason. Moral assessment must equally, or at least appropriately, consider the object, end, and circumstance(s) involved in a moral act; they are each morally relevant.[24]

For Fuchs[25] and Schüller[26] moral decisions are so critically important because they penetrate to the essential character of human existence and do not remain in the merely factual or empirical domain. Moral decisions do not define human nature, which is the pre-given status of our being, that part of our being which is not subject to human control. Human nature is an abstract concept portraying what human beings would be like without grace. Moral decisions create and demonstrate human personhood and culture. Indeed the basic absolute is God, and the secondary absolutes pertain to analytic or formal norms such as "be honest" and "be just." Concrete moral decisions, however, involve human persons in a world which is contingent and which therefore can be different than it is. As we actualize ourselves and our culture in relation to ontic or premoral goods and evils we create the concrete persons whom we are as well as the specific societies and cultures in which we live.

## III. Commensurate Reason

The ultimate question for proportionalists is the proper specification of what is meant by proportionate or commensurate reason. Knauer associates commensurate reason with one basic characteristic which he then expresses in two manners. First, the evaluation of commensurate reason "rests on the foundation that the value sought is commensurate when it is achieved in the highest possible measure for the whole."[27] What is most significant here, and will remain important in the contributions of other proportionalists, is the notion of the "whole" or "totality." Knauer does not give us a synonym for commensurate, but I would suggest it implies "fitting" or "consistent" with the values contained within the whole. If a nonmoral evil is to be chosen as a means to a nonmoral good, or as the lesser of two nonmoral evils, then the nonmoral good or evil realized must be consistent with the values of the whole. The specification of a speed limit which would likely tolerate a significant number of fatalities and yet allow for the reasonable transportation needs of a society would permit the nonmoral disvalue of death for some citizens as the price for sustaining commerce in a modern state. If a nation is invaded and faced with the alternative of loss of nationhood or the loss of a large number of its citizens in military conflict, two ontic evils, its decision to fight or surrender must be consistent with the values or meaning of that society as a whole.

The second manner in which Knauer expressed the basic nature of the commensurate reason which might permit an act which involves ontic evil requires that in the long run the act cannot fundamentally contradict, through the manner of achieving it, the value sought.[28] The central issue in the above examples is how to compare two different nonmoral values: life and commerce, surrender or the death of many citizens. This can be done, Knauer argued, if one can determine the manner in which one value serves the other. If the speed limit were set so high that accidents occurred at such a rate as to impede commerce, proportionate reason would be lacking. In the same way, if a nation surrendered to an invader in order to protect its population while knowing that the invader would kill a large number of them simply because they were Jews, the decision would be lacking in commensurate reason.

Following St. Thomas, Janssens maintains that the means or the external action, the material component of the moral act, must be well disposed, *materia bene disposita*, or in due proportion to the end.[29] Thus some means or actions might not be appropriate to specific ends. But how is the appropriateness of the means or action to be ascertained? "If ontic evil is *per se* intended, the end itself (object of the inner act of the will) is morally bad and, being the formal element (reason and cause of the exterior action), vitiates the entire action."[30] The premise of Janssens' position is that moral evil should never be willed for and in itself, i.e. *per se*. One can never intend an ontic evil for its own sake. Note that in choosing the lesser evil, one does not choose evil in and for itself, but only to avoid an even greater evil.

According to Janssens, an act is morally good when there is no intrinsic contradiction between the means and the morally good end of the inner act of the will.[31] I take this as asserting a position similar to Knauer's second expression of commensurate reason. The means or the external act cannot significantly contradict the good intended in the act. The means or act must have a due proportion to the end sought. The means must be consistent with the value of the end.

As do proportionalists in general, Janssens widens the scope of moral investigation in a manner which might have shocked neo-Thomists. "In the actualization of a good end and the deliberation about the means to this end, the genuinely important question is what place this end has in the totality of human existence."[32] Thus acts must be evaluated not just in terms of personal ends or goals, although these remain important, but also in terms of the goals of a society or culture; indeed one would seem to need to acquire an international and intercultural perspective. An action which directly intends to vitiate legitimate social and cultural values would be an immoral act because it has an immoral end.

Janssens has also carefully indicated the manner in which the order of charity and order of goods can further clarify ambiguous moral choices. First, the Christian demand of love of neighbor requires an impartiality which acknowledges the basic dignity of all persons, including one's self, and which can discern the legitimate grounds on which persons can be treated differently. This impartiality is the basis of key characteristics of our social world: co-existence, co-operation and co-participation.[33] Second, the order of goods provides specific guidelines for the values which are to be sought in the light of the totality of human existence as well as the manner of determining the legitimate needs of one's neighbor. All things being equal, the higher value ought to be given priority. Third, the urgency of a value has to be taken into account. The poverty which threatens death to my neighbor is more urgent than my desire for superfluous goods. The degree of probability in achieving a goal is important. The realistic goal has priority over the utopian ideal. Finally, special attention must be given to those cases in which an act is placed contrary to a good protected by a social institution. What are the implications of my failure to pay legitimate taxes—does the institution of governmental taxation itself become jeopardized? Janssens' discussion of the orders of love and goods provides an important nuance to his notion of proportionate reason. The order of love specifies the kinds of ends which proportionate reason needs to consider and provides some clarification of the relationship between such ends.[34]

In his most recent contribution to the discussion of proportionalism, Janssens has illuminated the role which character, the sorts of persons that we are, plays in enabling us to discern moral values adequately. Drawing upon dynamic psychology he has attempted to demonstrate the manner in which our intentional feelings orient us to values and disvalues; he suggests that human aspirations impel us to engage a world in which these values can be realized. Janssens' essay addressed the central feature of morality: how persons perceive values and are driven to realize them in the concrete world. His position is somewhat similar to McCormick's concept of the way in which faith keeps the Christian focused on the basic human goods, it is similar as well to the role Curran attributes to a theological stance.

Schüller develops his position in relation to a preference principle which requires that we minimize ontic disvalues and maximize the realization of ontic values. The principle which is most illuminative of the specific manners in which we are to love our neighbor, and which is therefore the fundamental norm of morality, is the Golden Rule: treat others as you wish to be treated. Schüller considers the traditional formulation of this rule too egoistic and so he has reformulated it to read: you ought to impose the same moral norm on yourself as you impose on the other.[35] This formulation, he argues, is based on a view of persons *qua* persons and strictly imposes the norm of impartiality required by the Golden Rule.

This basic formulation is open to yet further specification. When one finds oneself facing concurrent nonmoral goods, one ought to give preference to the alternative which promises to bring more moral good into existence.[36] Schüller's position clearly illuminates the teleological character of the proportionalist moral theory. Given a choice between two non-moral goods, one ought to choose what will maximize the good in the world.

Further, the rule of impartiality requires that a conflict between two ontic goods, e.g. the lives of two people, be resolved so that the life of the one that can be saved be preferred over that of the one which is already irretrievably lost. The complexities of life may force persons to choose between two goods, between the lives of two persons, but such decisions ought to be made in a manner which is consistent with the good sought and in a manner which is not inconsistent with a higher good. In either letting a person die or in the direct killing of an innocent person the value of life and respect for life must be maintained. A partisan captured by the Nazis during World War II, for example, might know that eventually, as a result of either torture or drugs, he will reveal secrets which will lead to the deaths of many of his colleagues and the possible destruction of the resistance movement. Proportionate reason might lead the partisan to kill himself or, if possible, to ask a colleague to kill him. The intention of such an act is to protect the lives of his colleagues as well as to secure the eventual triumph of the resistance. His death is intended to have significant social and cultural ramifications. The ontic evil of his death might well be construed as a lesser evil when compared to the death of many colleagues and to the permanent loss of the values associated with his culture and nation. Although his death is regretted, and although it involves neither despair on his part nor malice on the part of the one who kills him, it is directly intended and he is an innocent person.

Like his fellow proportionalists McCormick maintains that in conflict situations proportionate reason dictates that the lesser non-moral evil be chosen. The will remains fixed on a moral good and tolerates the non-moral evil only for a proportionate reason. One may intend a non-moral evil as a means if it is the only way of protecting a good which is proportionate to or greater than the non-moral evil.[37]

According to McCormick, proportionate reason is "a structure of moral reasoning and moral norming, teleological in character, whose thrust is that those concrete norms understood as exceptionless because they propose certain interventions dealing with nonmoral goods as intrinsic evils cannot be sustained."[38] McCormick of all these authors is perhaps the most exhaustive in unpacking the meaning of this structure.

The use of proportionate reason requires that a value at least equal to that sacrificed be at stake; that there be no less harmful way of protecting the value here and now; and that the manner of its protection will not undermine the value in the long run.[39] What proportionate reason accomplishes is a clarification of what the will intends in causing or permitting non-moral evil. A significant value is at stake, there is no alternative way of protecting the value at this time, and the value is being protected in a manner which will not endanger it in the long run. The circumstances provide the context in which each of these determinations must be made. Proportionate reason examines an act involving non-moral evil within its specific circumstances in order to determine whether the act is proportionate to its end.

A first characteristic of McCormick's theory of proportionalism is that it would attempt to minimize the non-moral evil in the world and to maximize the non-moral good. Thus proportionalism is deeply concerned with the consequences, both personal and social, of human action. One of the dangers latent within this position is that proportionalists might be mistakenly understood as pure consequentialists or even utilitarians.[40] For this reason they run the further risk of being accused of extrinsicism, i.e. of basing their moral theory on grounds extrinsic to morality, the consequences of moral acts.[41] McCormick has been clear in pointing out, however, that consequences can only serve as indicators that there was a disproportion within an action. Consequences can reveal that the value sought was not the equal of the non-moral value sacrificed. Therefore American and Soviet leaders might reconsider other involvements similar to that of the United States in Vietnam or that of the Soviets in Afghanistan. Why? Because the values sought in these engagements were not proportionate to the non-moral evils, i.e. deaths, wounding, and the destruction of property which resulted from them. It is not inconceivable that one form of direct killing, capital punishment, might be determined to be an inappropriate means of protecting the value of life. Consequences do not determine the moral rightness or wrongness of an act; only proportionate reason and the end intended can make an act morally good or evil. However, consequences can enable us to perceive how effective we have been in maximizing non-moral values supportive of human flourishing.

Thus the second characteristic of McCormick's theory of proportionalism acknowledges it as a form of moderate teleology. Proportionalists, however, "insist that other elements than consequences function in moral rightness and wrongness."[42] Certainly the nature of non-moral values and disvalues would be one such element. Moral absolutes which deal with our relationship to God as well as analytic norms which orient us towards basic values are not irrelevant to determinations of proportionate reason. McCormick's understanding of the manner in which religious faith helps to keep our attention directed towards the basic human goods would be another such factor influencing moral determinations. Janssens' emphasis on the order of charity and the order of goods is yet another factor in moral reasoning. The common insistence among the proportionalists that a fundamental characteristic of proportionalism is right reason would be still another factor. Consequences are important for this theory but they are not decisive.

Proportionalism maintains that concrete moral norms need to be determined within a teleological frame of reference. Its advocates contend that non-moral evils can be permitted, and even directly willed, where a proportionate reason exists. If McCormick, as the principal American spokesperson for the proportionalists, is correct, as I believe him to be, each of the chief characteristics of proportionalism needs to be seen as an attempt to reform the tradition from within the tradition. Neo-Thomist moral theologians would undoubtedly have rejected proportionalism, but they would have understood the concepts of "proportionate reason," "nonmoral evil," and the teleological nature of concrete rule-making (see Chapters Four and Five). Where I believe they would have been totally at a loss is with respect to the sweep of morally relevant factors. Interpersonal relations, social and cultural factors are seen by the proportionalists as elements which contribute to the moral assessment of specific actions. This requires a scope and breadth of moral vision which the neo-Thomists were reluctant to admit.

## IV. The Results of the Situation Ethics and Proportionalism Debates

Neo-Thomist moral theory was fundamentally challenged on at least three issues by situation ethics and proportionalism. Both of these recent theological debates questioned and then rejected the notion of intrinsic moral evil. This point has been sufficiently elaborated in the present and the previous chapters. Neo-Thomist natural law theory and its understanding of the role of the ordinary papal magisterium were also issues which would be altered by the emergence of situation ethics and proportionalism.

### (A) Natural Law

Many of the objections to the traditional understanding of natural law as well as several new manners of conceiving it were at least indirectly alluded to in the two previous chapters. What needs to be added here, therefore, is clarification and specification of the current discussion of the natural law.

The writings of Charles Curran point out quite clearly what many recent theologians have found problematic in the manualist presentation of the natural law.[43] First, natural law tended to be seen as a monolithic system. The manualists failed to notice the diversity of understandings of the natural law on which St. Thomas had depended as well as the diversity within the tradition stemming from him. The term "natural law" was simply not the univocal concept that many manualists supposed.

Second, traditional presentations of the natural law tended to be physicalist. The moral significance of human acts, particularly sexual acts, tended to be determined in relation to the physical structure of the acts. This was the case especially in terms of the classification of some sexual sins as "in accord with" or "contrary to" nature. In particular the moral assessment of contraception seemed to be based on a physical interpretation. Any artificial barriers to conception, any artificial means of altering ovulation or insemination for contraceptive purposes, were considered immoral because they violated a natural process.

Third, traditional natural law positions were ahistorical. They were based on a static understanding of human nature and a metaphysical conception of essences as unchanging. Intrinsically evil acts were determined to be such in an abstract manner, apart from the circumstances in which they occurred or the reasons for which they might have been performed. The morality of acts was judged apart from the totality of the social, cultural, and interpersonal contexts in which they occurred. The dictates of the natural law, therefore, remained unchanged. The moral requirements of 1970 were, for the most part, the same as those of 1870 or 1370.

Recent theological developments (see Chapter Ten) have shifted attention away from human nature as the basis of the natural law and have focused instead on the human person or individual. This basic reinterpretation has had a number of significant implications. "Person" possesses many connotations not associated with "human nature." Persons are conscious and historical. Persons are social and many of their obligations arise specifically from their relationships to others. The call and invitation of Christ is extended to persons who then respond out of their free determination. From the perspective of Christian personalism, the "natural" began to be seen in a manner inconsistent with the position of the manualists. Reflecting upon these developments, Louis Monden was able to write in the early 1960s that the natural law ought not to be associated with a physical or biological view of human nature nor with a collection of abstract principles, but rather, natural law means:

> . . . a dynamic existing reality, an ordering of man towards his self-perfection and his self-realization, through all the concrete situations of his life and in intersubjective dialogue with his fellow man and with God.[44]

In the late 1960s and early 1970s two Dutch theologians, William Van der Marck, O.P.,[45] and Cornelius Van der Poel, C.S.Sp.,[46] developed phenomenological interpretations of the natural law which emphasized its intersubjective and historical aspects. The natural law, Van der Poel informed his readers, "is not an independent entity which confronts man, but human reality itself with its essential ability of unfolding its capacities."[47] Van der Poel's view of human nature was significantly different from what one finds in the manualist literature. Whereas neo-Thomism focused on a metaphysical understanding of human nature and viewed a person's relationships, other than that to God, as accidental, the Dutch theologians stressed the centrality and concreteness of human relationships. "Man is not alone, either as to his corporeity or his intersubjectivity, his love, the humanity he shares with others—all of which constitute the particular nature of man and, therefore, his life task."[48]

Theologians who have accepted these more recent notions of the natural law are also associated with proportionalism. Proportionalism has vastly extended the range of factors which have significance for the determination of the moral goodness or moral evil of specific acts. So also have these more recent interpretations of the natural law. Persons as, in the language of

Janssens, living in a world characterized by co-existence, cooperation and co-participation must seriously consider these aspects of human existence as they ponder their moral duties. Or, in the same vein, recall Fuchs' insistence that moral decisions ought to be made with a view toward their significance for the total reality of persons, their society and their culture.

One further, perhaps obvious, comment needs to be made. Neo-Thomist natural law theory stressed the role of right reason. Curran continues to stress that this is the abiding and fundamental meaning of the natural law. In the language of proportionalism "right reason" has been transformed into "proportionate reason." Right reason for the neo-Thomists meant the proximate, objective norm of morality; right reason enabled a person to determine whether an act was in accord with or contrary to the divinely established moral order. This is precisely what proportionate reason strives to accomplish for the proportionalists. The key difference between these two positions is how they understand the phrase "objective norm." For the neo-Thomists this basically meant that an act was consistent with the natural law as the objective measure of human acts. For the proportionalists there are no ready-made moral rules which are always applicable. Proportionate reason is a means of creating moral rules and assessing their applicability. Its function, to recall the title of Knauer's essay, is hermeneutical.

### (B) The Magisterium

The first chapter of this study examined the manner in which Gratian codified the decretals of the early medieval papacy. The fourth and fifth chapters alluded to the manner in which Roman responses to specific questions continued to provide the criteria which the neo-Thomist manualists employed to resolve new and difficult moral issues. This gave rise, as we have seen, to the charge of ecclesiastical positivism, the ready acceptance of papal norms as the resolutions of complex moral issues. The modern high point of ecclesiastical positivism was the reign of Pius XII. Our concern here is not with the wide spectrum of teachings proposed by Pius XII which, as Robert Springer once quipped, ranged from astronomy to street cleaning,[49] but rather with the manner in which theologians interpreted and continue to interpret statements of the ordinary magisterium.

In *Theological Studies'* "Notes on Moral Theology, 1952," Gerald Kelly reported that the question of the doctrinal value of papal allocutions, radio messages, etc. had been raised by the Roman theologian Francis Hürth, S.J. Kelly noted that Hürth believed that:

> . . . in view of the content, audience, and speaker, these messages and addresses have substantially the same doctrinal value as encyclicals; they are a part of the *ordinarium magisterium* of the

Pope, and as such, though not infallible, they command both internal and external acceptance.[50]

In the same year *The American Ecclesiastical Review* carried an essay by Joseph Clifford Fenton which argued that the contents of encyclical letters, even of those in which the pope made no claim to be speaking *ex cathedra*, should be interpreted as containing infallible statements.[51] Two years later, Gerald Kelly reviewed the statements of Pius XII dealing with the principle of totality in order to:

> . . . study his use of the principle and to try to determine how it must or may be applied not only to certain ordinary problems of medical ethics but also to some specifically modern questions.[52]

The first three chapters of *Contemporary Moral Theology*, published in 1958 by John Ford, S.J. and Gerald Kelly, S.J., dealt with the manner in which the magisterium determines the content of moral theology.[53] All this attention to the binding force of papal statements occurred well before the publication of *Humanae Vitae*. Note also that all of these authors understood papal statements as normative for Christian life; *Roma locuta est, causa finita est* (Rome has spoken, the issue is now resolved).

Several years later John Reed, S.J., addressed the relation of natural law morality to the teaching authority of the church.[54] His essay reflected what were probably the generally accepted theological understandings of the role of the papal teaching office prior to the publication of *Humanae Vitae*. The popes were understood to teach the natural law as part of their mission to instruct Christians in the moral order as the way to God, holiness and sanctification. Although the natural law could be known by reason, the value of papal teaching did not depend upon or come from the inherent force or logic of the argument. The authority of the authentic magisterium rested not on the reasons it gave for a specific teaching, but rather on the mission of Christ and the guidance of the Holy Spirit. A natural law teaching of the magisterium could be infallible as a result of a solemn definition (*ex cathedra*) or because it had been the constant and universal position of the ordinary magisterium. Non-infallible papal teachings were to be treated as authentic and binding. In the external order non-infallible papal teaching imposed the obligation not to contradict the doctrine in speech or writings, although theologians might still discuss the question privately. Such papal statements also imposed the obligation of intellectual assent to and acceptance of the teaching. Only an exceptionally qualified person could legitimately deny such assent. These were essentially the same characteristics of the ordinary magisterium which had been developed by Joseph Kleutgen, S.J., and which had been assimilated into papal teaching.[55]

The morality of the regulation of births had been an issue among Catholics since the 1930s. In the post-World War II era it was to become a growing issue in both Europe and the United States.[56] The debate first focused on the moral acceptability of the rhythm method. In 1946, Gerald Kelly, S.J. opined that:

Only exceptional couples can take up the practice of the "rhythm-theory" without exposing their married lives to grave danger; and even these couples usually need the special grace of God.[57]

Pius XII, however, gave limited approval to the rhythm method in two addresses in 1951. The rhythm method could be employed if the intention to restrict intercourse to sterile periods was based on adequate moral grounds; some couples might even need to restrict intercourse to the safe period for long periods of time or even for the entire duration of their marriage.[58]

In the 1950s the first birth control pills were being introduced. The response of Catholic moral theologians to this new means of birth control was virtually unanimous. The use of such pharmaceuticals was, according to John J. Lynch, first a violation of the fifth commandment because direct sterilization was a form of self-mutilation. Intercourse during the period of sterilization was also a violation of the sixth commandment because by intent, and in effect, the act of intercourse was contraceptive, onanistic, illicit birth prevention.[59] The question of the use of the pill was the subject of an allocution of Pius XII in 1958. To use the pill for the direct intention of sterilization, he concluded, was immoral. However if there were legitimate therapeutic reasons which were the direct intention of the pill's use, the indirect sterilization which resulted was morally permissible.[60]

On July 25, 1968 Paul VI issued his encyclical *Humanae Vitae*. This letter was in part the result of a papal commission established by John XXIII and enlarged by Paul VI. The encyclical specifically excluded "every action which, either in anticipation of the conjugal act, or in its accomplishment, or in the development of its natural consequences, proposes, whether as an end or as a means, to render procreation impossible."[61] Consistent with the understanding of the ordinary papal teaching office stemming from the writings of Kleutgen, Pope Paul again asserted that the papal teaching authority was "competent to interpret even the natural moral law," that it was not restricted to the law of the gospels.[62] In a manner similar to Pius XII's admonition in *Humanae Generis*, Pope Paul instructed professors of moral theology that "the example of loyal internal and external obedience obliges not by reasons adduced, but rather because of the light of the Holy Spirit."[63] Theological response to *Humanae Vitae* was lightning-fast. The next day, July 30, 1968, Charles Curran read a statement at a press conference in Washington, D. C., which represented the opinion of eighty-seven theologians. The theologians objected to the ecclesiology of the letter, its method and specific conclusions. Even more importantly, however, the theologians alluded to their *duty* to dissent from authoritative, non-infallible teachings of the magisterium.[64] From 1968 to the present, theological journals on a regular basis have continued to publish essays discussing aspects of the ordinary magisterium and the relation of theologians to the magisterium. What has been the substance of these articles?

One side of the debate has emphasized the binding force of the papal teaching and its authority. John C. Ford and Germain Grisez have argued that, although not defined as an *ex cathedra* statement, the conclusions of *Humanae Vitae* have been "proposed infallibly by the ordinary magisterium."[65] They contend that *Humanae Vitae* fulfills the conditions for the infallibility of a statement stipulated by *Lumen Gentium*: 1) the bishops remain in communion with one another and the pope; 2) they teach authoritatively on a matter of faith or morals; 3) they agree in one judgment; 4) they propose this judgment as one to be held definitively.[66] Ford and Grisez contend that the encyclical and the responses of the various episcopal conferences proclaim Christ's doctrine infallibly. They further contended that because the condemnation of birth control had been infallibly proclaimed, it was irreformable Catholic teaching.

The following year, Grisez argued that:

> The bishops ought not to condone this dissent, and should make clear that theologians and teachers who adopt consequentialism teach and speak without authorization from the bishops and, therefore, not as Catholic theologians and teachers.[67]

Grisez went on to state that it was a requirement of charity to "resist trends which threaten essential aspects of faith and Christian life."[68] The encyclical contained irreformable doctrine; the role of theologians was to transmit to their students essential elements of the Catholic faith. They were not to dissent from or to critique an irreformable doctrine.

In a much more tempered yet still impassioned vein, John Connery has attempted to indicate the issues involved in continued dissent.[69] Connery's principal point is that the Holy Spirit, not the argument given, is the principal reason for accepting papal teaching. Although the possibility of error is not absolutely ruled out, the guidance of the Holy Spirit ensures, for the most part, that error will not actually occur. Repeated dissent, Connery continued, throws doubt on this kind of teaching. Reason, not the rule of faith, tends to become the standard by which moral teachings are accepted. He then turns his attention directly to the proportionalists and suggests that their dissent not just from *Humanae Vitae*, but also from traditional Catholic teachings on adultery, premarital sex, and direct killing of the innocent as intrinsically evil acts demonstrates their implicit rejection of the role of the Holy Spirit in the teaching office.

Revisionist theologians contend that the ordinary magisterium is due respect and, in Rahner's words, must be taken seriously, but that its teaching is capable of error and in fact has erred in the past. According to Rahner, authentic but non-definitive teaching is reformable.[70] Curran has indicated that errors in papal teaching have stimulated theological reflection and thus led to the reversal of the error.[71] Vatican II's decree on religious freedom is clearly different from the views of the papacy during the late nineteenth and early twentieth century. Recent papal directives concerning the interpretation of scripture are inconsistent with the requirements imposed by Pius X in his defense against modernism.

The theologians who defend legitimate dissent maintain that papal interpretations of the natural law require a reasoned argument if they are to be accepted. Rahner proposed that it would have been "desirable for the material grounds for holding the papal thesis to have been justified by more precise arguments."[72] Without such a reasoned argument acceptance of papal teaching is simply obedience to authority. However, such statements should not be interpreted as suggesting that the teaching of the ordinary magisterium should be evaluated as simply another theological argument which fails or is sustained by its logic. There is always a presumption of truth with regard to papal statements. The importance of papal teaching lies in the guidance of the Holy Spirit, but whom is it that the Spirit guides?

One of the primary objections to *Humanae Vitae* was that it was inconsistent with the ecclesiology of Vatican II. To many the letter was excessively authoritarian in tone, but the key issue was the question posed by Charles Curran:

Does the authoritative hierarchical magisterium always constitute the only factor or always the decisive factor in the total magisterial activity in the Church?[73]

Curran clearly believes that this is not the case. All baptized persons share in the total teaching office. Theologians attempt "to understand and interpret the reality of the Christian mystery in the world in which we live . . . the hierarchical teaching office proclaims, makes creatively present, and safeguards the Christian faith."[74] Theology is a scientific and intellectual pursuit, the teaching office a pastoral function. Heresy is possible among theologians as is error within the hierarchy. Both the theologians and the hierarchy teach. The Holy Spirit works in both. Thus if theologians believe that a proposition of the ordinary magisterium is in error they have not only the right but the duty to oppose it.[75]

John Connery would probably have accepted much of this argument. What appears to have been at the center of his response to the dissenters were the frequency and the number of issues which were in dispute. Curran believes, however, that it is possible to explain at least partially the scope of current dissent. First, contemporary theology has assumed a more historically conscious methodology which in turn has led to an inductive methodology. Such a method will never produce the amount of certitude that the traditional, deductive methodologies claimed. Second, some theologians, primarily proportionalists, maintain the non-identification of the physical structure of an act with its moral description. Therefore the morality of some acts as compared to others will be much more difficult to assess, and will thus lead to differing opinions.

The proportionalist debate, as had the situation ethics discussion before it, found the manualist understanding of intrinsically evil acts unconvincing. A number of important Catholic theologians have come to maintain that the morality of an act can only be properly determined in relation to its object, end, and circumstances. But their investigations into this key issue of moral theory required that eventually they address the traditional sources which determined the intrinsically evil character of certain acts. Their understanding of the natural law rejects the notion of an ahistorical understanding of human nature and instead emphasizes its historical, social, and cultural dimensions. In place of right reason, they are more likely to speak of proportionate reason. They have also been compelled to grapple with the manner in which the ordinary magisterium might be a source of moral absolutes. If *Humanae Vitae* had never been published, proportionalists would still have had to face this issue. If this had been the case, however, the entire discussion might have been much more peaceful and the stakes not seen as quite so high. But *Humanae Vitae* was in fact published, and the discussion has not been placid. The ecclesiology of Vatican II has undoubtedly assisted the proportionalists in propounding their case. Although many issues remain to be resolved regarding the manner in which the ordinary teaching office is to be understood, at least this much is clear: there is a significant body of Catholic theological ethicists whose conception of the magisterium is decisively different from that of Joseph Kleutgen.

## NOTES

1. Richard A. McCormick, S.J., "Ambiguity in Moral Choice," in *Doing Evil To Achieve Good*, eds. Richard A. McCormick and Paul Ramsey (Chicago: Loyola University Press, 1978).

2. Peter Knauer, "The Hermeneutic Function of the Principle of Double Effect," *The Natural Law Forum* 12 (1967):132–162.

3. Ibid., 133.

4. McCormick, "Ambiguity in Moral Choice," 7–11.

5. Bruno Schüller, "Directe Tötung-indirecte Tötung," *Theologie und Philosophie* 47 (1972):341–357.

6. Charles Curran, *Themes in Fundamental Moral Theology* (Notre Dame: University of Notre Dame Press, 1977), 139.

7. Josef Fuchs, S.J., *Personal Responsibility and Christian Morality* (Washington: Georgetown University Press,1983), 169. See also Louis Janssens, "Ontic Evil and Moral Evil," in *Readings in Moral Theology #1*, eds. Richard A. McCormick and Charles E. Curran (New York: Paulist Press, 1979), 61–66; Janssens, "Ontic Good and Evil—Premoral Values and Disvalues," *Louvain Studies* 12 (1987):63–70; McCormick and Ramsey, *Doing Evil to Achieve Good*, 194–195.

8. Bruno Schüller, S.J., "Can Moral Theology Ignore Natural Law?" *Theology Digest* 15 (1967):99.

9. Bruno Schüller, S.J., "Zur Problematik allgemein verbindlicher ethischer Grundsätze, " *Theologie und Philosophie* 1 (1970):9.

10. Ibid.

11. Schüller, "Direkte Tötung-indirecte Tötung," 341–357.

12. Janssens, "Ontic Evil and Moral Evil," 49.

13. Josef Fuchs, S.J., "The Absoluteness of Moral Terms," *Gregorianum* 59 (1971):415–433.

14. Janssens ,"Ontic Evil and Moral Evil," 60.

15. Ibid., 69.

16. Fuchs, "The Absoluteness of Moral Norms," 443.

17. Richard McCormick, S.J., *How Brave a New World?* (Garden City: Doubleday and Company, Inc., 1981), 4–5.

18. Bruno Schüller, S.J., *Die Begrundung sittlicher Urteile: Typen ethische Argumentation in der katholischer Moraltheologie* (Düsseldorf: Patmos-Verlag, 1973), 42.

19. Knauer, "Hermeneutic Function," 133.

20. Ibid., 135.

21. Janssens, "Ontic Evil and Moral Evil," 79–80; see also his "Norms and Priorities in Love Ethics," *Louvain Studies* 6 (1976–77):213.

22. Janssens, "Ontic Good and Evil," 81.
23. Fuchs, "The Absoluteness of Moral Terms," 437.
24. Ibid., 444–447.
25. Ibid., 481.
26. Schüller, "Can Moral Theology," 98; see also his *Die Begrundung*, 95.
27. Knauer, "Hermeneutic Function," 142.
28. Ibid., 143.
29. Janssens, "Ontic Evil and Moral Evil," 68.
30. Ibid., 69.
31. Ibid., 71.
32. Ibid., 81.
33. Janssens, "Norms and Priorities," 219–228.
34. Ibid. 229–230.
35. Schüller, *Die Begrundung*, 58.
36. Ibid., 120–121.
37. McCormick,"Ambiguity in Moral Choice," 38–41.
38. Richard A. McCormick, "A Commentary on the Commentaries," in *Doing Evil to Achieve Good*, eds. Richard A. McCormick and Paul Ramsey (Chicago: Loyola University Press, 1978), 232.
39. McCormick, "Ambiguity in Moral Choice," 45.
40. John Connery, S.J., "Morality of Consequences," *Theological Studies* 34 (1973):396–414; "Catholic Ethics: Has the Norm for Rule Making Changed?," *Theological Studies* 42 (1981):232–250.
41. William E. May, "Ethics and Human Identity: The Challenge of the New Biology," *Horizons* 3 (1976):17–37; "The Moral Meaning of Human Acts," *Homiletic and Pastoral Review* 79 (1978–79):10–21.
42. Connery, "Catholic Ethics," 245.
43. Charles Curran, *Contemporary Problems In Moral Theology*, (Notre Dame: Fides Publishers, Inc.,1970), 97–158.
44. Louis Monden, *Sin, Liberty, and Law*, trans. Joseph Donceel, S.J. (New York: Sheed and Ward, 1965), 89.
45. Cornelius Van der Marck, O.P., *Toward A Christian Ethic*, trans. Denis Barrett (Westminster: Newman Press, 1967).
46. Cornelius Van der Poel, *The Search For Human Values* (New York: Newman Press, 1971).
47. Ibid., 83.
48. Van der Marck, *Toward a Christian Ethic*, 28.
49. Robert Springer, S.J., "Current Theology," *Theological Studies* 28 (1967):309.
50. Gerald Kelly, "Notes On Moral Theology, 1952," *Theological Studies* 14 (1953):33.

51. Joseph Clifford Fenton, "Infallibility In The Encyclicals," *American Ecclesiastical Review* 128 (1953):177-198.
52. Gerald Kelly, S.J., "Pius XII and the Principle of Totality," *Theological Studies* 16 (1955):373-396.
53. John C. Ford, S.J. and Gerald Kelly, S.J., *Contemporary Moral Theology* (Westminster: The Newman Press, 1958).
54. John Reed, S.J., "Natural Law, Theology, and the Church," *Theological Studies* 26 (1965):40-64.
55. John P. Boyle, "The Ordinary Magisterium: Towards a History of the Concept," *Heythrop Journal* 20 (1979):380-398; 21 (1980):14-29.
56. William H. Shannon, *The Lively Debate* (New York: Sheed and Ward, 1970), 3-75.
57. Gerald Kelly, S.J., "Notes on Moral Theology," *Theological Studies* 7 (1946):105-106.
58. Pius XII, "Apostolate of the Midwife," *Catholic Mind* 50 (1952):56-57.
59. John J. Lynch, S.J., "Fertility Control and the Moral Law," *Linacre Quarterly* 20 (1953):83-89; John J. Lynch, S.J., "Another Moral Aspect of Fertility Control," *Linacre Quarterly* 20 (1953): 118-122.
60. Pius XII, "Morality and Eugenics," *The Pope Speaks* 6 (1960):395.
61. Paul VI, *Humanae Vitae*, (Washington: United States Catholic Conference, ND), #14.
62. Ibid., #4.
63. Ibid., #12.
64. The statement is reprinted in *Dissent In and For the Church*, ed. Charles E. Curran and Robert E. Hunt (New York: Sheed and Ward, 1969), 24-26.
65. John C. Ford, S.J. and Germain Grisez, "Contraception and the Infallibility of the Ordinary Magisterium," *Theological Studies* 39 (1978):259.
66. Ibid., 272.
67. Germain Grisez, "Charity and Dissenting Theologians," *Homiletic and Pastoral Review* 79 (1979):12.
68. Ibid., 15.
69. John Connery, S.J., "The Non-Infallible Moral Teaching of the Church," *Thomist* 51 (1987): 1-16.
70. Karl Rahner, "On The Encyclical Humanae Vitae," in *Confrontations*, vol. 11 of *Theological Investigations*, trans. David Bourke (New York: The Seabury Press, 1974), 263-287.
71. Charles Curran, *Moral Theology: A Continuing Journey* (Notre Dame: University of Notre Dame Press, 1982), 4.
72. Rahner "On the Encyclical," 266.

73. Curran, *Moral Theology: A Continuing Journey*, 4.
74. Ibid., 5.
75. Rahner, "On the Encyclical," 271; see also Bruno Schüller, S.J., "Remarks on the Authentic Teaching of the Magisterium of the Church," in *Readings In Moral Theology No. 3*, ed. Charles Curran and Richard McCormick, S.J. (New York: Paulist Press, 1982), 23.

# Afterword.

A number of specific conclusions have been drawn in the course of this study. Rather than repeat them individually, I would prefer to draw together some general comments with regard to the nature of the discipline of moral theology as well as some implications for developments in the areas of theology and moral theory.

## I. Moral Theology as a Discipline

The first five chapters of this study investigated the origins, the social and pastoral contexts, the structure and content of the neo-Thomist manuals of moral theology. These manuals had an identifiable theology and moral theory, to a large extent derived from the writings of Joseph Kleutgen, S.J. From approximately 1879 to sometime in the post-Vatican II era, when persons referred to moral theology, they were usually alluding to the genre created by the neo-Thomist manualists. However there were always competitors offering somewhat different versions of what purported to be moral theology. There were the neo-scholastic moralists such as Bouquillon and Lottin as well as the Tübingen theologians such as Tillmann.

As the neo-Thomist genre began to decline in influence, Bernard Häring and Josef Fuchs, and still later Bruno Schüller, Charles Curran, Richard McCormick and other revisionist theologians continued to use the term "moral theology" to depict their area of research. As now employed the term can be used to depict a body of theological writings which were produced over a three hundred year period, writings which have employed significantly different theological paradigms and different moral theories. If "moral theology" can be used to refer to such a wide variety of methods, theological presuppositions, and moral theories, one must begin to query what the name specifically indicates. At best it is an analogical term, and neo-Thomist moral theology is its prime analogue.

"Moral theology" is, I believe, no longer a helpful term with which to categorize the work of Curran, Schüller, McCormick, Fuchs, Häring or other revisionist theologians. Their theological positions and moral theories are simply too distinct from the prime analogue. It creates more confusion than precision to attempt to join such a plurality of positions under a common name. Further, the work of these theologians should no longer be understood as a revision of the past, be that past neo-Thomism, neo-scholasticism, or the writings of Aquinas himself, but rather as new expressions of a living tradition.

Second, and at least as important, a steadily increasing number of persons working in this area are doing so from a university as opposed to a seminary context. As the intellectual world of Thomas Aquinas was markedly different from that of Raymond of Penafort, so the intellectual and theological interests of university professors are different from those of seminary professors. But as was the case in the relationship between Aquinas and Raymond the work of the university theologian can be of immense importance to the practical or pastoral theologian. And indeed the practical theologian's concrete understanding of a given culture and sensitivity to the questions and topics which are alive in the minds of the people can force reality upon the theoretical and abstract speculations of a university professor. The difference between the university theologian and the practical theologian arises from the fact that the two fields of scholarship are focused on different projects. The goals of the university are academic; the goals of the seminary are pastoral. The purpose of the seminary is not to produce scholars, but to produce well-educated, professional ministers. Unlike the university, the seminary is deeply involved in the pastoral function of the church.

Perhaps Bernard Lonergan's distinction between major and minor authenticity can further clarify the distinction I wish to draw between the theology of the university and that of the seminary. Lonergan spoke first of the major authenticity "that justifies or condemns the tradition itself."[1] The authenticity of a culture or tradition refers to its ability to mediate a set of symbols and acts of meaning which can nurture, enhance, and make meaningful the lives of persons who live within the world of mediated meaning which such symbols create. An authentic culture produces the concrete acts of meaning which create the physical and intellectual habitats in which human life is lived. The notion of major authenticity provides the same sort of support for a life of virtue and the production of goods capable of nurturing a way of life as that which Alasdair MacIntyre described in *After Virtue*.[2]

Lonergan described minor authenticity as the authenticity of the "subject with respect to the tradition that nourishes him." Minor authenticity pertains to the intellectual, moral, and religious capacities of persons to live in a manner consistent with the culture and traditions that shape their lives. But note the important point: the authenticity of the subject is dependent upon and conditioned by the authenticity of the culture and tradition. A morally deficient culture or tradition cannot sustain, cannot nurture a morally sensitive population.

I understand university theology to be concerned with the major authenticity of a theological tradition, in my case Roman Catholicism. In what set of symbols, what acts of meaning, what specific values can this tradition express itself so that it can nurture and support a Catholic way of life in American society? The task of university theology is not to discern acts of meaning which can exist alongside those of American society, but rather the effort must be to penetrate and fecundate the symbol system of society itself. Such, I believe, was the vision of Bouquillon and the accomplishment of John A. Ryan. But note that the exchange can be in the other direction as well—American culture can also contribute to Catholic theology. Such was the vision of cultural Catholicism and the accomplishment of John Courtney Murray and Gustave Weigel.

Practical theology pertains to the body of knowledge and skills which can facilitate minor authenticity. An authentic tradition is as alive and vibrant as that portrayed by the modernists and the theologians of the *nouvelle théologie*. Such a tradition possesses the dynamism which Aquinas associated with the new law and Häring associates with conversion. The God of Christian belief thrives within such a tradition. Such a tradition is not primarily a series of abstract doctrines, but rather, as permeating the lives of persons, it is concrete and lived. Such an understanding of tradition reflects the concern for immanence associated with the modernism of Laberthonniere and the theologies of Hecker and DeLubac. The Christian lives in accord with the will of God when he or she lives in accord with such an authentic tradition. The sacraments are quintessential acts of meaning within the Catholic tradition, but they are necessarily supported by the preaching, healing, teaching, and caring functions of pastoral ministry. Each of these aspects of the pastoral office are means to assist individuals to embody in their lives a way of life consistent with the tradition to which they choose to adhere.

I would propose the use of the term "Catholic theological ethics" to denote the work of ethicists working within the university context. Such a theological ethic would be "Catholic" in at least two senses. First, I presume that these theologians have a loyalty and commitment to the tradition of Catholic theology. The work of these theologians is also "Catholic" in the related sense that their conclusions, their ideas have a past and a present. There can be no new beginning which does not understand itself in relation to the past as well as the future. Ideas are never totally fresh, they are the result of unanswered questions posed by our ancestors or the result of the fact that answers proposed by our ancestors are no longer adequate to the viewpoint of a yet further developed culture. Or, indeed, problems may arise because a current generation has been unable to sustain the authenticity of the tradition created by their predecessors. In either case, the archeology of the mind always has a past which reaches back into the creativity and ingenuity and frustrations of previous generations. But a living theological tradition must also look to the present in order to discern the possible meaning of that tradition for the present and the future.

Catholic theological ethics is a university-based academic discipline which seeks to mediate between a living religious tradition and a culture. It needs to discover and articulate as clearly as possible the anomic phenomena in a culture. Modernism, the *nouvelle théologie*, the situation ethics discussion in post World War II Germany were, each in their own way, attempting to do this. Contemporary discussions of how we should care for the dying, whether there are occasions in which we ought to directly kill the dying, debates over artificial means of initiating human life and the significance of surrogate parenting are certainly some of the key anomic issues in contemporary American life. Part of the genius of a Reinhold Niebuhr or a John Courtney Murray was the ability of each of these men to excavate key issues in American life and to address these topics from their respective religious traditions.

The university is the particularly appropriate context for the pursuit of such investigations. Its literature and history departments, its departments of economics, sociology and political science, its science departments, schools of medicine and law are enormous resources which enable theologians to garner detailed knowledge of their culture and specific topics of investigation. They provide potential colleagues for collaborative research. But above all the university is the place where the past and the present clash, where traditions are confronted by current questions and new problems. The function of the university, and thus of Catholic theological ethics, is to be involved in this intellectual ferment.

The term "moral theology" is, I believe, as anachronistic in the seminary as in the university. In fact nowhere is the term less appropriate than in the seminary. The manuals of moral theology intended to prepare ministers of the sacraments. The ministry of priests for the entire period during which the neo-Thomists manuals existed was principally a sacramental ministry. Although the celebration of the sacraments will always hold a privileged and sacred place within any notion of Catholic ministry, we must also acknowledge that ministry within American Catholicism is no longer so exclusively sacramental. The good works of generations of religious men and women, their roles as educators and comforters of the sick, their work with the orphan, the widow, and the poor are now seen as integral aspects of the ministry of the church. Laity are involved in the preparation of catechumens, they visit the sick, they work with the youth, they are involved in a plethora of tasks which are essential elements of the ministry of the church. Future lay ministers, like their priestly counterparts, seek professional preparation for their ministry within the seminary setting. To prepare Catholic ministers, ordained or non-ordained, by means of moral theology would simply not prepare them for what the church will expect them to do. In a subsequent work, I hope to indicate a sort of hybrid of practical theology[3] and communications[4] which might serve the ethical needs of Catholic students preparing for such diverse and complex ministries.

## II. Theology

Neo-Thomism was the dominant theology of the pre-Vatican II church. It was also the theology of the papacy from Leo XIII to Pius XII. During its almost one hundred year hegemony, it had competitors: modernism, the Tübingen school, the *nouvelle théologie*, as well as its "kissing cousin," neo-scholasticism. Neo-Thomism attempted to destroy modernism and the *nouvelle théologie*. Kleutgen had written in direct opposition to Tübingen theology and his successors largely ignored it. Neo-Thomism lived in relative harmony with neo-scholasticism. But the days of such a unified theology for an international and multicultural religion are now a thing of the past. The Catholic world is today one of theological pluralism.

Rahner has pointed out, as I have attempted to do throughout this study, that there has always been theological pluralism within Catholicism. The difference today is the result of the accumulation of vast historical materials, different theological methods, and above all differing philosophical presuppositions. Theologies exist side by side "one another as disparate and mutually incommensurable."[5] Latin American liberation theology is, I believe, one of the most innovative, insightful, religiously sensitive theologies to be developed in the post-Vatican II era. It legitimately imposes upon North Americans a sense of moral duty in terms of the impact of our policy decisions upon the nations of Latin America. We need to keep listening to, learning from, and being challenged by liberation theology. However, I do not think that some version of liberation theology will be a major component of American Catholic theology. The life of the American Catholic Church is not in base communities. Its theological reflection mainly occurs in universities and seminaries. The contemporary theologies of Europe will continue to stimulate discussion and provoke innovation in their American readers. At some point, however, American theologians must contribute to the current pluralism by developing a theology which is reflective of the culture and society from which it stems.

## III. Moral Theory

Proportionalism will continue to play an important role in Catholic theological ethics. Not only is proportionalism a fitting tool for the evaluations of specific actions, it can also serve as a critique of public policy. Proportionalism attempts to assess the significance of ontic goods and evils in relation to the whole of a culture and a religious tradition. Increasingly public policy is determining the context and setting the parameters of important moral decisions. Public policy determines what Medicare and Medicaid will pay for; the selection of treatments for many of our citizens is limited by public policy. Those of us who are parents have a responsibility for the education of our children; public policies deeply influence the educational options which are available to us. A university-based theological ethic needs to be able to critique both actions and policies. Proportionalism can do both.

Proportionalism is also capable of engaging in some of the basic theoretical controversies among American ethicists. Much of the American ethical tradition, largely following upon the work of William James and John Dewey, has embraced pragmatism; it assesses the meaning of an act within a social context. For many contemporary ethicians subjectivism is the major premise of their position. The customary Catholic allegation against such a philosophy is that it is a form of relativism. The neo-Thomist manualists, on the other hand, represented a rigid form of objective ethics. Proportionalism, especially when grounded in a transcendental theology, is capable of assimilating the riches of both relativism and objectivism. But an amplification of this claim must wait for another day.

Loyola University of Chicago
February 20, 1989

### NOTES

1. Bernard Lonergan, S.J., *Method In Theology*, (New York: Herder and Herder, 1972), 80.
2. Alasdair MacIntyre, *After Virtue* (Notre Dame: University of Notre Dame Press, 1981).
3. Don S. Browning, *Practical Theology*, (San Francisco: Harper Forum Books, 1980); Regis Duffy, O.F.M., *A Roman Catholic Theology of Pastoral Care*, (Philadelphia: Fortress Press, 1983).
4. Lonergan, *Method In Theology*, 355–368.
5. Karl Rahner, S.J., *Confrontations*, vol. 11 of *Theological Investigations*, trans. David Bourke, (New York: The Seabury Press, 1974), 7.

# Index

Abelard, 17
*Aeterni Patris*, 31, 32, 38, 49, 51,
   123, 141, 151, 191, 195, 196
Alphonsus Liguori, 32, 35, 36, 51,
   83, 106
American Catholic Theology,
   185–199
Americanism, 130–132, 194
Aquinas, St. Thomas, 5, 7, 20–25,
   29, 30, 34, 37, 40, 49, 53, 56,
   58, 59, 60, 62, 63, 65–70, 84,
   85, 86, 90, 93, 99–100, 102,
   123, 128, 141, 148, 150, 152,
   154, 168, 204, 249, 252, 270,
   271
Aristotle, 22, 24, 42, 53, 62, 65,
   67, 68, 94, 107, 148
Augustine, 7, 13, 18, 51, 83, 86, 100

Barth, Karl, 140, 234, 236
Berman, Harold, 10, 11, 14, 15
Blondel, Maurice, 125–126
Bonaventure, St., 24, 141, 152
Bonhoeffer, Dietrich, 234, 236
Bouquillon, Thomas, 123, 134–138,
   152, 162, 167, 188, 191, 196,
   269, 271
Bourke, Vernon, 90–91

Brown, Peter, 12–13
Brunner, Emile, 140, 234
Bultmann, Rudolf, 140, 234

Canon Law, 5, 16–17, 35, 52
Carroll, John, 185–186, 188
Casuistry, 36–37, 52, 98, 166–206,
   246
Cathedral Schools, 22–24, 34
Catholic University of America,
   134, 190–193, 194, 198
Charity, 102, 112–114
Chenu, M.-D, 13n27, 22, 66–67,
   69, 70, 143, 144–146, 152
Commensurate reason, 246,
   252–257
*Concordance of Discordant
   Canons*, 15–16
Congar Yves, 38, 143
Connery, John, 236, 262–263, 264
Conscience, 81–84
Copleston, Frederick, 23–24, 71
Council of Trent, 29, 33, 34
Curran, Charles, 52, 204, 217–219,
   224, 245, 257, 263, 269

Daly, Gabriel, 184
Danielou, Jean, 141–142, 143

Davis, Henry, 50, 51, 54, 60, 61,
    77, 80, 81, 84, 86, 88, 93, 94,
    102, 103, 105, 107–108, 109,
    110, 111, 115, 116, 117, 118
Dolan, Jay, 184, 186, 194, 196
Double Effect, Principle of, 99–104,
    246–247

Ellis, John Tracy, 195, 196
Enlightenment, 38–39, 185–186
Eternal Law, 86–87, 89

Finnis, John, 90, 216
Fletcher, John, 224, 236–238, 239
Ford, John, 260, 262
Fogarty, Gerald, 188, 194
Fuchs, Joseph, 158, 162, 176–180,
    203, 212–214, 218, 224,
    233–235, 245, 249, 251–252,
    269, 270

Gilson, Etienne, 30, 49, 65, 75, 79–
    80, 140
Grisez, Germaine, 90, 176, 216, 262
Gustafson, James, 52, 216

Häring, Bernard, 11, 36, 158, 162,
    163, 169–176, 178, 180, 203,
    204–207, 217, 224, 270
Hecker, Isaac, 130, 190
Hennessey, James, 186, 187, 196,
    197, 198
Hewit, Augustine, 190, 193–194
*Humani Generis*, 149–151,
    197–198, 225–226
*Humanae Vitae*, 115, 223–224,
    261–264
Hürth/Abellan, 52, 57, 59, 76, 81

Ireland, John, 188, 190

Jansenism, 36, 83
Janssens, Louis, 245, 249,
    250–251, 252–254, 258–259

Kant, Immanuel, 154–156, 184, 209
Kelly, Gerald, 105, 235, 260
Kleutgen, Joseph, 48, 49, 50,
    62–65, 70–71, 123, 137, 148,
    151, 154, 177, 179, 196, 261,
    264, 269, 274
Knauer, Peter, 99, 245, 246, 250
Koch, Preuss, 52, 53, 60, 77, 81,
    85, 86, 88, 103, 108, 111
Konings, A., 85, 87

Laberthonniere, Lucien, 124–126,
    128, 129, 132, 133
*Lamentabile*, 132, 140
Leclerq, Jacques, 143
Leo XIII, 30, 38, 49, 123, 132, 141,
    151, 184, 192, 195, 223, 273
Liberatore, Matteo, 41, 48, 62
Loisy, Alfred, 124, 126–129
Lonergan, Bernard, 38, 43, 123,
    141, 151, 152–157, 168,
    184–185, 224, 270–271
Lottin, Dom Odon, 75, 77, 123,
    152, 158, 162, 166–169, 176,
    180, 269
Lubac, Henri de, 143, 146–149, 263
Lynch, John, 235, 261

Magisterium, 249, 259–264
Mahoney, John, 1, 7, 223
Marechal, Joseph, 48, 65, 152
Maritain, Jacques, 30, 48, 49, 65,
    75, 91–92
McCool, Gerald, 48, 50, 62, 75, 208
McCormick, Richard, 203,
    214–217, 218, 224, 245, 246,
    250, 255–257, 270

McHugh, John/Callan, Charles, 50,
    53, 59, 76, 82, 86, 90, 92,
    102, 103, 105, 106, 117, 118
McNeill, John, 8
Milhaven, John Giles, 236, 238–240
Modernism, 124–134, 141, 142, 272

Natural law, 87–92, 99, 100,
    104–105, 175, 206–207,
    207–209, 213–214, 257–259
Neo-scholasticism, 49, 152, 197,
    269, 270, 273
Neo-Thomism, 31, 37–41, 48–65,
    75–93, 98–119, 123–124, 140,
    151, 165–166, 167, 169–170,
    175, 177, 179, 181, 185,
    195–198, 203–204, 209, 212,
    217, 219, 223, 224, 231–232,
    241, 257, 269, 270, 272, 273,
    274
New Law, 58–60, 92–93
Niebuhr, H. Richard, 196, 206,
    217–218, 236
Noldin/Schmitt, 51, 56, 78, 82, 84,
    86, 90, 93, 102, 108, 110, 116,
    117
Nouvelle théologie, 141–151, 152,
    153, 157–158, 170, 175, 225,
    271, 272, 273

O'Connell, Francis, 76, 77, 78

Pelikan, Jaroslav, 21, 24
Penitentials, 7–11, 19–20
Pius X, 52, 129, 132, 149, 150,
    152, 223
Pius XII, 52, 149, 150, 151, 152,
    223, 225–226, 260, 261, 273
Probabilism, 36–37, 83–84

Proportionalism, 223, 224,
    245–249, 255–257, 258, 274
Proportionate reason, 102–104
Prummer, Dominic, 54, 57, 58, 60,
    80, 82, 86, 88, 93, 94, 107, 114

Rahner, Karl, 6, 123, 141, 151,
    152–153, 155–156, 168, 203,
    207–209, 227–228, 232, 235,
    263, 273
*Ratio Studiorum*, 34–35
Raymond of Penaforte, 18–20, 270
Revisionist theologians, 203–204,
    224, 269

Sabetti/Barrett, 41, 51, 59, 76, 93,
    94
Schüller, Bruno, 78, 203, 209–212,
    224, 245, 248–249, 251,
    254–255, 270
Situation Ethics, 223–224, 225–241
Slater, Thomas, 22, 55, 56, 87, 93,
    102, 103, 105, 109, 110, 113,
    116
Suarez, Francisco, 85, 99
*Summae Confessorum*, 5, 6,
    18–20, 21, 29, 30, 45, 98
*Summa Contra Gentiles*, 68–70
*Summa Theologica*, 5, 20, 21, 29,
    32, 34, 36, 44, 53, 58, 65–70,
    84, 99, 101, 168

Tillmann, Fritz, 162–166, 167,
    170–172, 176, 177, 178, 179,
    180
Todorov, Tzvatan, 32, 44
Totality, Principle of, 98, 104–106
Tracy, David, 43, 151, 185
Transcendental Thomism, 141,
    151–158, 168, 170

Tübingen Theology, 40, 64, 119, 123
Tyrrell, George, 124, 129–130, 132

Vatican I, 38, 51
Vatican II, 5, 29, 32, 48, 49, 158,
   196, 197, 198, 199, 223, 263,
   269

Wassmer, Thomas, 237–238
Weigel, Gustave, 197, 198

Zahm, John, 192, 193
Zalba, Marcellinus, 58, 60, 76, 79,
   83, 85, 86, 88, 93, 102, 105,
   107, 108, 109, 110